AF323712

REAPPRAISALS IN THE LAW OF PROPERTY

Law, Property and Society

Series Editor:
Robin Paul Malloy

The Law, Property and Society series examines property in terms of its ability to foster democratic forms of governance, and to advance social justice. The series explores the legal infrastructure of property in broad terms, encompassing concerns for real, personal, intangible, intellectual and cultural property, as well as looking at property related financial markets. The series is edited by Robin Paul Malloy, and book proposals are welcome from all interested authors.

Robin Paul Malloy is E.I. White Chair and Distinguished Professor of Law at Syracuse University College of Law, USA. He is Director of the Center on Property, Citizenship, and Social Entrepreneurism. He is also Professor of Economics (by courtesy appointment) in the Maxwell School of Citizenship and Public Affairs, Syracuse University. Professor Malloy writes extensively on law and market theory and on real estate transactions and development. He has authored six books (one now in its third edition and another in its second edition), and edited five additional books. He has also written more than 25 scholarly articles, and contributed to 12 other books. His recent books include: LAW AND MARKET ECONOMY (2000, in English and translated into Spanish and Chinese); LAW IN A MARKET CONTEXT (2004); and REAL ESTATE TRANSACTIONS 3RD EDITION (with James C. Smith, 2007).

Reappraisals in the Law of Property

JOHN V. ORTH
University of North Carolina School of Law, USA

ASHGATE

Published by
Ashgate Publishing Limited
Wey Court East
Union Road
Farnham
Surrey, GU9 7PT
England

Ashgate Publishing Company
Suite 420
101 Cherry Street
Burlington
VT 05401-4405
USA

www.ashgate.com

British Library Cataloguing in Publication Data
Orth, John V.
Reappraisals in the law of property. -- (Law, property and society)
1. Real property--Interpretation and construction.
I. Title II. Series
346'.043'01-dc22

Library of Congress Cataloging-in-Publication Data
Orth, John V.
Reappraisals in the law of property / by John V. Orth.
p. cm. -- (Law, property and society)
Includes index.
ISBN 978-0-7546-7731-4 (hardback) -- ISBN 978-0-7546-9449-6 (ebook)
1. Real property--United States--History. 2. Land tenure--Law and legislation-- United States--History. 3. Property--United States--History. I. Title.

KF570.O78 2010
346.7304'3--dc22

2010007975

ISBN 9780754677314 (hbk)
ISBN 9780754694496 (ebk)

Printed and bound in Great Britain by
TJ International Ltd, Padstow, Cornwall

Contents

Afterword   137

Preface

This book began ten years ago as a series of articles on property law published in the *Green Bag 2d*, self-described as "an entertaining journal of law" – entertaining, not in the sense of comic, but in the sense of lively and engaging. Whether my articles, or indeed any articles on law, can measure up is not for me to decide. For all my professional life, more than thirty years, I have found property law fascinating, a mixture of history, economics, language, logic, politics, and sheer self-interest. Sir William Blackstone was onto something two hundred and fifty years ago when he wrote that "there is nothing that so generally strikes the imagination, and engages the affections of mankind, as the right of property." At least, it is so with me.

My original proposal was for a series of three articles, one each year for three years. As the final installment was in press, a further idea or two came to me, and with the encouragement of the *Bag*'s editor-in-chief, Ross Davies, I continued the series. And so it has gone on, year after year, for ten years, until it became what may be the longest-running, single-author series in law review history. At first, I had no particular agenda, other than to re-examine traditional doctrines of basic property law and the forces that tugged and pulled at that law. What attracted me to topics was a perhaps perverse interest in those areas of the law where the join between old and new seemed most obvious, where the ideal and the real seemed most at odds, or where the claims made for reforms of one kind or another seemed particularly overstated.

This hit-or-miss approach suited the *Bag*'s editor and suited me, because I did not, and do not, think there is an overall plan for or unifying theory of the law of property – or of the law of anything else, for that matter. But as entries in the series accumulated, I began to see not a unifying theme, but rather a unifying question – a single quest – that inspired all my investigations. How did this hodge-podge of ancient rules and modern conveniences that make up the "American law of property" come to be assembled? And how well does this contraption work to serve the needs of contemporary society?

This book is the result of trying to answer those questions, not comprehensively but by examining a wide range of property rules and some of the most important forces that shaped them. The *Green Bag* articles are here, refocused, rearranged, and (more or less) consolidated. In addition, a couple of articles along the same lines, but that were not, for one reason or another, part of the original series, are included, and one previously unpublished entry is added – the whole bound together by an introduction and, if not a conclusion, at least an afterword on what I think it all means.

As I re-examine – reappraise – what I have written, I am struck by two things in particular. The first is the extensive use I have made of citations to North Carolina cases and statutes and to the North Carolina State Constitution. Although the tables at the back of the book contain references to authorities drawn from just about every American jurisdiction, as well as to English cases and statutes, North Carolina is obviously over-represented. There is no mystery about why this is so. I have lived and taught in this state for more than three decades and written about its law and constitution. All property law is local, the law of the *situs*, the place where the land lies or where the owner of personal property is domiciled. There is very little national law of property, and what there is is mostly incident to federal taxation or financial regulation, which is why I earlier put quotation marks around the phrase "American law of property." Nonetheless, it is possible to write about property law in general, derived as our system is mainly from English common law. The citations are there not to document the law of any particular state, but to illustrate my points and demonstrate that I am writing about what was really the law at some specific time and place.

The second thing I noticed on rereading these pages is that I sometimes use the same examples to illustrate different points. I have done my best to eliminate needless duplication and to insert cross-references to other chapters in which the subject is more fully examined, but I am aware that some repetition remains. I can only hope it reinforces the argument and does not detract from it. In the end, there is no better way to describe my own appraisal of what I have done than to repeat the words used by H.W. Fowler in the preface to his book on proper English usage: "I think of it as it should have been, with its prolixities docked, its dullnesses enlivened, its fads eliminated, its truths multiplied."

J.V.O.

Chapel Hill, N.C.

May, 2010

List of Abbreviations

Note: In a few instances, an edition other than the one listed below is cited. In those cases, a full citation appears in the footnotes.

Am. L. Prop.   *The American Law of Property* (A. James Casner ed. 1952).

Atkinson, *Wills* Thomas E. Atkinson, *Handbook of the Law of Wills* § 62, p. 293 (2nd ed. 1953).

Bl. Com.   William Blackstone, *Commentaries on the Laws of England: A Facsimile of the First Edition of 1765–1769* (1979).

Broom, *Maxims* Herbert Broom, *A Selection of Legal Maxims* (8th ed. 1882).

Brown, *Personal Property*
     Ray Andrews Brown, *The Law of Personal Property* (2nd ed. 1955).

Bruce & Ely, *Easements*
     Jon W. Bruce & James W. Ely, Jr., *The Law of Easements and Licenses in Land* (2001 and annual supplements).

Cardozo, *Judicial Process*
     Benjamin N. Cardozo, *The Nature of the Judicial Process* (1921).

Carter, *Law*   James C. Carter, *Law: Its Origin, Growth and Function* (1907).

Co. Litt.   Edward Coke, *Commentary upon Littleton*, 16th ed. by Francis Hargrave & Charles Butler (1809).

Cribbet, *Property*
     John E. Cribbet et al., *Cases & Materials on Property* (9th ed. 2008).

Dicey, *Law and Opinion*
     A.V. Dicey, *Lectures on the Relation Between Law and Public Opinion in England During the Nineteenth Century* (1905).

Digby, *History of the Law of Real Property*
     Kenelm Edward Digby, *An Introduction to the History of the Law of Real Property* (5th ed. 1897).

Dukeminier, *Wills, Trusts, and Estates*
     Jesse Dukeminier et al., *Wills, Trusts, and Estates* (7th ed. 2005).

Fifoot, *Mansfield*
     C.H.S. Fifoot, Lord Mansfield (1936).

Geldart, *Introduction to English Law*
     William Geldart, Introduction to English Law (D.C.M. Yardley ed., 9th ed. 1984).

Gray, *Rule Against Perpetuities*
> John Chipman Gray, *The Rule Against Perpetuities* (4th ed., Roland Gray ed. 1942).

Gray, *Nature and Sources of Law*
> John Chipman Gray, *The Nature and Sources of the Law* (2nd ed., Roland Gray ed., 1927).

H.E.L.			William Holdsworth, *A History of English Law*, ed. by A.L. Goodhart and H.G. Hanbury (1966).

Holmes, *Common Law*
> O.W. Holmes, Jr., *The Common Law* (1881).

Kent Com.			James Kent, *Commentaries on American Law* (12th ed., O.W. Holmes, Jr., ed., 1873).

Litt.			Thomas Littleton, *Tenures*, in Edward Coke, *Commentary upon Littleton* (16th ed., Francis Hargrave & Charles Butler eds, 1809).

Plucknett, *History of the Common Law*
> Theodore F.T. Plucknett, *A Concise History of the Common Law* (5th ed. 1956).

Pollock & Maitland, *History of English Law*
> Frederick Pollock & Frederic William Maitland, *The History of English Law* (2nd ed. 1898).

Schoshinski, *Am. Law L. & T.*
> Robert S. Schoshinski, *American Law of Landlord and Tenant* (1980).

Simes, *Future Interests*
> Lewis M. Simes, *Handbook of the Law of Future Interests* (2nd ed. 1966).

Simpson, *History of the Land Law*
> A.W.B. Simpson, *A History of the Land Law* (2nd ed. 1986).

Simpson, *Leading Cases*
> A.W. Brian Simpson, *Leading Cases in the Common Law* (1995).

Thompson on Real Property
> *Thompson on Real Property: Thomas Edition* (2nd ed., David Thomas ed., 2004 and annual supplements).

Webster's Real Estate Law in North Carolina
> *Webster's Real Estate Law in North Carolina* (5th ed., Patrick K. Hetrick & James B. McLaughlin, Jr. eds, 1999 and annual supplements).

*Private property began the instant
somebody had a mind of his own.*
e.e. cummings

Introduction

Property law is a large subject, and getting larger all the time. In the mid-eighteenth century, when Americans were beginning to think about independence, Sir William Blackstone filled one volume, and that the thickest, of his four-volume *Commentaries on the Laws of England* with the law of property. By the middle of the twentieth century, the magisterial treatise on the *American Law of Property*, edited by Professor A. James Casner, required eight volumes. The latest edition of *Thompson on Real Property*, edited by Professor David A. Thomas, runs to more than twice that length. On so vast a subject it is difficult to gain perspective.

In consequence, this book makes no attempt to summarize the entire body of property law. The author has neither the time nor the patience – and probably not the skill – for that task. Instead, it is an attempt to think critically about a number of representative topics drawn from that body of law. Abstracted from the mass, they may be seen entire – and fresh. Reappraisals of parts of the whole, worthwhile on their own account, may also develop skills useful for other projects and may even suggest new approaches to the larger subject. In other words, this is not a reappraisal of the law of property, in the sense of a rethinking of property law in all its aspects. It is, rather, a series of reappraisals in the law of property.

The chapters are arranged in two parts. "Getting down to cases" is what lawyers trained in the common law tradition do best, so Part I is devoted to individual subjects chosen from categories familiar to every student of property law. It begins with one of the most ordinary, yet most intractable problems in the law of personal property: the rights of finders of lost articles. The inquiry then moves through successive topics in the law of real property: estates and future interests, concurrent estates, landlord and tenant, servitudes, and conveyancing. The first part ends, literally, at the end of the line, with the law of escheat, when private property in both land and chattels ends, and the state takes over. The specific topics are meant as examples illustrating the forces that made and continue to make the law of property. If the topics are well chosen, they will act like leading cases, teaching more than a specific rule by demonstrating the law's approach to problems of that kind.

The second part, "driving forces," covers more general topics, spanning the whole law of property: trying to respect intention while maintaining a rule-based system, the pressure of jurisdictional competition, the use of legal fictions and clever labels to facilitate legal change, and, finally, the seemingly endless search for the most enlightened legal rules. The primary purpose of this part is to take a close and critical look at forces that affect broad areas of property law.

If there is any unifying theme, it is that property law today is no more than a collection of legal rules accumulated over many centuries. Rules embodying outmoded social policies are slow to disappear, sometimes lingering in obscurity, sometimes gradually modified to serve purposes they were never designed for. New rules, supposedly better suited to new needs, are awkwardly inserted. The preservation of continuity, sometimes merely verbal; the demand for predictability, in order to allow counseling and planning; the pressure to recognize new social realities, ever appearing and disappearing; the imperative to respond to economic necessities, as perceived by one group or another – make property law a bundle of rules rather than a bundle of rights. The only constant is the need to resolve the seemingly endless parade of disputes, petty as well as grand, brought to the judges for final resolution.

PART I
Getting Down To Cases

Chapter 1

Finding: Asking the Wrong Question

The law of finders is supposed to govern cases in which persons assert rights to presently unowned or unclaimed items of personal property.[1] A finder acquires a right in a found item by taking possession of it,[2] but the finder's right remains subordinate to the right of the owner, if any, until the owner's right is terminated by abandonment or the running of the statute of limitations.[3] The law determines whether a chattel is unowned by asking whether the owner has abandoned it, that is, has relinquished physical control of the item with the intention of no longer owning it.[4] An unclaimed chattel is one, the owner of which has relinquished control without intending to surrender ownership.

As between competing persons each claiming to be a finder of unclaimed property, the law may require a determination of whether the item was originally lost or mislaid. Lost property is property that the owner unintentionally left behind and still wishes to recover,[5] while mislaid property is property the owner intentionally placed somewhere and, for an unknown reason, is slow to reclaim.[6] The classic examples of lost and mislaid property, drawn from the leading cases,

---

1   The unowned or unclaimed items that are discussed here are the type that ordinarily end up in a lost-and-found department; that is, usually small items of tangible personal property, such as umbrellas or, occasionally, money or pieces of jewelry. Items of property on deposit, held for named owners who have not taken any action with respect to them for a significant period of time, such as the balance of inactive bank accounts or uncashed dividend checks, are "presumed abandoned" and taken into the state's custody. They are discussed in Chapter 8, Escheat: Picking Up the Pieces.

2   Possession may be defined as taking physical possession of an item with the intention to assert a right to it. A valuable review of the history of the concept of possession is in C.H.S. Fifoot, *Judge and Jurist in the Reign of Victoria* chap. 4 (1959). For modern concepts, see Carol M. Rose, Possession as the Origin of Property, 52 *U. Chi. L. Rev.* 73 (1985), and Richard A. Posner, Savigny, Holmes, and the Law and Economics of Possession, 10 *Geo. Mason U. Civ. Rts. L. J.* 121 (1999).

3   The finder's right may also be subordinate to the rights of others, such as the owner's bailee or even a prior finder.

4   1 *Am. Jur.* 2d, Abandoned, Lost, and Unclaimed Property, § 10 (2005).

5   Id. § 4.

6   Id. § 6.

are respectively: a package containing money found on the floor of a shop (lost)[7] and a wallet left on a table in a barbershop (mislaid).[8] The right to possess lost property belongs to the finder,[9] while the right to possess mislaid property belongs to the owner of the place in which (*locus in quo*) the item was left.[10]

One problem with the law of finders is that the legal definitions of the terms it uses, particularly the terms "lost" and "mislaid," are not congruent with popular usage. As illustrated by a quotation from Oscar Wilde's famous play, *The Importance of Being Earnest*, the words may be used interchangeably by a person unable to locate a missing item. "The manuscript unfortunately was abandoned," said Miss Prism, "I use the word in the sense of lost or mislaid."[11] From the point of view of disappointed finders, legal results turning on a choice of words necessarily lack credibility.[12]

The principal problem with the law of finders, however, is that too often it requires a determination of the one thing always unknown and unknowable under the circumstances: the intention of the owner. Before the law considers property abandoned, there must be proof not only that the owner lost physical control of it but also that the owner manifested an intention to relinquish title as well. In the usual finding case, of course, the owner is not only absent but unknown. The only evidence of the owner's intention is typically the location of the item when found and the apparent length of time the item remained unclaimed. In order to protect ownership, the law never presumes abandonment. Loss of physical control, even for a long period of time, is generally not conclusive of an intention to abandon ownership.[13] In one case it was held that a state had not abandoned documents it had lost in colonial times;[14] in another, that the government of Spain had not abandoned its sunken galleons.[15] Unless the owner is joined in the proceeding, of course, it is unlikely that any judgment of abandonment would be conclusive.

---

7   *Bridges v. Hawkesworth*, 21 *L.J.*, N.S. 75 (Q.B. 1851). For an historical perspective, see A.E.S. Tay, *Bridges v. Hawkesworth* and the Early History of Finding, 8 *Am. J. Legal Hist.* 224 (1964).

8   *McAvoy v. Medina*, 11 Allen (Mass.) 548 (1866).

9   1 *Am. Jur.* 2d, Abandoned, Lost, and Unclaimed Property, § 18 (2005).

10   Id. § 24. The rule as stated treats the ownership of the *locus* as unproblematic, but in fact the ownership may be divided between present and future interest owners, co-owners, or landlord and tenant; it may also, of course, be contested between an adverse possessor and a legal title-holder or between disputing title-holders.

11   Oscar Wilde, *The Importance of Being Earnest*, act II (1895).

12   For another example of legal results turning on a choice of words, see Chapter 6, The Burden of an Easement: Playing a Word Game.

13   See *Columbus-America Discovery Group v. Atlantic Mut. Ins. Co.*, 974 F.2d 450, 467-68 (4th Cir. 1992) ("the law is hesitant to find abandonment and such must be proved with clear and convincing evidence").

14   *State v. West*, 235 S.E.2d 150 (N.C. 1977).

15   *Sea Hunt, Inc. v. Unidentified Shipwrecked Vessel*, 221 F.3d 634 (4th Cir. 2000).

As with abandonment, so with the distinction between lost and mislaid property: the decisive issue is the owner's intention.[16] Whether the item accidentally escaped the owner's control and was then inadvertently left behind or whether it was knowingly deposited before being unknowingly left is impossible to determine in the ordinary case without evidence concerning the owner's intention, which in the nature of things is never available. So the fact-finder in such cases is left to deduce the owner's state of mind from the facts about where and when the item was discovered. A package of money on the floor is more likely to have been dropped rather than placed, and a wallet on a table is more likely to have been placed rather than dropped, though in neither case can the degree of confidence in the conclusion be high. Packages may be placed on floors and wallets may fall on tables. Needless to say, when an item is discovered in an intermediate location, as on a chair pushed partially under a table, the matter becomes still more speculative.[17]

The indeterminacy of the fact supposedly determinative of the outcome in many finders' cases inevitably invites manipulation. Because finders have rights to lost property and landowners to mislaid property, it is tempting when characterizing the property to keep at least one eye on the relative merits of the claimants. Analyzing the result in a case in which a soldier in the course of duty found a cobweb-covered brooch in a crevice on the top of a window frame in a house requisitioned from an absentee landowner,[18] one commentator observed:

> Under the particular circumstances of this case where the owner of the pin is very unlikely to reclaim it, where the owner of the house had never lived there and knew nothing about it, where the finder is an honest serviceman whose conduct should be rewarded and encouraged, the better solution is to classify the jewelry as lost property.[19]

By which is meant, of course, that the better outcome of the case is to give the item to the finder rather than to the landowner, which can be done by characterizing the property as lost. A disinterested observer, if asked whether a brooch in that particular situation would more likely have been intentionally placed and, for whatever reason, not reclaimed (mislaid) or inadvertently left behind (lost), would probably have chosen the former. More likely still, a person innocent of the legal categories might imagine a story in which the jewelry was concealed by one, whether the owner or not, who did not want its existence to be known.

English common law actually had a category for property that was hidden and not retrieved: "treasure trove," defined by Sir William Blackstone in the

---

16   1 *Am. Jur.* 2d, Abandoned, Lost, and Unclaimed Property, § 4 (2005).

17   *Paset v. Old Orchard Bank & Trust Co.*, 378 N.E.2d 1264 (Ill. 1978) (holding that the item was "lost" within the meaning of a statute).

18   *Hannah v. Peel*, 1 K.B. 509 (1945).

19   Ralph E. Boyer et al., *The Law of Property: An Introductory Survey* 10–11 (4th ed. 1991).

mid-eighteenth century as "any money or coin, gold, silver, plate, or bullion" that is found "hidden in the earth, or other private place, the owner thereof being unknown."[20] To qualify as treasure trove, in other words, two elements were required: in addition to a certain intention on the part of the owner (to conceal), the property had to be of a certain type ("money or coin, gold, silver, plate, or bullion"). In Blackstone's day, banknotes were not legal tender, so his reference to "money" has generally been limited to specie,[21] and, depending on its composition, the brooch in question might or might not qualify. Blackstone explained the origin of treasure trove as dating to the fall of the Roman Empire:

> When the Romans, and other inhabitants of the respective countries which composed their empire, were driven out by the northern nations, they concealed their money under-ground; with a view of resorting to it again when the heat of the irruption should be over, and the invaders driven back to their desarts. But as this never happened, the treasures were never claimed; and on the death of the owners the secret also died along with them.[22]

Although English common law never made ancient concealment an actual element of the legal definition of treasure trove, some modern American courts have done so. Treasure trove, it is said, requires a "thought of antiquity."[23]

Once discovered, treasure trove went neither to the finder nor to the owner of the *locus in quo*, but to the king, although the royal right remained subordinate to the owner's. As Blackstone explained, "If he that hid it be known, or afterwards found out, the owner and not the king is entitled to it"[24] – further evidence that Roman origin was not required. Since American states never claimed this royal prerogative, in the states that still recognize the category, "the rule is that title to treasure trove belongs to the finder, against all the world except the true owner."[25] Treasure trove in America, in other words, is assimilated to lost property in that it is awarded to the finder, despite the fact that it resembles mislaid property in that it was intentionally placed and not reclaimed.

Dissatisfaction with the traditional law of finders has led a number of states to legislate on the matter. The principal object of these statutes seems to be to improve the owners' chances of recovering their property by providing for a public depository. Typically, found property of more than minimal value is to be deposited with the police, who are charged with holding it for a designated period of time. If unclaimed by the owner during the relevant period, the property is to be returned to the finder, who may even be given title to it by the statute.[26]

---

20 1 *Bl. Com.* 285.
21 See 1 *Am. Jur.* 2d, Abandoned, Lost, and Unclaimed Property, § 7 (2005).
22 1 *Bl. Com.* 286.
23 *Hill v. Schrunk*, 292 P.2d 141 (Or. 1956).
24 1 *Bl. Com.* 285.
25 1 *Am. Jur.* 2d, Abandoned, Lost, and Unclaimed Property, § 26 (2005).
26 E.g., N.Y. Personal Property Law, §§ 251-58 (McKinney 1997).

The designation of a public depository is certainly an improvement on the common law, which left the found item either with the finder if it was lost or with the owner of the *locus in quo* if it was mislaid. Developed by the judges in the determination of individual cases, the common law was institutionally incapable of doing more than resolving a dispute in favor of one or the other of the parties. Indeed, it seems likely that the common law's development of the category of mislaid property, which is to be left at the place of finding, was an attempt to aid an owner searching for the property by stabilizing its location, rather than confiding it to a transient finder.[27] The New York statute on Lost and Found Property, for example, expressly recognizes the fact that, having created a public depository, it no longer needs the common law categories and accordingly defines "lost property" tautologically – and unhelpfully to those not already versed in the law of finding – as "lost *or mislaid* property."[28]

The statutes may be faulted for setting too low a minimum value for coverage and thereby encompassing too many found items of small value. Is it reasonable to require New Yorkers who find items worth as little as twenty dollars to deposit them with the police?[29] And is it reasonable to impose on the police the record-keeping and warehousing duties that are involved? In addition, appraising the value of found items other than current cash or coin may be difficult; expert appraisers and their concomitant fees may be necessary.

Of more moment is the objection that elaborate statutory schemes may be unknown to the public at large and consequently ignored. Leaving aside any provision for criminal punishment in case of noncompliance with the statute,[30] one may ask who, in the case of noncompliance, has a right to the found item? In New York, for example, where the statute defines the term "lost property," "as used in this article," to include mislaid as well as lost property, do the common law categories (and their associated results) still apply if the finder does not comply with the statute and therefore is arguably not subject to "this article," but to the common law instead?[31]

That the common law of finders may remain relevant despite compliance with a statute is demonstrated by a 1995 Iowa case, *Benjamin v. Lindner Aviation,*

---

27   See *McAvoy v. Medina,* 11 Allen (Mass.) 548 (1866) (categorizing the property as mislaid and describing that result as "better adapted to secure the rights of the true owner").

28   N.Y. Personal Property Law, § 251 (3) (italics added). Abandoned property and treasure trove are conclusively presumed to be "lost property" unless in an action commenced within six months of the finding they are determined not to be lost property. Id.

29   Id. § 252 (1). See also Iowa Code, §§ 556F.6-556F.8 (requiring finder of goods worth five dollars or more to report the find to the county auditor and to advertise the find).

30   See, e.g., N.Y. Personal Property Law, § 252 (3) (making willful failure to comply a misdemeanor punishable by a fine of not more than one hundred dollars or imprisonment of no more than six months).

31   See *Hurley v. City of Niagara Falls,* 254 N.E.2d 917 (N.Y. 1969) (holding that failure to report finding to police as required by the statute did not affect the statutorily vested rights of the finder).

Inc.[32] In *Benjamin*, money concealed in the wing of a private airplane was found by a mechanic in the course of servicing the plane. The Iowa Lost Property Law requires that found property of more than five dollars in value be reported to the county auditor and advertised.[33] The finder complied with the statute, even depositing the money with the police, which is not required. When the owner of the money failed to come forward, the owner of the plane, a bank that had recently repossessed it, claimed the property, as did the mechanic who found the money. Unlike the New York statute, which expressly preempts the common law of mislaid property, the Iowa statute refers simply to "lost property."[34] As a matter of statutory construction, the Iowa Supreme Court held, over a vigorous dissent, that the Lost Property Law did not cover mislaid property, that the money concealed in the airplane was mislaid rather than lost, and that therefore the owner of the plane, as the owner of the *locus in quo*, was entitled to the money.

What is objectionable about this result is that the unknown owner's legitimate concerns with respect to the property – reporting, publicity, and opportunity to reclaim – were all protected in the statutorily prescribed manner. The legislative concern is purely practical: that the owner be given a fair chance to recover. If the owner fails to do so, the property may as well be left with the finder. The court's concern, on the contrary, is purely theoretic. The common law of finders is comprised of categories dependent on the presumed intention of owners, and the results are determined by those categories. Concealed property, like money hidden in the wing of an airplane, could hardly have been parted with unwittingly; more likely, it was intentionally put in its hiding place. The court rejected the finder's argument that the money was treasure trove on the ground that it had not been concealed long enough to qualify for that category.[35] Under the logic of the categories, since the property could not have been lost; it must have been "mislaid."

What's wrong with the law of finders is that it routinely starts at the wrong end, asking the wrong question: How did the property get where it was found? What

---

32   543 N.W.2d 400 (Iowa 1995). See Jennifer S. Moorman, Comment, Finders Weepers, Losers Weepers?: *Benjamin v. Lindner Aviation, Inc.*, 82 *Iowa L. Rev.* 717 (1997).

33   Iowa Code §§ 556F.6 to 556F.8. A finder of goods worth five dollars or more is required to advertise the find by posting a notice at the door of the courthouse in the county where the property was found and in three other public places in the county; in addition, in case the property is worth more than ten dollars, three weekly advertisements must be placed in a county newspaper. Id. § 556F.8.

34   Id. § 556F.6. It is more than likely that the failure to address the distinction between lost and mislaid property in the Iowa statute is due to the fact that the statute was originally adopted before the modern categories had emerged. See Moorman, Comment, 82 *Iowa L. Rev.* at 725 (citing Iowa Statute Laws of the Territory of Iowa, Water Crafts, Lost Goods, and Estrays (1838–39)). See also id. 730 (noting that *Benjamin* court erroneously stated the adoption date as 1843). The earliest American case to draw the distinction between lost and mislaid property was apparently *Lawrence v. State*, 20 Tenn. (1 Humph.) 228 (1839) (prosecution for larceny).

35   *Benjamin*, 534 N.W.2d at 406.

follows is entirely logical, but largely irrelevant to the matter to be decided. The categories of abandoned, treasure trove, lost, and mislaid property correlate with different states of mind among owners: to give up ownership (abandonment), to conceal with the intention to return (treasure trove), to be unable to locate property involuntarily parted with (lost), and to be unable to recall or unable to return to the location of property intentionally placed (mislaid). From the owners' point of view these abstractions are meaningful. To one theorizing about how title or possession is lost they are useful.

But from the point of view of the finders – and those who must decide disputes among competing persons claiming to be finders – these categories are worse than useless. The identity of the person or persons claiming to be the finder is knowable, as is the place of finding, the right of the finder to be there, the ownership of the place, and the behavior of the finder and other persons involved. A practical law of finders would be based on these fundamentals. As a general rule, the right of the finder ought always to be recognized. If a court must resolve disputes about intention, it is much to be preferred that it involve the intention of parties actually before the court and not the intention of the absent owner.

Although a rule favoring finders is utilitarian, in that it encourages them not to conceal their discoveries out of fear that they will lose possession, the principal argument in its favor is that it enhances the integrity of the judicial process by presenting the fact-finder with a manageable issue.[36] Exceptions should be made only if the finder was not lawfully present at the place of finding, as for example if the finder was intentionally trespassing on private property,[37] or if the finder was acting at the time on behalf of another, as for example if the finding occurred in the course of employment.[38] Whether an employee is under a duty to deliver found property to the employer may be difficult to discern; very often the question will have to be answered by reference to an implied term of the contract of employment.

---

36 Legal rules are often concerned with shaping social behavior in desirable ways. See Chapter 7, Covenants of Habitability: Doing the Right Thing. But for rules to have the desired effect they must be generally known and relied on. Only rules that people consult *before* taking specific action will shape that action. Persons who lose (or mislay) their property never do so in reliance upon any particular understanding of the law of finders, except that they expect the law to protect their right to the property; nor do finders usually determine their actions with the law of finders in mind.

37 Cf. N.Y. Personal Property Law, § 256 (1) (giving the person in possession of the premises the right of the finder if the finding took place on the premises when the finder's presence there was a crime). The New York statute seems to draw a distinction between civil and criminal trespass. It is possible that the line should be drawn instead between willful and innocent trespass; that is, a mere technical trespass ought not defeat the finder's right.

38 Cf. id. (2) (giving the finder's employer the right of the finder if the finding occurred while the finder was employed "under a duty to deliver the lost property to the employer").

In the absence of a statute it must be conceded that the right of the owner is protected only by the judicial recognition that the finder's right remains subordinate to the owner's. This is demonstrated in dramatic fashion in the *Benjamin* case. The airplane in which the money was found (the *locus in quo*) had a record chain of title, but neither of the parties apparently made any attempt to contact the plane's prior owners.[39] And the court seems to have felt itself without the capacity to initiate contact on its own motion. The failure to contact known prior owners makes a mockery of the supposed rationale underlying the category of mislaid property, that it is "better adapted to secure the rights of the true owner."[40]

In case of a dispute between persons each claiming to be the sole finder, doubts should be resolved against any claimant whose behavior has not been completely honest in dealing with the found object, as by attempting to conceal it. The result in *Benjamin* may have been influenced by the fact that the finder's initial impulse was not to inform the plane's owner of the find but to offer to split the money with the finder's supervisor.[41] Where more than one good faith claimant exists, the possibility of recognizing a joint finding should be explored.[42] In finder's cases, it should always be kept in mind that the award of possession to either party is a windfall. As a practical matter, in cases that reach litigation, particularly appellate review, the likelihood of the owner's return is remote. Also in such cases, in which the value of the property at issue makes litigation worthwhile, the accompanying notoriety will be more likely to alert the owner than the usual public posting or legal advertisement.

The proposed solution for what's wrong with the law of finders is in keeping with the common law's tradition of practicality, resolving disputes as they arise, rather than trying to answer abstract questions. An analogy may be found in the history of the law of real property. The most ancient form of action concerning title to land, the writ of right, was designed to determine who actually owned the land. It was supplanted in the course of time by a new form of action, the assize of novel disseisin, designed to answer a much simpler question: which of the two litigants first possessed (was seised of) the land?[43] Eventually, the action of ejectment provided an even more efficient means to determine the right to present possession.[44]

In the law of finding, the proper question is: which of the two litigants first found the item? Speculation about the supposed intention of absent owners is out of place. Focusing on the parties actually before the court and the facts

---

39   *Benjamin*, 534 N.W.2d at 407–08.

40   *McAvoy*, 11 Allen (Mass.) 548 (1866).

41   *Benjamin*, 534 N.W.2d 403.

42   See, e.g., *Keron v. Cashman*, 33 A. 1055 (N.J. Eq. 1896). See also R.H. Helmholz, Equitable Division and the Law of Finders, 52 *Fordham L. Rev.* 313 (1983).

43   See Simpson, *Land Law* 29–30.

44   For a brief discussion of the mechanics of the action of ejectment, see Chapter 11, Fiction: Pious Fraud.

actually known or knowable will produce results that are more defensible and more in line with public expectations. As restated, the law of finders will also relate better with statutes, where they exist. Whatever their flaws, the statutes have the sensible aim of improving protection for the rights of owners; they are not generally concerned with the rights of finders, except that the latter might interfere with the former. Finally, a reformed law of finders offers the benefit of bringing to conscious and express consideration what is now often masked behind the outcome-determinative question of whether property is abandoned, treasure trove, lost, or mislaid. Attention to the question of the absent owner's presumed state of mind is what is truly misplaced.

Chapter 2

The Rule in Shelley's Case:
Staying Too Long

The rule in Shelley's Case, the Don Quixote of the law, the last knight errant of
chivalry, has long survived every cause that gave it birth and now wanders aimlessly
through the reports, still vigorous, but equally useless and dangerous.

Robert M. Douglas, J. (1897)

What the Rule in Shelley's Case is, is not a mystery, although its famed obscurity
has been the subject of many legal jokes. "Did the student answer with a correct
guess, when, on being asked the meaning of the Rule, he said: 'The Rule in
Shelley's case is very simple if you understand it. It means that the same law
which was applied in that case applies equally to every other case just like it.'?"[1]
In fact, the Rule in Shelley's Case did not originate with Shelley's Case, properly
Wolfe v. Shelley (1581),[2] but gained its name and fame from Sir Edward Coke's
elaborate report of that case. The statement of the Rule, refined over two and a
half centuries, attained classic form for American lawyers in New York Chancellor
James Kent's *Commentaries on American Law*:

> When a person takes an estate of freehold, legally or equitably, under a deed,
> will, or other writing, and in the same instrument there is a limitation by way of
> remainder, either with or without the interposition of another remainder, of an
> interest of the same legal or equitable quality, to his heirs, or heirs of his body,
> as a class of persons to take in succession, from generation to generation, the
> limitation to the heirs entitles the ancestor to the whole estate.[3]

Once the terms are defined, the Rule is not particularly difficult, certainly not in
comparison to other legal rules that lawyers are routinely expected to master. In
the simplest possible case, a grant of land "to A for life, then to A's heirs," the
result under the Rule in Shelley's Case is that A gets a fee simple absolute. The
Rule vests in A the remainder in fee simple that is apparently granted to A's heirs,

---

1   *Welch* v. *Gibson*, 138 S.E. 25, 28 (N.C. 1927) (Stacy, C.J.).

2   1 Co. Rep. 93b, 76 Eng. Rep. 206 (C.P. 1581). For a detailed examination of the
facts that led to Shelley's Case, see Simpson, *Leading Cases* 13–44.

3   4 *Kent Com.* 215 (based on 1 *Preston on Estates* 263–419 (1828)).

which then merges – since there is no intervening vested interest – with A's life estate to produce a present possessory fee simple.[4]

Nor is the reason for the Rule mysterious. A charge called a relief was due to the feudal overlord on inheritance, and medieval lawyers tried to structure their clients' transfers of wealth from one generation to the next so as to avoid any unnecessary charges – just as modern estate planners do. If an heir could take by remainder instead of by inheritance, no relief would be owed. More than two hundred years before Shelley's Case and before statutes had become the preferred means of law reform, English judges had closed this particular loophole. Ruling in the case of a son, "A's heir," who sought to avoid this form of medieval estate tax, Chief Justice Thorpe commented:

> I know very well what you want to say. You have pleaded that you ought not to have to pay relief since you are in as purchaser, being the first in whom the remainder takes effect according to the words of the deed; but you are in as heir to your father… and the remainder was not entailed to you by your proper name but under the description of heir….[5]

Ruling that relief was payable despite the fact that the form of the grant was a life-estate-and-remainder-to-heirs was to rule that the estate passed by inheritance; in effect, to equate such a grant with an outright grant in fee simple. In other words, "to A for life, then to A's heirs" was the functional equivalent of "to A and heirs." From this tiny kernel, the elaborate Rule in Shelley's Case was to grow. Today, of course, those who collect tolls in the form of inheritance or estate taxes on the inter-generational transmission of wealth have learned not to make payment depend on the form of the transfer. All successions, whether by way of remainder or inheritance (or by will, right of survivorship, or any other will substitute) are treated by the tax collector more or less the same, and there is no longer any reason to unsettle the property lawyers' tidy system of estates and future interests.

The mystery of the Rule in Shelley's Case is not what it is or why it came to be, but why it stayed so long. In 1660 the Statute of Tenures[6] reformed the English system of landholding and in the process did away with the relief, along with all other feudal dues. Why, once its reason for being had ceased, did the rule continue? It was not because the common law had lost its vigor. In 1682 in the

---

4   See Simes, *Future Interests* § 21, p. 45 (2nd ed. 1966).

5   Provost of Beverley's Case, Y.B. 40 Edw. 3, f. 9, no. 18 (1366), quoted in Plucknett, *History of the Common Law* 565. "Purchaser" is used in its narrow legal sense to describe the grantee of an estate, not necessarily a "purchaser for valuable consideration." The Provost of Beverley's Case involved a purported remainder in fee tail rather than in fee simple, i.e., "to the heirs of A's body" rather than "to A's heirs," but the Rule in Shelley's Case applies just the same.

6   12 Car. 2, c. 24 (1660).

Duke of Norfolk's Case[7] the Chancery Court laid the foundation for an even more famous rule, the Rule Against Perpetuities, which the courts of law and equity together elaborated over the next 250 years.[8] At the same time, English judges were actively collaborating with conveyancers in the development of the strict settlement of land, an extraordinary combination of life estates, remainders in fee tail (usually in fee tail male), and – crucially – remainders to trustees to preserve contingent remainders (necessary because of their destructibility).[9] The validity of covenants for title in deeds of real property was also established,[10] and the use upon a use was accepted as an evasion of the venerable Statute of Uses.[11] It is notable that all these departures were elaborations on the received tradition. Perhaps the genius of the common law at this time could add but not subtract.

Nor did the Rule in Shelley's Case outlive its usefulness simply because nobody noticed or cared. Lord Mansfield, the reforming Chief Justice of King's Bench, seized the initiative in 1770, the hundredth anniversary of the Statute of Tenures. In *Perrin v. Blake*, construing a will that ran afoul of the rule, Mansfield observed:

> as the law had allowed a free communication to the testator, it would be a strange law to say, "Now you have communicated that intention so as everybody understands what you mean, yet because you have used a certain expression of art, we will cross your intention and give your will a different construction; though what you mean to have done is perfectly legal, and the only reason for contravening you is because you have not expressed yourself as a lawyer".... I admit that there is a devise to [A] for life, and in the same will a devise to the heirs of his body, and I agree that this is within the letter of Shelley's Case; and I do not doubt but there are, and have been always, lawyers of a different bent of genius and different course of education, who have chosen to adhere to the strict letter of the law. They will say that Shelley's Case is uncontrollable authority....[12]

But, Mansfield continued, *he* would say otherwise. No medieval anachronism should be allowed to stand in the way of clearly expressed intention.

---

7   3 Ch. Cas. 1, 22 Eng. Rep. 931 (Ch. 1682). See George L. Haskins, Extending the Grasp of the Dead Hand: Reflections on the Origins of the Rule Against Perpetuities, 126 *U. Pa. L. Rev.* 19 (1977).

8   See *Scatterwood* v. *Edge*, 1 Salk. 229, 91 Eng. Rep. 203 (K.B. 1699); *Thellusson* v. *Wood*, 11 Ves. 112, 32 Eng. Rep. 1030 (Ch. 1805); *Jee* v. *Audley*, 1 Cox 324, 29 Eng. Rep. 1186 (Ch. 1787); *Cadell* v. *Palmer*, 1 Cl. & Fin. 372, 6 Eng. Rep. 956 (H.L. 1832, 1833); *In re Villar*, [1929] 1 Ch. 243.

9   On the rise of the strict settlement, see Lloyd Bonfield, *Marriage Settlements, 1601–1740: The Adoption of the Strict Settlement* (1983); Eileen Spring, *Law, Land, and Family: Aristocratic Inheritance in England, 1300–1800* (1993).

10   See 3 *H.E.L.* 163.

11   *Hopkins* v. *Hopkins*, 1 Atk. 591, 26 Eng. Rep. 371–72 (Ch. 1738).

12   Quoted in Fifoot, *Mansfield* 174. Like the Provost of Beverley's Case, *Perrin* involved a purported remainder in fee tail rather than in fee simple.

Even on his own court, Mansfield encountered opposition.[13] Dissenting in *Perrin*, Mr. Justice Yates pointed out that in construing a will it was not only the intention of the testator that mattered: "After you have fixed the intention, it then becomes a question, whether such intention can be executed consistently with the established rules of law."[14] Admitting that the original reason for the rule was obsolete, Yates nonetheless felt bound to apply it. Shelley's Case was, he thought, "uncontrollable authority" – uncontrollable, that is, by the courts. Here we can detect a countercurrent to the continued activism of the common law judges, an early indication of the idea of separation of powers: what the judges had made, they could not unmake. The initiative in law reform was now passing, however haltingly, to the legislature. For centuries, lawyers of a certain "bent of genius" would continue to defer to the legislature in the matter of the Rule in Shelley's Case. In the middle of the twentieth century, a Texas judge would solemnly repeat: "Repeal is the duty of the legislative branch of our government, and the judiciary cannot legislate by refusing to follow the Rule."[15] Latterly, legal commentators have encouraged the judges to reassert their medieval powers over the common law and do away with the Rule without waiting for the legislature.[16]

So momentous was the majority's decision in *Perrin* that it was appealed to the extraordinary Court of Exchequer Chamber,[17] which agreed with Yates and handed Mansfield one of his rare reversals.[18] Among the judges who overruled Mansfield was Sir William Blackstone, recently raised to the bench from his Oxford professorship.[19] Blackstone's defense of the rule came as no surprise. In

---

13   Dissents were rare in King's Bench during Mansfield's long tenure as Chief Justice; no more than twenty instances are reported, Fifoot, *Mansfield* 46, a record that rivals John Marshall's as Chief Justice of the United States Supreme Court. See Herbert A. Johnson, *The Chief Justiceship of John Marshall, 1801–1835*, figure 2, p. 91 (1997).

14   Quoted in 12 *H.E.L.* 484.

15   *Sybert* v. *Sybert*, 254 S.W.2d 999, 1002 (Tex. 1953) (Griffin, J., concurring).

16   See, e.g., Rest. (2d) of Prop.: Donative Transfers § 30.1 (3) ("The Rule in Shelley's Case has been abolished prospectively in practically all the States and should be abolished prospectively by judicial decision to the extent it has not been abolished prospectively by statute.").

17   A writ of error, a proceeding in the nature of an appeal, lay from King's Bench to the Court of Exchequer Chamber, which consisted of the four judges of the Court of Common Pleas and the four barons of the Court of Exchequer. 3 *Bl. Com.* 56.

18   4 Burr. 2579, 98 Eng. Rep. 355; 1 Collectanea Juridica 283 (Exch. Ch. 1772). For the history of *Perrin*, a case that "divided the profession of law into bitter factions for many years," see 3 Lord Campbell, *Lives of the Chief Justices* 329–37 (1873). Mansfield suffered only six reversals during his chief justiceship. Fifoot, *Mansfield* 47.

19   The disagreement over the Rule in Shelley's Case may have affected the relationship between two of the greatest English lawyers of the eighteenth century. "It would not be surprising if Mansfield had allowed resentment of the major rebuff he and his court received in *Perrin* v. *Blake* to affect his attitude toward Blackstone." Wilfrid Prest, *William Blackstone: Law and Letters in the Eighteenth Century* 268 (2008).

his lectures on the common law he had emphatically adopted Sir Edward Coke's position that the common law, as it was, was "the perfection of reason."[20]

> And [Blackstone continued] it hath been an antient observation in the laws of England, that whenever a standing rule of law, of which the reason perhaps could not be remembered or discerned, hath been wantonly broke in upon by statutes or new resolutions, the wisdom of the rule hath in the end appeared from the inconveniences that have followed the innovation.[21]

As an unintended consequence of Mansfield's attempt to eliminate it, the Rule in Shelley's Case emerged with a renewed lease on life. Only in the final decision in *Perrin* was it held to be a rule of law, not of construction; that is, a rule to be applied as the Rule Against Perpetuities was applied, "remorselessly" without regard to intention.[22] In consequence, even a statement in the creating instrument that the ancestor is to take no more than a life estate does not preclude its operation.[23] As Dean Samuel Mordecai of Trinity (later Duke) Law School quipped (quoting W.S. Gilbert): intentions, "like 'The flowers that bloom in the spring! Tra-la!! Have nothing to do with the case.'"[24]

Not only was the ruling case law established, but Charles Fearne, a conveyancer of genius, was inspired to write his classic treatise, *Essay on the Learning of Contingent Remainders and Executory Devises* (1772), embedding the Rule firmly in legal literature. As one American court rather gloatingly put it, referring to the Rule in Shelley's Case:

> This "ancient landmark of the law" was, we believe, on a celebrated occasion, shown but slight respect by so great a judge as Lord Mansfield, but the controversy which immediately sprang up between his Lordship and Mr. Fearne did not, it is said, result to the advantage of the former, and the rule was more firmly settled than ever in the jurisprudence of England.[25]

Maintaining the Rule in Shelley's Case could always be justified because, in the hands of experienced conveyancers, it could do little harm. The problem in *Perrin* was not, as Lord Mansfield observed, that the law would not allow the testator to do what he wished with his own, but that he had not expressed himself "as a lawyer."

---

20   1 *Bl. Com.* 70. Cf. *Co. Litt.* § 138, p. 97b.

21   1 *Bl. Com.* 70.

22   See Gray, *Rule Against Perpetuities* § 629, p. 599. See also Chapter 9, Intention: The Law of Unintended Consequences.

23   See Simes, *Future Interests* § 24, pp. 51–52 (citing *Perrin*).

24   Samuel Mordecai, *Law Lectures* 594 (1907) (quoting W.S. Gilbert, *The Mikado*, act II, ll. 644–46 (1885), in *The Complete Annotated Gilbert and Sullivan* 639 (Ian Bradley ed. 1996)).

25   *Starnes* v. *Hill*, 16 S.E. 1011, 1016 (N.C. 1893).

Strange as it may seem, had the devise been "to A for 100 years if he so long live, then to A's heirs," the Rule in Shelley's Case would not have interfered: it applies only where a grantee takes "an estate of freehold" followed by a remainder to his heirs.[26] A term of years defeasible on death is not a life estate and what follows is not technically a remainder, although of course it functions very much the same. Or, making use of the power of equity, one could convey "to T in trust for the life of A, then to A's heirs." On this grant, too, the Rule gained no purchase: the interests of A and his heirs are not "of the same legal or equitable quality."[27]

In a striking passage in his lectures on the Common Law, Oliver Wendell Holmes outlined what he described as a "very common phenomenon," "one very familiar to students of history":

> The customs, beliefs, or needs of a primitive time establish a rule or a formula. In the course of centuries the custom, belief, or necessity disappears, but the rule remains. The reason which gave rise to the rule has been forgotten, and ingenious minds set themselves to inquire how it is to be accounted for. Some ground of policy is thought of, which seems to explain it and to reconcile it with the present state of things; and then the rule adapts itself to the new reasons which have been found for it, and enters on a new career.[28]

Long after its initial formulation, the Rule in Shelley's Case acquired a new rationale, one suitable to a new "state of things": to promote alienability. The longer title to property remains in the form of life-estate-and-remainder, the longer it is, as a practical matter, inalienable. Indeed, in a curious way the medieval Rule in Shelley's Case seemed to fall in with a later judicial preference for the unencumbered fee simple absolute.[29]

Sometimes American judges had to work hard to keep the Rule. In North Carolina, for example, an early statute declared that grants and devises "to the heirs of a living person" were to be construed to be "to the children of such person."[30] A moment's reflection will reveal that that simple change could have spelled the end for the Rule in Shelley's Case. If "to A for life, then to A's heirs" means "to A for life, then to A's children," the Rule has no effect. It applies only when the remainder is to the life tenant's heirs "as a class of persons to take in succession, from generation to generation"; that is, it applies only when the word "heirs" is used in its technical sense.[31] To avoid this result, the North Carolina Supreme Court held that the statute

---

26   See Simes, *Future Interests* § 21, p. 45.

27   See id. § 24, p. 54. Even if T later conveyed the legal life estate to A, the Rule still would not apply because the life estate and the remainder were not created by "the same instrument." Id.

28   Holmes, *Common Law* 8.

29   See, e.g., *Doyle v. Andis*, 102 N.W. 177 (Iowa 1905).

30   N.C. Gen. Stat. § 41–6. Similar statutes exist in other states. See Simes, *Future Interests* § 107, p. 221, n. 5.

31   See Simes, *Future Interests* § 24, p. 50.

did not apply if the living person in question takes a precedent freehold estate; that is, "to A for life, then to A's heirs" means just what it says despite the statute, and the Rule in Shelley's Case works its accustomed magic.[32]

If the Rule in Shelley's Case was a positively good thing, not merely a relic of a bygone age, then there was no reason not to extend its reach. Having begun as a means to avoid a feudal charge on succession to land, the Rule was historically limited to real property ("estates of freehold"). Even as it was fading throughout the common law world, the Rule was extended in a few American states to personal as well as real property.[33] If accelerated alienability was desirable for owners of interests in land, it was just as desirable for beneficiaries of trusts of personal property – perhaps even more so, as wealth shifted increasingly from tangible to intangible forms.

But the Rule in Shelley's Case had become more than a mere rule of property; it had become part of the mystique of the common law. A badge of professional attainment, it helped justify the lawyers' claimed monopoly on the lucrative art of drafting deeds and wills. Above all, it added to the majesty of the common law tradition. Emerging from the remote past, "time whereof the memory of man runneth not to the contrary," the common law bore visible signs of its long history.[34] Born in feudalism, it retained remnants of the feudal past, even as it adapted to the needs of the modern world.

* * *

I have said that the mystery of the Rule in Shelley's Case is why it stayed so long, but equally mysterious is why, having stayed so long, it left when it did – and fairly quickly by historical standards. The Rule in Shelley's Case was abrogated by statute in England, its original home, in 1926.[35] In the American states the process had begun earlier and lasted longer, but with North Carolina's abolition of the Rule in 1987, it is nearly gone.[36] The manner of its passing is worth noting. As Lord Mansfield had feared, abolition required legislative action, and for long the legislative branch was uninterested in the intricate details of property law. But change, when it came, did not represent the defeat of the legal establishment. What the lawyers on the bench had lost, lawyers elsewhere gained. Lawyers in

---

32   *Starnes* v. *Hill*, 16 S.E. 1011 (N.C. 1893).

33   *Riegel* v. *Lyerly*, 143 S.E.2d 65 (N.C. 1965); *Society Nat'l Bank* v. *Jacobson*, 560 N.E.2d 217 (Ohio 1990). See generally William A. Reppy, Judicial Overkill in Applying the Rule in Shelley's Case, 73 *Notre Dame L. Rev.* 83 (1997).

34   1 *Bl. Com.* 67 ("In our law the goodness of a custom depends upon it's having been used time out of mind; or, in the solemnity of our legal phrase, time whereof the memory of man runneth not to the contrary.").

35   15 & 16 Geo. 5, c. 20, § 131 (1925).

36   N.C. Gen. Stat. § 41-6.3. See John v. Orth, Requiem for the Rule in Shelley's Case, 67 *N.C. L. Rev.* 681 (1988).

the legislative branch, usually acting on the advice of legal specialists outside – practitioners and law professors – now assumed the leading role in law reform.

The statutes abolishing the Rule in Shelley's Case represent a bewildering array of statements of the rule in order to extirpate it. The 1852 Code of Alabama, for example, provided:

> Where a remainder created by a deed or will is limited to the heirs, issue, or heirs of the body of a person to whom a life estate in the same property is given, the persons who, on termination of the life estate, are the heirs, issue, or heirs of the body of such tenant for life are entitled to take as purchasers by virtue of the remainder so limited to them.[37]

North Carolina tried a more direct approach: "The rule of property known as the rule in Shelley's case is abolished."[38] Certainly in the latter instance and probably in the former as well, lawyers and law students are doomed to continue to study the Rule in order to know what is being done away with.

To convince the public of the value of legal advice no longer requires anachronisms like the Rule in Shelley's Case. The modern tax code is more than sufficient for that purpose. And justifying the retention of an obsolete rule with the argument that elites with access to skilled professionals will not be hindered by it is unseemly in a democratic society, although certain provisions of the tax code survive for just that reason. More important, the trappings of history no longer lend an air of authority. In an increasingly positivistic age, the ancient grandeur of the common law seems more of an inconvenience than an advantage.

There had, of course, been another possibility for the Rule in Shelley's Case – one that appears from the history of the Rule's fraternal twin, the Doctrine of Worthier Title.[39] The latter, more descriptively labeled "the rule against remainders to the grantor's heirs" or the "conveyor-heir rule," was originally designed to close a loophole similar to the one plugged by the Rule in Shelley's Case: avoiding the payment of the feudal relief by structuring succession at the grantor's death as a remainder rather than an inheritance. While the Rule in Shelley's Case applies to grants in the form "to A for life, then to A's heirs," the Doctrine of Worthier Title applies to grants in the form "to A for life, then to the grantor's heirs."[40] For those

---

37   Codified in Ala. Code § 35-4-230. See *Lusk* v. *Broyles*, 694 So.2d 4 (Ala. 1997) (applying statute). Again, the word "purchaser" is used in the technical sense of "grantee."

38   N.C. Gen. Stat. § 41-6.3.

39   Despite its origin in feudal England, the Doctrine acquired the label of "Worthier Title" in America. See David Thomas, Anglo-American Land Law: Diverging Developments From a Shared History – Part II: How Anglo-American Land Law Diverged After American Colonization and Independence, 34 *Real Prop., Prob. & Trust J.* 295, 307 (1999) (citing *Ellis* v. *Page*, 61 Mass. (7 Cush.) 161 (1851)).

40   The Doctrine of Worthier Title is usually described as having two branches: the deeds (or *inter vivos*) branch and the wills branch. See Joseph W. Morris, The *Inter Vivos*

grants, the Doctrine operates to convert the apparent remainder in the grantor's heirs into an outright reversion in the grantor. In other words, "to A for life, then to the grantor's heirs" has the same effect as "to A for life," and the grantor remains free to direct the succession away from his heirs by deed or devise.

Although the Doctrine of Worthier Title also began as a rule of law,[41] it was never the object of premature law reform such as Mansfield's celebrated assault on the Rule in Shelley's Case. In consequence, it was not so firmly established in the case law or treatises, and reform, when it came in the twentieth century at the hands of another famous judge, Benjamin Cardozo, was widely accepted. Cardozo held that the doctrine raised a presumption only, one rebuttable by evidence of intention to the contrary;[42] as such, it could more readily be squared with the modern emphasis on effectuating intention. Perhaps because it is less menacing, the Doctrine of Worthier Title has been treated more generously, not cabined by restrictive interpretations. It applies to personal as well as real property, is not confined to future interests in the form of remainders, and applies even if the present and future interests are not of the same legal or equitable quality.[43]

Perhaps the very inflexibility of the Rule in Shelley's Case as it came down from the past meant that it had to be abolished, and could not be reformed. If it was bent, it would break. At last, intention seems to have triumphed. "To A for life, then to A's heirs" now means just what it says; that is, A's interest is for life only, with a remainder to his heirs. Of course, the remainder is a contingent one, since A's heirs are unascertainable until A's death. *Nemo est haeres viventis.* (No one is the heir of the living.)[44] Or, in Lord Coke's more colorful phrase: "*Solus Deus haeredem facere potest, non homo*" (God alone makes the heir, not man).[45] Interests in unascertainable persons are often inconvenient, however, and states have legislated to remedy the problem. A North Carolina statute, for example, allows the grantor of a deed that creates a contingent remainder in persons not yet ascertained (such as the heirs of a living person) to revoke the grant at any time prior to the vesting of the remainder,[46] an uncomfortable reminder that Blackstone

---

Branch of the Worthier Title Doctrine, 2 *Okla. L. Rev.* 133 (1949); Joseph W. Morris, The Wills Branch of the Worthier Title Doctrine, 54 *Mich. L. Rev.* 451 (1955).

41   *Co. Litt.* § 19, p. 22b ("If a man make a gift in taile, or a lease for life, the remainder to his own right heirs, this remainder is void, and he hath the reversion in him....").

42   *Doctor* v. *Hughes*, 122 N.E. 221 (N.Y. 1919).

43   See Simes, *Future Interests* § 27, pp. 58–59. Even here the desire not to be seen to defeat intention has led many states to abolish the Doctrine of Worthier Title. See Dukeminier, *Wills, Trusts, and Estates* 661 ("a majority of states have jettisoned the doctrine by statute or by judicial decision, both as a rule of law and as a rule of construction").

44   *Co. Litt.* § 19, p. 22b; Broom, *Maxims* 522.

45   *Co. Litt.* § 1, p. 7b.

46   N.C. Gen. Stat. §§ 39-6. Professor Link has rightly called this "a kind of statutory destructibility [of contingent remainders]." Ronald Link, The Rule Against Perpetuities in North Carolina, 57 *N.C.L. Rev.* 727, 728 n. 7 (1979). Statutes in some states that have abolished the Doctrine of Worthier Title provide that a trust may be revoked by the settlor

might have had a point when he warned about the unforeseen consequences of wantonly breaking in upon the common law.

Assuming the grantor intended to give A an estate that could not be effectively mortgaged or sold, an estate that A could not grant or devise away from his heirs at law, whoever they may be at his death and whatever they may have done during his life, then intention has indeed triumphed. One may wonder, however, whether grantors and testators fully understand the legal meaning of the word "heirs." Of course, if competent counsel was consulted, then it was explained to them. But then, if competent counsel had been consulted, they would never have encountered a Rule-in-Shelley's-Case problem in the first place!

---

and the ascertained beneficiaries when the only other interested persons are the settlor's heirs. See, e.g., N.Y. Est., Powers & Trusts Law § 7-1.9 (b).

Chapter 3

Joint Tenancy: Accounting for Continuity

The law's treatment of the survivorship philosophy has made a circle. Its origin has been ascribed to the needs of the feudal system. So as the idols of seisin were overthrown, so did the law develop a distaste for the right of survivorship, but the expense and delay incident upon administration of a decedent's estate today has led to a widespread revival of the survivorship tool as a means of effecting a simple and economical transfer of property on death.

Thompson on Real Property

Common law doctrines display remarkable stability. The intellectual apparatus used in many areas of law, including terminology, basic concepts, and fundamental assumptions, were developed centuries ago. Sir William Blackstone's *Commentaries on the Laws of England*, written in the mid-eighteenth century, on the eve of American Independence, continues to provide a useful starting-point for many legal disciplines. The United States Constitution and attached Bill of Rights, durable eighteenth-century documents only slightly younger than the *Commentaries*, perpetuate many common law distinctions.[1] While it is fashionable today to underline the up-to-date parts of the law and to stress legal change, it was once more common to insist upon the law's rootedness in the past and emphasize legal continuity. Until well into the twentieth century, it was still customary to learn the law from annotated editions of Blackstone.[2] Modern legal materials – law school casebooks, scholarly treatises, even judicial opinions – are less likely to reveal the connection between current results and ancient traditions. The effect is to obscure an important inquiry: how verbal formulae centuries old can continue to do useful service in the modern world. Historians have begun to realize that it is just as important to account for continuity as it is to account for change.

---

1 See, e.g., U.S. Const. art I, § 9 ("writ of habeas corpus"; "ex post facto law"). Id. amend. VII ("In suits at common law, where the value in controversy shall exceed twenty dollars, the right of trial by jury shall be preserved, and no fact tried by a jury shall be otherwise re-examined in any court of the United States, than according to the rules of the common law.").

2 William Draper Lewis, a distinguished legal scholar, published an updated edition of Blackstone's *Commentaries* in 1911. William Blackstone, *Commentaries on the Laws of England*, 4 vols. (William Draper Lewis ed., 1911). Influential twentieth-century lawyers often began their legal education with Blackstone. See, e.g., Arthur E. Sutherland, *The Law at Harvard: A History of Men and Ideas, 1817–1967*, at 200 (Roscoe Pound), id. 219 (Austin Wakeman Scott).

Essential elements of the law of joint tenancy, for example, remain today largely what they were hundreds of years ago.[3] Two or more persons may hold property concurrently as joint tenants. Each theoretically holds the entire estate, subject only to the equal right of the other or others. Each may alienate an undivided share, or demand a partition by which the estate is severed into separate shares or sold and the proceeds divided; but none may devise a share or leave it to pass by intestacy. The distinctive incident of the estate is the right of survivorship, sometimes referred to by its Latin name *jus accrescendi*. No true right, the right of survivorship is merely a label indicating that on the death of one joint tenant, that tenant's share vanishes and the surviving tenant or tenants own the whole.

With or without direct attribution, courts today continue to resolve disputes concerning the creation and severance of joint tenancies by reference to Blackstone's classic formulation of the Doctrine of the Four Unities:

> The *properties* of a joint estate are derived from it's unity, which is fourfold; the unity of *interest*, the unity of *title*, the unity of *time*, and the unity of *possession*: or, in other words, joint-tenants have one and the same interest, accruing by one and the same conveyance, commencing at one and the same time, and held by one and the same undivided possession.[4]

Older than Blackstone, the basics of joint tenancy law may be found in Sir Thomas Littleton's fifteenth-century treatise on *Tenures*,[5] the earliest printed book on English law – so early in fact that it was written in French – or, rather, in what was left of the French language brought over by the Norman Conquerors four hundred years earlier.[6] Twentieth-century cases have been decided on the authority of Littleton,[7] usually in the form of Sir Edward Coke's seventeenth-century *Commentaries on Littleton*.[8]

---

3   For a statement of the modern law of joint tenancy, see 4 *Thompson on Real Property* 1–61.

4   2 *Bl. Com.* 180 (emphasis in original). In Blackstone's day proper usage for the possessive of "it" was "it's," not, as it would be today, "its."

5   *Litt.* §§ 277–91.

6   French remained the language of the law courts until in 1362 a statute required that court proceedings should be in English. 36 Ed. 3, c. 15 (1362). Nonetheless, the lawyers, as Blackstone observed, "being used to the Norman language, and therefore imagining they could express their thoughts more aptly and concisely in that than in any other, still continued to take their notes in law French." 3 *Bl. Com.* 318.

7   E.g., *Jackson v. O'Connell*, 177 N.E.2d 194 (Ill. 1961) (holding that severance by one of three joint tenants by conveyance to one of the other two did not sever the joint tenancy as to the two-thirds held by those two) (citing *Co. Litt.* § 312, p. 196a).

8   Coke's admiration for Littleton's *Tenures* knew no bounds: "it is the most perfect and absolute work that ever was written in any humane science." *Co. Litt.* Preface. *Coke on Littleton* quickly became itself a classic of the common law. It reached definitive form in the sixteenth edition edited by Francis Hargrave & Charles Butler (London 1809).

The received history of the law of joint tenancy traces its origin to a sort of medieval conceptualism.[9] Feudal overlords were entitled to certain services which were thought of as issuing from the land of their vassals. The land itself, or rather its associated legal concept, "the estate," owed the services, not the transient persons who happened to occupy the land or hold the estate at any particular time. There was then a legal reason for keeping estates undivided, the same reason that supported a policy of primogenitary inheritance. An estate that was granted to two or more persons was, therefore, presumed to remain intact. The legal expression of this presumption was the joint tenancy which, by means of its associated right of survivorship, preserved the undivided estate until there was only one survivor. As Chief Justice Holt expressed it: "Joint tenancies were favoured, for the law loves not fractions of estates, nor to divide and multiply tenures."[10] Not until statutes were passed during the reign of King Henry VIII was a joint tenant able to compel a partition in kind, that is, a separation of the estate into divided shares, thereby eliminating the right of survivorship.[11]

As feudalism decayed, the joint tenancy found a new role, one that also favored the right of survivorship. Among the services owed by feudal estates were charges payable to the overlord on succession at death (relief),[12] as well as opportunities for profit by the overlord in case the heir was underage (wardship[13] and marriage[14]). Other disadvantages of feudal landholding included lack of the power to devise and inflexibility in the types of future interests, as well as a widow's right to dower.[15] All these could be avoided by the feoffment to uses in which equitable ownership was separated from legal ownership; the estate was transferred to a legal owner who held "for the use of" the beneficial owner, who thereby avoided the onerous duties and restraints.

Since feudal incidents still attached to the legal owner, it was necessary to avoid succession on death and inheritance by a minor, as well as dower rights. Here the

---

9   See generally Anne L. Spitzer, Joint Tenancy with Right of Survivorship: A Legacy from Thirteenth Century England, 16 *Tex. Tech. L. Rev.* 629 (1985).

10   *Fisher v. Wigg*, 1 Salk. 391, 392, 91 Eng. Rep. 339, 340 (K.B. 1701).

11   31 Hen. 8, c. 1 (1539); 32 Hen. 8, c.32 (1540).

12   2 *Bl. Com.* 65–66.

13   The overlord was entitled to "the custody of the body and lands of such heir, without any account of the profits, till the age of twenty one in males, and sixteen in females." 2 *Bl. Com.* 67.

14   The overlord had "the power of disposing of his infant ward in matrimony." That this was seen as primarily a profit-making opportunity is demonstrated by the rule that wards who refused suitable matches "forfeited the value of the marriage, *valorem maritagii*, to their guardian; that is, so much as a jury would assess, or any one would *bona fide* give to the guardian for such an alliance: and, if the infants married themselves without the guardian's consent, they forfeited double the value, *duplicem valorem maritagii*." 2 *Bl. Com.* 70.

15   Dower entitled a widow to "the third part of all the lands and tenements whereof [her husband] was seized during the coverture, to hold to herself for the term of her natural life." 2 *Bl. Com.* 129.

joint tenancy could be of service. By enfeoffing a group of joint tenants, one could postpone succession at death; the right of survivorship maintained the estate until the death of the last to die.[16] Indeed, by periodic transfers to still more joint tenants, one could – barring bungling or major catastrophes – keep the legal estate from passing at death indefinitely. The arrangement resembles modern trusts, for which, incidentally, joint tenancies remain useful.[17] The prevalence of joint tenancies in feoffments to uses reinforced the older expectation that concurrent ownership would be accompanied by a right of survivorship. Ironically, while the original preference for survivorship was based on a desire to maintain feudalism, the subsequent frequency of joint tenancies in feoffments to uses was designed to subvert it.

The Statute of Uses (1535),[18] which transformed ("executed") equitable estates into legal ones,[19] and the final extinction of feudal dues by the Statute of Tenures (1660)[20] eliminated the justification for the presumption in favor of joint tenancies. And the Statute of Wills (1540),[21] which provided a reliable way to direct succession at death, offered an alternative to the traditional device of creating a present interest with an associated right of survivorship. Nonetheless, legal inertia was sufficient to maintain the presumption in favor of the joint tenancy, just as it preserved the Rule in Shelley's Case, despite the lawyers' recognition that the situation had changed.[22] Lord Chancellor Hardwicke noted that "Lord Coke says that jointenancy is favoured because the law is against the division of tenures, but as tenures are many of them taken away, and in a great measure abolished, that reason ceases."[23] During these centuries neither the law courts nor parliament were active law reformers. The common law's antiquity was prized; continuity was favored over change. Practical lawyers served their clients in these years by knowing the rules and using them to achieve their purposes, by indirection if necessary.

---

16   See Plucknett, *History of the Common Law* 580 ("The commonest way of creating a use was by conveying the land to a number of joint-tenants; the advantage of this was greater security, since it was less likely that several feoffees would all turn out to be dishonest, while at the same time the rule of survivorship was a great convenience since neither dower nor feudal incidents attached upon the death of a joint-tenant....").

17   Most states today recognize a presumption in favor of joint tenancy when legal title is held by two or more trustees. See, e.g., Ind. Code Ann. § 32-1-2-8; Mich. Comp. Laws Ann. § 554.45; N.Y. Estates, Powers and Trusts Law § 6-2.2(a); Vt. Stat. Ann. tit. 27, § 2.

18   27 Hen. 8, c. 10 (1535).

19   The Statute of Uses specifically provided that dower could still be barred by a jointure, an estate for life held by a wife jointly with her husband (or a wife's sole life estate). 27 Hen. 8, c. 10, § 6.

20   12 Car. 2, c. 24 (1660).

21   32 Hen. 8, c. 1 (1540).

22   Sir Edward Coke explained the priority of the right of survivorship over the freedom of testation by saying that "the survivour claymeth by the first feoffor... and therefore in judgment of law his title is paramount the title of the devisee." *Co. Litt.* § 287, p. 185b. See also 4 *Kent Com.* 513 (same).

23   *Hawes v. Hawes*, 1 Wils. 165, 165, 95 Eng. Rep. 552, 552 (Ch. 1747).

By the time of Blackstone, the law concerning joint tenancy could be confidently laid down: "Now, if an estate be given to a plurality of persons, without adding any restrictive, exclusive, or explanatory words, as if an estate be granted to A and B and their heirs, this makes them immediately joint-tenants in fee of the lands."[24] By the mid-eighteenth century, however, social and legal conditions had so changed that Blackstone readily conceded that "in general it is advantageous for the joint-tenants to dissolve the jointure; since thereby the right of survivorship is taken away, and each may transmit his own part to his own heirs."[25] Voluntary partition was the simplest and most efficient means, but the Henrician legislation provided for compulsory partition on demand as well.

By the time of American Independence, common law lawyers had expended considerable ingenuity in preventing the creation of joint tenancies despite the formal presumption in their favor, and several remnants of these efforts remain to puzzle lawyers to this day. The common law presumption in favor of joint tenancies was not applied with equal force to wills, which achieved legal recognition after the basic law of joint tenancy was settled and for which the primary rule was to effectuate the testator's intention. In the case of a will, Blackstone could recognize a counter-presumption: "The devisor may be presumed to have meant what is most beneficial to both the devisees,"[26] that is, something other than a joint tenancy.

The phrase "share and share alike," still frequently encountered in deeds and wills creating an interest in two or more persons, was construed to be an expression of intention against joint tenancy.[27] The reason, which may well escape modern lawyers, was that it could be considered inconsistent with an intention that each grantee or devisee holds the whole interest, a requirement for a joint tenancy.[28] The rigors of the Doctrine of the Four Unities, today often taken to exemplify the excessive formalism of earlier law, actually served a practical purpose in its day. Although the presumption in favor of joint tenancy could not at the time be overturned by direct means, it could be undermined by a strict application of the letter of the law. The slightest deviation from any of the required unities was used to defeat – in effect, to reverse – the presumption, so the phrase "share and share alike" could be taken to indicate a preference for a tenancy in common.

Thus the law of joint tenancy stood on the eve of the American Revolution: an historically embedded presumption in favor of joint tenancy, undercut by

---

24   2 *Bl. Com.* 180. Blackstone took it for granted that A and B were not a married couple. For the common law marital estate, see Chapter 4, Tenancy by the Entirety: Adapting to Change.

25   2 *Bl. Com.* 187. "Jointure" here means simply "joint tenancy," not the provision made for a widow in the form of an estate for life held by a wife jointly with her husband.

26   Id. 193.

27   See, e.g., 1 *Webster's Real Estate Law in North Carolina* § 7-3, p. 187 ("where an instrument provides that land shall be held by the tenants 'equally' or that they are to 'share and share alike,' a tenancy in common is created").

28   See Thomas M. Cooley, What Constitutes a Gift to a Class, 49 *Harv. L. Rev.* 903, 922 (1936).

hypertechnical requirements that in many cases nullified the effect of that presumption. So complex a system could be handled with success only by a highly skilled corps of legal operatives. In the newly independent American states, legal advice was less readily available and less technically competent than in England; in addition, landholdings were smaller and more dispersed, and landholders less likely routinely to rely on professional counselors. Finally, the political break caused by the Revolution created an opening for sweeping law reform.[29] Inherited legal practices such as primogeniture and joint tenancies attracted particular criticism. Primogeniture, where it still existed in America, was speedily abolished.[30] Partible inheritance, giving equal shares to all heirs of the same degree of kinship, greatly increased the potential for plural ownership; no consideration was given to recognizing joint tenancies in such cases.

Joint tenancy law, as such, was speedily reformed in some states by statutes abolishing the right of survivorship. A wide-ranging North Carolina statute of 1784 that ended primogeniture and altered many other common law rules explained the motive for remodeling what had long been the premier form of concurrent ownership: "In real and personal estate held in join-tenancy the benefit of survivorship is a manifest injustice to the families of such as may happen to die first,"[31] which can only mean that widows and orphans were deprived of what they (and the larger political community) thought were their reasonable expectations, probably because the presumption in favor of joint tenancies had caused the deceased to hold the property with another or others in joint tenancy. In an early Ohio case refusing to recognize the estate of joint tenancy, the court declared: "The reasons which gave rise to this description of estate in England, never existed with us. The *jus accrescendi* is not founded in principles of natural justice, nor in any reasons of policy applicable to our society or institutions."[32] Similar concerns seem to have motivated a judge in Connecticut, where the right of survivorship had been abolished,[33] to denounce it as "odious and unjust."[34] Without the associated right of survivorship, of course, there existed, as the same Connecticut judge observed, "no essential difference between the rights of joint tenants and tenants in common."[35]

---

29   See John v. Orth, After the Revolution: "Reform" of the Law of Inheritance, 10 *Law & Hist. Rev.* 33 (1992); Stanley Katz, Republicanism and the Law of Inheritance in the American Revolutionary Era, 76 *Mich. L. Rev.* 1 (1977).

30   See C. Shammas, M. Salmon & M. Dahlin, *Inheritance in America: From Colonial Times to the Present* 32–33 (1987).

31   Act of 1784, ch. 22, § 6, reprinted in 24 *The State Records of North Carolina* 574 (Walter Clark ed. 1904). In early sources the estate of joint tenancy was referred to as "jointenancy" or "joyntenancy." See *Co. Litt.* § 277, p. 180a; Joseph Story, *Commentaries on the Law of Partnership* 4 (1841).

32   *Seargent v. Steinberger*, 2 Ohio 305 (1826).

33   Conn. Gen. Stat. § 47-14a.

34   *Whittelsey v. Fuller*, 11 Conn. 337, 339 (1836).

35   Id. Technically, it is not true that the right of survivorship is the *only* essential difference between joint tenancy and tenancy in common. Each joint tenant theoretically

The rout of the joint tenancy was never complete. The North Carolina statute abolishing the right of survivorship in general nonetheless preserved it in cases of business partnerships,[36] where it provided useful continuity of title to property, a function today performed by the tenancy in partnership under the Uniform Partnership Act.[37] In all states trustees, like the old feoffees to uses, are still presumed to hold title as joint tenants for the same reason; likewise for joint executors, joint administrators, and other joint fiduciaries.

Even outside the business context the right of survivorship proved almost impossible to extirpate. The Pennsylvania Act of 1812,[38] for example, which seemed to do away with the right of survivorship in the most unqualified terms (except as to trust estates), was soon construed not to prevent its creation if the grantor plainly expressed the necessary intention.[39] In Connecticut, the statute abolishing the "odious and unjust" right of survivorship was held to apply to the estate only as it arose by operation of law from unqualified grants to a plurality of persons. A right of survivorship could still be intentionally created by adding to the grant the phrase "as joint tenants."[40] For example, to use the hypothetical conveyance given by Blackstone, a grant "to A and B and their heirs," which would have created a joint tenancy with right of survivorship at common law, no longer did so; but a grant "to A and B and their heirs *as joint tenants*" would create a fully functional joint tenancy. To paraphrase a famous quip about the judicial interpretation of the Statute of Uses: this reform of the law of joint tenancy had no more effect than to add three words to the form of the grant.[41] In North Carolina, courts came to

---

holds the entire estate, subject to the equal right of all other joint tenants, while the tenant in common holds only a share of the common estate, albeit an undivided share. It would probably be true to say, however, that the right of survivorship is the only *practical* difference.

36   N.C. Gen. Stat. § 41-2 (2007). This proviso apparently incorporates pre-existing common law. See *Lake v. Craddock*, 3 P. Wms. 158, 24 Eng. Rep. 1011 (Ch. 1732). See also Chantal Stebbings, Jus Accrescendi Inter Mercatores Locum Non Habet, 5 *J. Legal Hist.* 152 (1984).

37   6 U.L.A. 1 (1969).

38   Act of 1812, codified in Pa. Stat. Ann. tit. 68, § 110. Credit for the adoption of the Act of 1812 was attributed to John Bannister Gibson, then serving in the Pennsylvania legislature, later an influential chief justice of the Pennsylvania Supreme Court. *Dictionary of American Biography* 254 (Allen Johnson & Dumas Malone eds 1931).

39   *In re Lowry's Estate*, 171 A. 878 (Pa. 1934) (construing Act of 1812 as rule of construction not rule of law). The phrase normally used to create a survivorship estate in Pennsylvania is "to the grantees as joint tenants with right of survivorship and not as tenants in common." *In re Estate of Michael*, 218 A.2d 338 (Pa. 1966).

40   Conn. Gen. Stat. Ann. § 47-14a.

41   Referring to the Statute of Uses (1535), Lord Hardwicke had quipped:

> Yet the judges still adhered to the doctrine, that there could be no such thing as an use upon an use, but where the first use was declared, there it was executed, and must rest for that estate: therefore, on a limitation to A. and his heirs, to the use

recognize an anomalous right of survivorship created by a so-called "contract,"[42] a theory abandoned only in 1990 when legislation expressly resurrected the joint tenancy, so long as the grantor used the words "in joint tenancy with the right of survivorship"[43] – adding yet a few more words to the form of the grant.

In jurisdictions that have truly abolished the common law right of survivorship, courts have permitted parties to create a functional equivalent, usually in the form of alternative contingent remainders following an estate for joint lives.[44] In schematic form, the grant would run "to A and B for their joint lives, then to the survivor of them and to the survivor's heirs." The estate thus created resembles a joint tenancy in that possession is shared during life and the survivor ends up with the entire estate. The difference is that so long as both are alive, neither can eliminate the survivorship right of the other. In such cases, the statutes are construed not to prohibit the right of survivorship *and anything like it*, but simply to eliminate the right of survivorship that once arose by operation of law as an incident of joint tenancy. These decisions seem to be influenced by a desire to effectuate expressed intention and to facilitate a reasonable arrangement. They may also reflect the residual influence of the common law: what the common law permitted, even encouraged, for so many centuries cannot be so bad that willing parties should be denied its equivalent, in the absence of a clear legislative prohibition. Ironically, the effect is somewhat like returning to the condition before the time of King Henry VIII, when joint tenancies were not subject to partition.

States that did not address the problem of the joint tenancy until later tended to favor a different solution: rather than trying to do away with the right of survivorship, they simply reversed the common law presumption in favor of joint tenancies.[45] Grants to a plurality of persons, "to A and B and their heirs," are presumed in such states not to be in joint tenancy, but in tenancy in common. In these

---

of B. and his heirs, in trust for D., B.'s estate was held there to be executed by the statute, and D. took nothing.

Of this construction equity took hold, and said that the intention was to be supported. It is plain B. was not intended to take, his conscience was affected. To this the reason of mankind assented, and it has stood on this foot ever since, and by this means a statute made upon great consideration, introduced in a solemn and pompous manner, by this strict construction, has had no other effect than to add at most three words to a conveyance.

Hopkins v. Hopkins, 1 Atk. 591, 26 Eng. Rep. 371–72 (Ch. 1738). See also 2 *Bl. Com.* 336.

42   E.g., *Vettori v. Fay*, 137 S.E.2d 810 (N.C. 1964).

43   N.C. Gen. Stat. § 41-2 (2007). See John *v.* Orth, The Joint Tenancy Makes a Comeback in North Carolina, 69 *N.C. L. Rev.* 491 (1991). Arguably the North Carolina "joint tenancy with the right of survivorship" is not the common law joint tenancy, which lost its right of survivorship in 1784, but a new, statutorily created concurrent estate. Id. 499, n. 34.

44   E.g., *Runions v. Runions*, 207 S.W.2d 1016 (Tenn. 1948).

45   See, e.g., Ill. Ann. Stat. ch. 76, para. 1 (originally adopted in 1827).

jurisdictions, courts have faced the question how far to take the new presumption. While insisting on clear expressions of intention by parties seeking joint tenancies, often in the form of the stereotyped phrases used in the statutes, these courts have not displayed a generalized hostility to joint tenancies as such. Other technical requirements for the creation of joint tenancies, notably the Doctrine of the Four Unities, have not in such cases been aggressively applied.[46]

The newfound sympathy for the old joint tenancy, specifically for the right of survivorship, is explained by the popularity of devices, commonly referred to as "will substitutes," that provide a convenient method of transmitting property at death, avoiding the delays and expenses incident to probate.[47] Joint tenancies in real estate are not alone: joint accounts at financial institutions and securities firms are commonplace. Joint-and-survivor bank accounts, in particular, have been hailed as a simple and inexpensive means of arranging for succession at death, as (in short) "the poor man's will."[48] It may be, too, that the increasing prevalence of unmarried persons holding property together contributes to the renewed demand for joint tenancy. For married couples, the tenancy by the entirety (usually limited to realty) was historically available and remains an option in about half the states.[49] Again, the familiarity with joint tenancies derived from study of the common law seems to have influenced the result.

The law of joint tenancy has outlasted feudalism and the commercial, industrial, and social revolutions that succeeded it. This remarkable stability suggests that joint tenancy law, at least its essential feature of the right of survivorship, satisfies some near-permanent societal demand, although the exact nature of that demand has changed over time.[50] Secondary factors also account for the perceived continuity. Long familiarity with joint tenancy as an integral part of the common law of property helps to perpetuate the estate. Also, while the general features of joint tenancy law may satisfy societal demands, the details of that law in individual, highly particularized cases are relatively undetermined. One specific result may relate to general doctrine as well as another, permitting judges in individual cases to do justice as they see fit.

When the demands of justice or the felt needs of society do not influence the result, the judges sensibly fall back on well-established precedent. Precedent's

---

46   See, e.g., *Tindall v. Yeats*, 64 N.E.2d 903 (Ill. 1946) (agreement concerning exclusive use by one joint tenant did not sever joint tenancy); *Biggers v. Crook*, 656 S.E.2d 835 (Ga. 2008) (deed to secure debt executed by one joint tenant did not sever joint tenancy); *Estate of Quick*, 905 A.2d 471 (Pa. 2006) (severance not implied from separate leases executed individually by all joint tenants).

47   See 4 *Thompson on Real Property* § 1779, p. 29 (1979 replacement ed. by John S. Grimes).

48   See *In re Estate of Michaels*, 132 N.W.2d 557 (Wis. 1965). See also Note, Disposition of Bank Accounts: The Poor Man's Will, 53 *Colum. L. Rev.* 103 (1953).

49   For a listing see 4 *Thompson on Real Property* § 33.06, n. 110.

50   Recent threats to the joint tenancy and their rebuff are described in John v. Orth, The Perils of Joint Tenancies, 44 *Real Prop., Tr. & Est. L.J.* 427 (2009).

principal purpose in the decision of individual cases is to direct the attention of the judge away from the particularities of the parties and the specifics of the given dispute. Its broader social purpose, of course, is to secure the first rule of justice, that like cases be decided alike. Application of a rule dating to Coke and Littleton resolves the case without obvious judicial creativity and reinforces in the process legal predictability. It also, of course, reinforces the stability of doctrine.

Chapter 4
Tenancy by the Entirety: Adapting to Change[1]

> Now, although we act as one person, we are, in point of fact, two persons….
> It is a legal fiction, and legal fictions are solemn things….
> It's all very well to say we act as one person, but when you supply us with only one
> ration between us, I should describe it as a legal fiction carried a little too far.
>
> W.S. Gilbert

Sir William Blackstone entitled one chapter of his survey of English property law in the mid-eighteenth century "Estates in Severalty, Joint-Tenancy, Coparcenary, and Common."[2] "We come now to treat of estates," he magisterially commenced, "with respect to the number and connexions of their owners, the tenants who occupy and hold them."[3] Considered in this regard, estates, Blackstone observed, "may be held in four different ways: in severalty, in joint-tenancy, in coparcenary, and in common."[4] Tenancy in severalty was sole ownership, for Blackstone "the most common and usual way of holding an estate."[5] To this form of ownership he devoted few words: "There is little or nothing peculiar to be remarked concerning it, since all estates are supposed to be of this sort, unless where they are expressly declared to be otherwise."[6] Most of his remarks were therefore directed to estates with more than one owner, what today would be called concurrent estates, which Blackstone explicitly described as "the other three species of estates, in which there are always a plurality of tenants":[7] joint tenancy, tenancy in coparcenary, and tenancy in common.

---

1   An earlier version of this chapter appeared under the title Tenancy by the Entirety: The Strange Career of the Common Law Marital Estate in 1996 *BYU L. Rev.* 35.

2   *2 Bl. Com.* 179.

3   Id. The common law did not at first use the concept of "ownership" with respect to land, preferring to describe those with interests in real property as "tenants" a word derived from the Latin for "holders." What was held was, therefore, a "tenancy." See Simpson, *History of the Land Law* 47–48.

4   *2 Bl. Com.* 179.

5   Id. Despite the Commentator's unqualified assertion that ownership in severalty is "the most common and usual way of holding an estate," aristocratic estates were in fact usually tied up in strict settlements, by which legal title to land was held by trustees as joint tenants for the benefit of family members.

6   Id. According to the pioneering legal anthropologist, Sir Henry Maine, "It is more than likely that joint-ownership, and not separate ownership, is the really archaic institution." Henry Maine, *Ancient Law* 152–53 (1861).

7   *2 Bl. Com.* 179.

Of the three concurrent estates, Blackstone gave pride of place to the historic joint tenancy, at common law the preferred and presumed form of concurrent ownership. Blackstone catalogued the four unities of the joint tenancy, usually summarized as time, title, interest, and possession. The unities remain relevant to this day wherever joint tenancies are found, not only for determining whether a joint tenancy has been created but also for determining whether a severing event has occurred, one that transforms the joint tenancy into a tenancy in common. Describing the unity of possession, he repeated a time-hallowed phrase in the archaic dialect of Law French: "Joint tenants are said to be seised *per my et per tout*,"[8] by the share and by all. "That is," he explained, "they each of them have the entire possession, as well of every *parcel* as of the *whole*."[9] From the unity of the joint tenancy comes what Blackstone labeled the "grand incident of joint estates; *viz*. the doctrine of *survivorship*,"[10] by which the entire estate continues in the surviving joint tenants until only one remains and the estate returns to a severalty.

The ancient estate in coparcenary occupied Blackstone next. This estate arose when land descended from an ancestor to two or more persons, an eventuality which, apart from the prevalence of wills, occurred only about half as often in his day as in ours because the first-born male then inherited to the exclusion of all others.[11] At common law, multiple heirs meant inheritance by or through females: daughters, sisters, aunts, female cousins, or their representatives. Today the tenancy in coparcenary is subsumed in the tenancy in common.[12]

At last, the Commentator reached the third form of concurrent ownership, the tenancy in common. For him, it was a sort of default tenancy, what multiple owners had when either a joint tenancy or a tenancy in coparcenary was destroyed, or when a special limitation in a deed or will to two or more persons managed to escape the common law presumption in favor of a joint tenancy. For the latter, incidentally, Blackstone recommended a seemingly redundant form of words still commonly used: "*as tenants in common, and not as joint-tenants*."[13]

---

8   Id. 182. The Law French word *my*, equivalent to the English *moiety*, means generally "share" or, more particularly, "half." Because joint tenants at common law hold equal interests, Blackstone translated the phrase *per my et per tout* as "by the *half* or *moiety*, and by *all*." Id. If there are more than two joint tenants, however, each holds "by the equal share and by the whole" (author's translation).

9   Id.

10   Id. 183.

11   Of the seven common-law canons of inheritance, the first three operated together to produce the result in favor of the first-born male, often described as the law of primogeniture: (1) "inheritances shall lineally descend to the issue of the person last actually seised, *in infinitum*; but shall never lineally ascend," id. 208; (2) "the male issue shall be admitted before the female," id. 212; (3) "where there are two or more males in equal degree, the eldest only shall inherit; but the females all together," id. 214.

12   See 4 *Thompson on Real Property* § 35.08.

13   2 *Bl. Com.* 194 (italics in original).

In the first edition of the *Commentaries* in 1765–1769, as apparently in the decade of lectures that preceded it, and in all the editions that followed it during his lifetime, Blackstone made mention of no other concurrent estate. Only in the posthumous edition of 1783, prepared by Richard Burn, did another estate intrude and then only in a single sentence, awkwardly inserted in the discussion of the joint tenancy:

> And therefore, if an estate in fee be given to a man and his wife, they are neither properly joint-tenants, nor tenants in common: for husband and wife being considered as one person in law, they cannot take the estate by moieties, but both are seised of the entirety, *per tout et non per my*; the consequence of which is, that neither the husband nor the wife can dispose of any part without the assent of the other, but the whole must remain to the survivor.[14]

The unnamed estate here referred to by Blackstone for the first time later became commonly known as the tenancy by the entirety because of its undivided and indivisible seisin. Over the years that followed, in all the multitude of editions of the *Commentaries* prepared by a myriad of editors, the developing body of law concerning the tenancy by the entirety had to appear as a gloss on this solitary sentence.

The fractured foundation on which the law of tenancy by the entirety was subsequently built is revealed in Blackstone's one-sentence afterthought. The reason the logical Commentator had excluded the marital estate from his original discussion of concurrent ownership was simply that he did not think of it as an estate with a "plurality of tenants." Husband and wife were "one person in law," so the marital estate was not a concurrent estate at all, but rather a peculiar form of tenancy in severalty, a legal fiction of the most solemn kind. Both husband and wife were seised of the entirety, which meant that there were no shares (moieties) to speak of. For this reason, the marital tenancy could not be a joint tenancy, let alone a tenancy in common.

The effect of this legal fiction was neatly summarized and the distinction from the joint tenancy clearly demarcated by the modification of the Law French tag that described the seisin of joint tenants as *per my et per tout*; tenants by the

---

14   2 William Blackstone, *Commentaries on the Laws of England* 182 (Richard Burn ed. 1783). Burn disclaimed making any changes of his own in the text:

> The editor judges it indispensable to preserve the author's text intire. The alterations which will be found therein, since the publication of the last edition, were made by the author himself, as may appear from a corrected copy in his own handwriting. What the editor hath chiefly attended to is, to note the alterations made by subsequent acts of parliament. These, together with some few other necessary observations, in order to prevent confusion, are inserted separate and distinct at the bottom of the page.

Richard Burn, *Advertisement* 1 id. xi (footnote omitted).

entirety held, by contrast, *per tout et non per my*. In consequence, "neither the husband nor the wife can dispose of any part without the assent of the other."[15] Not having a share at all, it necessarily followed that neither had an alienable share. In fact, the only reason shares are recognized in joint tenancies is that each joint tenant has something to alienate; title, interest, and possession in that estate are undivided. Finally, in the tenancy by the entirety, "the whole must remain to the survivor."[16] Functionally, this is a right of survivorship, but it is not the same as that "grand incident of joint estates" mentioned by Blackstone for the simple reason that the tenancy by the entirety was not for him a joint estate at all. It was in law always a severalty.

The marital estate was paradoxically a severalty with two owners. There was only one tenant, who happened to be a couple – what the literary lawyer W.S. Gilbert later mocked as "a legal fiction carried a little too far."[17] Although the concept could be thus encapsulated, it posed constant problems in practice – reminiscent of Lord Macnaghten's comment on Lord Thurlow's attempt to put the Rule in Shelley's Case in a nutshell: "It is one thing to put a case like Shelley's in a nutshell and another thing to keep it there."[18] Given that each owned all in a tenancy by the entirety, who had the right of use? And who was entitled to any rents or profits? In a joint tenancy the answer was simple: Each joint tenant has an equal right. Another question which was closely related and often of critical importance: What were the rights of creditors in a tenancy by the entirety? In a joint tenancy, creditors had all the rights of the indebted tenant, including the power to alienate or to compel a partition or a sale and division of the proceeds.

The conceptual difficulty in answering these quotidian questions with respect to the tenancy by the entirety stemmed from the fact that the law was trying to perform a particularly difficult form of doublethink: to think about two persons as though they were one. Although Blackstone elsewhere categorically declared that during marriage "the very being and existence of the woman is suspended,"[19] he could not consistently maintain that legal fiction, as he himself candidly admitted: "Neither the husband nor the wife can dispose of any part without the assent of the other."[20] She may have been a nonperson in some sense, but for a sale her separate assent was required.[21] The problem inevitably suggested comparison to

---

15   2 id. 182.

16   Id.

17   W.S. Gilbert, *The Gondoliers* act 2, 1. 44 (1889), in *The Complete Annotated Gilbert and Sullivan* 921 (Ian Bradley ed. 1996).

18   *Van Grutten v. Foxwell*, 1897 App. Cas. 658, 671 (Eng.).

19   2 *Bl. Com.* 433.

20   2 William Blackstone, *Commentaries on the Laws of England* 182 (Richard Burn ed. 1783).

21   2 *Bl. Com.* 432 ("But, though our law in general considers man and wife as one person, yet there are some instances in which she is separately considered; as inferior to him, and acting by his compulsion. And therefore all deeds executed, and acts done, by her, during her coverture, are void, or at least voidable; except it be a fine, or the like

that other great class of person-nonpersons: slaves – and antebellum feminists made the most of it.[22]

Whatever the theoretical deficiencies, answers to the practical questions had to be found. Courts recognized the right of use in the husband, even to the exclusion of the wife.[23] Rents and profits, too, were the husband's with no duty to account to the wife.[24] By marriage the two had become one, the cruel quip ran, and "the husband was the one."[25] From this point, it was just a small step to recognizing the rights of creditors, at least the husband's creditors. If the husband was entitled to rents and profits and if he had the exclusive right of use during his lifetime, why not extend these rights to his creditors? A few courts went that far.[26] The wife's interest was whittled down, in other words, from "seisin of the entirety" to a mere indefeasible right of survivorship. As one court frankly conceded, "It is possible that a wife might receive no benefits at all from land held by the entireties if she predeceases her husband."[27] Blackstone's tenancy by the entirety, in which "neither the husband nor the wife can dispose of any part without the assent of the other," became in some states an alienable estate in the husband subject only to the wife's contingent (but indestructible) future interest. These answers had to be accepted by the married woman because she had no cause of action against her husband. The law heard no complaints because the injured party could not speak in a legally audible voice.

This state of affairs could exist, however, only so long as a married woman's legal existence remained in suspended animation. Passage of the married women's property acts in the middle decades of the nineteenth century shook the unstable foundations of the tenancy by the entirety. In some states, courts took the entirely logical position that once the rights of married women to hold property were recognized, the two were no longer one and there was no longer any such estate as tenancy by the entirety.[28] In England, the original home of the estate, after the

---

matter of record, in which case she must be solely and secretly examined, to learn if her act be voluntary."). "Fine," in this sense, refers not to a criminal punishment, but to a legal procedure allowing a married woman to transfer her property.

22   See. e.g., Sarah M. Grimke, *Letters on the Equality of the Sexes and the Condition of Woman Addressed to Mary S. Parker, President of the Boston Female Anti-slavery Society* 74–83 (1838) (comparing the legal condition of free women to slaves). See also Elizabeth B. Clark, Matrimonial Bonds: Slavery and Divorce in Nineteenth-Century America, 8 *Law & Hist. Rev.* 25 (1990).

23   See, e.g., *Voight v. Voight,* 137 N.E. 887 (Mass. 1925).

24   See, e.g., *Pineo v. White,* 70 N.E.2d 294 (Mass. 1946); *Childs v. Childs,* 199 N.E. 383 (Mass. 1936); *North Carolina Bd. of Architecture v. Lee,* 142 S.E.2d 643 (N.C. 1965).

25   Cribbet, *Property* 377.

26   See, e.g., *Raptes v. Cheros,* 155 N.E. 787 (Mass. 1927); *Lewis v. Pate,* 193 S.E. 20 (N.C. 1937).

27   *Dearman v. Bruns,* 181 S.E.2d 809, 811 (N.C. Ct. App. 1971).

28   See, e.g., *Cooper v. Cooper,* 76 Ill. 57 (1875); *Appeal of Robinson,* 33 A. 652 (Me. 1895); *Clark v. Clark,* 56 N.H. 105 (1875).

1882 Married Women's Property Act,[29] husband and wife seemingly held as joint tenants.[30] In 1925 the flickering flame was snuffed out altogether when the tenancy by the entirety was abolished.[31]

"The life of the law," as Oliver Wendell Holmes famously reminded us, "has not been logic,"[32] and in about half the American states the tenancy by the entirety persists,[33] despite the recognition of the legal capacity of married women with respect to property. It is only in those states that the tenancy by the entirety is a true concurrent estate, one in which (to use Blackstone's words) "there are always a plurality of tenants."[34] Rather than being a peculiar form of tenancy in severalty, the tenancy by the entirety became a peculiar form of joint tenancy. "An estate in entirety is an estate in joint tenancy," a Massachusetts judge flatly declared in 1893, "but with the limitation that during their joint lives neither the husband nor the wife can destroy the right of survivorship without the assent of the other party."[35] So far had the common law come since 1783 when Blackstone with equal assurance had added in his afterthought: "If an estate in fee be given to a man and his wife, they are neither properly joint-tenants, nor tenants in common."[36]

The forces that carried the tenancy by the entirety into the modern world included more than simple inertia, although that undoubtedly played a part. Perhaps some judges thought that married women still needed the protection of a male-dominated tenancy, that men were in general better suited to decide property questions, or simply that some legal rule was required to resolve intraspousal property disputes. Marriage is, after all, a democracy in which each spouse has one vote, and the one with the most votes wins. Clearly, some judges were loath to end the tenancy by the entirety on the uncertain trumpet of the married women's property acts, which did not explicitly refer to the estate. Finally, there may even have been a forward-looking concern to provide protection to marital property – to build, in other words, out of the scraps of common law an analog to the civil law system of community property, in which property acquired with the earnings of either spouse during marriage is treated as owned in equal undivided shares by husband and wife.[37]

---

29   Married Women's Property Act, 45 & 46 Vict., ch. 75 (1882).

30   See *In re March*, 27 Ch. D. 166 (1884) (dictum); see also Joshua Williams, *Principles of the Law of Real Property* 365 (T. Cyprian Williams ed., 17th ed. 1894).

31   Law of Property Act, 15 & 16 Geo. 5, ch. 20, § 39(6), sch. I (1925) (converting tenancy by entirety into joint tenancy).

32   Holmes, *Common Law* 1.

33   See *Thompson on Real Property* § 33.06(e) n. 81 (listing states).

34   2 *Bl. Com.* at 179.

35   *Morris v. McCarty*, 32 N.E. 938, 939 (Mass. 1893) (Allen, J.) (Justice Holmes joined in the unanimous opinion of the court).

36   2 William Blackstone, *Commentaries on the Laws of England* 182 (Richard Burn ed. 1783).

37   On the system of community property, see William A. Reppy, Jr. & Cynthia A. Samuel, *Community Property in the United States* (4th ed. 1994). The rules of community property apply to personal as well as real property.

Although verbally the tenancy by the entirety was equated with the joint tenancy, subject to the significant exception of the indefeasible right of survivorship, it remained a concurrent estate with strikingly different qualities. Well past the middle of the twentieth century, it was still male-dominated in a number of states.[38] Despite the married women's property acts, for many married women holding property with their husbands as tenants by the entirety, the husband was still "the one." This, of course, defied logic. What could the unities of title, interest, and possession, essential to the existence of a joint tenancy, mean when the husband had the right of use, even to the exclusion of the wife, the other co-owner? One court candidly admitted that "husband and wife do not 'share equally' in an estate by the entireties. The husband has the exclusive right during coverture to possession, control, and use of the land."[39]

The creative juices of the common law courts had now seemingly dried up, and legislative solutions were required. With glacial slowness, in a process not completed until late in the twentieth century, state after state legislated to equalize the rights of the spouses over property held in the tenancy by the entirety. In what was probably the last law of its type in the United States, North Carolina adopted the Tenancy by the Entirety Reform Act in 1982, which provided: "A husband and wife shall have an equal right to the control, use, possession, rents, income, and profits of real property held by them in tenancy by the entirety."[40] As the tenancy by the entirety now truly does approximate the joint tenancy, one would expect, incidentally, to see the same sort of remedies provided to one tenant by the entirety whose interest is injured by the other. In the future there may be suits by one spouse against the other for trespass or waste or for an accounting, just as for centuries there have been such suits by one joint tenant or tenant in common against another. The dilemma lurking in this development, of course, is that a tenant by the entirety lacks the easy escape hatch provided the joint tenant by the power of alienation and the right to partition.

The reconceptualization of the tenancy by the entirety as a form of joint tenancy has left some unanswered questions. What, for example, should be the effect of divorce on property held in tenancy by the entirety? Absent a severance, the ex-spouses still hold the property together as concurrent owners, and the unities of time, title, interest, and possession remain intact. It would not be at all illogical,

---

38   See, e.g., *D'Ercole v. D'Ercole*, 407 F. Supp. 1377 (D. Mass. 1976) (In property held in tenancy by the entirety, "the spouses do not have an equal right to control and possession of the property. The husband during his lifetime has paramount rights in the property.").

39   *Dearman v. Bruns*, 181 S.E.2d 809, 811 (N.C. Ct. App. 1971).

40   N.C. Gen. Stat. § 39–13.6(a) (1984). The section preserves the common-law restraint on individual alienation: "Neither spouse may bargain, sell, lease, mortgage, transfer, convey or in any manner encumber any property so held without the written joinder of the other spouse." Id. For a discussion of issues raised by the reform, see William A. Reppy, Jr., North Carolina's Tenancy by the Entirety Reform Legislation of 1982, 5 *Campbell L. Rev.* 1 (1982).

although it would certainly be impractical, to find that the specialized form of joint tenancy limited to married persons permutates at divorce into the ordinary form of joint tenancy, complete with a right of survivorship in each ex-spouse. At least one court has so held,[41] and many state legislatures,[42] not to mention the drafters of the Uniform Probate Code,[43] have taken the possibility seriously enough to provide explicitly for conversion into the more realistic tenancy in common.

Two situations involving the creation (or attempted creation) of a tenancy by the entirety reveal the legal muddle. Where a grantor deeds property to a husband, a wife, and a third party, the result may be, in states still recognizing the tenancy by the entirety, a one-half interest in the married couple as tenants by the entirety and a one-half interest in the third party, the two shares being held in tenancy in common.[44] The reason, firmly rooted in the old law, is that marriage made the two one and that the marital unit shares equally with the other grantee, a true integer.[45] This is, perhaps, "a legal fiction carried a little too far," one likely to baffle the intention of a modern grantor.

Where, in a case of more common occurrence, one spouse deeds property once held in severalty to both spouses together (as when a husband deeds to himself and his wife, or a wife deeds to herself and her husband), the result may not be a tenancy by the entirety at all, even if the grantor plainly expresses the intention to create that estate. The reason here was once consistent with that in the last case: the two have become one, therefore one of the two cannot grant anything to the two of them. "A man cannot grant any thing to his wife," Blackstone bluntly explained, "for the grant would be to suppose her separate existence."[46] A grant by the wife, a legal nonentity, was simply unimaginable.

As the tenancy by the entirety is conflated (not to say confused) with the joint tenancy, this result continues to be reached, but the reason shifts. To create the tenancy by the entirety, the requirements for the creation of the joint tenancy

---

41   See *Shepherd v. Shepherd*, 336 So. 2d 497 (Miss. 1976). This rule was reaffirmed in *Ayers v. Petro*, 417 So. 2d 912 (Miss. 1982).

42   See *Thompson on Real Property* § 31.08(c) nn. 365–372 (listing states).

43   See Unif. Probate Code § 2-804(b)(2) (1993) (applying to interests held as "joint tenants with the right of survivorship"); id. § 1–201(26) (defining "joint tenants with the right of survivorship" to include "co-owners of property held under circumstances that entitle one... to the whole of the property on the death of the other," that is, tenants by the entirety).

44   See, e.g., *Jenni v. Gamel*, 602 S.W.2d 696 (Mo. Ct. App. 1980); *Mosser v. Dolsay*, 27 A.2d 155 (N.J. Ch. 1942); *In re Buttonow*, 49 Misc. 2d 445 (N.Y. Sup. Ct. 1966); *In re Gardner*, 202 S.E.2d 318 (N.C. Ct. App. 1974).

45   The principle is traceable to the fifteenth century. *Litt.* § 291 ("Also, if a joint estate be made of land to a husband and wife and to a third person, in this case, the husband and wife have in law in their right but the moity, and the third person shall have as much as the husband and wife, viz. the other moity, etc. And the cause is, for that the husband and wife are but one person in law....").

46   1 *Bl. Com.* at 430.

– specifically the four unities – must also be met. Since at common law a joint tenancy cannot be created by a transfer from a grantor to the grantor and another because a self-transfer does not create the unities of time and title in the new owners,[47] the grant by one spouse to the two of them cannot be effective to create a tenancy by the entirety. Giving a bizarre twist to the argument, a few judges, uncomfortable with the result which obviously defeats intention, suggested that the unities are in fact present because the grant is from one spouse as an individual to the two spouses as a unit.[48] Judicial improvisation, however ingenious, proved insufficient in most states. The problem is taken seriously enough that a large majority of the states still recognizing the tenancy by the entirety have adopted statutes explicitly authorizing conveyances by one spouse to both as tenants by the entirety.[49]

What about the all-important question of creditors' rights? Creditors of one joint tenant can compel alienation or partition or a sale and division of the proceeds. A few states still recognizing tenancy by the entirety, feeling bound by the married women's property acts to enforce complete equality between the sexes, have recognized creditors' rights in the wife's interest, even in her right of survivorship,[50] but a sizeable number of states refuse any rights in the entirety property to the creditors of either spouse.[51] The traditional justification of the latter result is rooted in the notion of the unity of the married couple. If the two have indeed become one, then the only creditors who matter are the creditors of that one. (Of course, in the *Alice-in-Wonderland* logic of the tenancy by the entirety, the *one* in this case means the *two*.) In states that had recognized the rights of the husband's creditors, the same result may today be reached by the paradoxical means of reforming the tenancy by the entirety to recognize the wife's co-equal rights of use and to rents and profits. The result is now justified as protection of the marital property from the profligacy of one member of the marital unit.[52]

---

47   See, e.g., *Dolley v. Powers*, 89 N.E.2d 412 (Ill. 1949); *Stuehm v. Mikulski*, 297 N.W. 595 (Neb. 1941). This result has been reversed by statute in many states. See *Thompson on Real Property* § 31.06(c) (summarizing 30 statutes).

48   See, e.g., *Wollard v. Smith*, 94 S.E.2d 466, 469 (N.C. 1956) (stating that a married couple is "an entity separate from the individuals"); *In re Klatzl's Estate*, 110 N.E. 181, 185 (N.Y. 1915) (Collin, J., dissenting) ("The husband did not convey to himself, but to a legal unity or entity which was the consolidation of himself and another.").

49   See *Thompson on Real Property* § 33.06(c) (summarizing 17 statutes).

50   See, e.g., *King v. Greene*, 153 A.2d 49 (N.J. 1959).

51   See, e.g., *Sawada v. Endo*, 561 P.2d 1291, 1294-97 (Haw. 1977) (listing states).

52   Id. at 1297 (quoting *In re Estate of Wall*, 440 F.2d 215, 218 (D.C. Cir. 1971)). See also *United States v. Craft*, 535 U.S. 274 (2002) (Scalia, J., dissenting) (describing tenancy by the entirety as "a form of ownership that was of particular benefit to the stay-at-home spouse or mother. She is overwhelmingly likely to be the survivor that obtains title to the unencumbered property; and she (as opposed to her business-world husband) is overwhelmingly unlikely to be the source of the individual indebtedness against which a tenancy by the entirety protects.").

As with all jerry-built structures run up with the materials at hand, the tenancy by the entirety as a device to protect marital property is a haphazard affair. The marks of its making remain all too obvious. Holmes once illustrated the process of common law development with a striking biological simile: "Just as the clavicle in the cat only tells of the existence of some earlier creature to which a collar-bone was useful, precedents survive in the law long after the use they once served is at an end and the reason for them has been forgotten."[53] The clavicle in this particular cat is laid bare in the answer to one simple question: Why is the tenancy by the entirety limited in most states to land? After all, a great amount of family wealth is today held in personal, as opposed to real, property; in community property states no such distinction is drawn. Why should the common law protect only marital real estate from one spouse's improvidence? The answer (but not the reason) is because at common law the husband had complete dominion over his wife's personalty, unlimited by even the modest restraints imposed by the tenancy by the entirety on his control of the marital realty. Once married women gained control over their own personal property through the married women's property acts, the matter was at an end.[54] Not so with land held by the entirety (at least in those states in which the tenancy persists).

Today, no discussion of the tenancy by the entirety would be complete without addressing one final question: Why is the tenancy by the entirety still limited to married persons? The unity now produced by matrimony is, after all, considerably attenuated in practice as well as in theory, and there are pairs today that function as couples but that are not, for one reason or another, legally united. Why should the law – to use fashionable jargon – "privilege" one relationship above others? No combination of joint tenancy or tenancy in common plus contracts not to partition and to make a will can give the unmarried couple all the benefits automatically conferred on spouses holding property as tenants by the entirety. In fairness, it should be said that this question applies with equal force to any form of marital property, both to the civil law system of community property as well as to the common law estate of tenancy by the entirety. Should unmarried persons ever be allowed the benefits of the tenancy by the entirety (perhaps calling it by some other name), it would only add a new twist to the estate's already strange career.[55] Having survived the earthquake of the married women's property acts (at least in some states), the tenancy by the entirety could probably survive the shock.

---

53   Holmes, *Common Law* 35.

54   An exception to the rule of no holding of personalty in tenancy by the entirety is recognized in cases in which realty held in that estate is converted into its money value without the consent of both owners. The usual case of "involuntary conversion" occurs when real property is taken by condemnation. *See, e.g., Ronan v. Ronan,* 159 N.E.2d 653 (Mass. 1959).

55   See John v. Orth, Night Thoughts: Reflections on the Debate Concerning Same-Sex Marriage, 3 *Nev. L. J.* 560 (2003); John v. Orth, *In re* Married Couples, Common Law Marriages, and Same-Sex Partners: *Orth v. Orth,* 85 *N. D. L. Rev.* 287 (2009).

Over the years, the common law marital estate has evolved into its present shape. The legal existence of married women and their capacity to handle their own property has everywhere been recognized. The unfairness inherent in a male-dominated tenancy has also now been eliminated; insofar as interest and possession are concerned, the tenancy by the entirety is today indistinguishable from the joint tenancy. With respect to alienability and the right of survivorship, however, the tenancy by the entirety remains distinct. One tenant by the entirety cannot, acting alone, sever the estate, in effect withdrawing a one-half share and terminating the right of survivorship; so much seems owing to the special relationship between the parties. Creditors' rights are more troublesome. In many states, land may be protected to an unlimited extent from the creditors of either tenant by the entirety, but, in most states, no amount of personal property may be so shielded. In practice, however, the real estate that is protected is usually the marital residence, often compensating for a miserly homestead exemption. The exclusion of personal property from the ambit of the estate means that creditors usually have adequate assets available to them.

The common law marital estate is by no means perfect. Holmes was, of course, right about the life of the law not being logic. The tenancy by the entirety since Blackstone has been an awkward compromise, renegotiated in each generation, and only belatedly catching up with social reality. Today, no doubt, further adjustments are required. The only justification for the present system must be that people are familiar with it and that, by and large, it works. Perhaps we may console ourselves with the reflection that while Tabby may be endowed with a needless clavicle, she more often than not catches the mice.

Chapter 5
Leases: Misled by a Simile

O ye sons of men…,
how long will ye love vanity,
and seek after leasing.

Psalm 4

Leases of residential real estate nowadays include an implied covenant of habitability because leases "should be interpreted and construed like any other contract"[1] and contracts for the sale of consumer goods now include an implied warranty of fitness for use.[2] Because they are obligated under the covenant of habitability to keep the premises "fit and habitable" throughout the term, landlords today can be held liable in tort for injuries occurring on the leased premises.[3] Because contracts in violation of statutes are void, leases of premises in violation of applicable housing codes are also void, there being no reason "to treat a lease agreement differently from any other contract."[4] And landlords faced with an abandoning tenant have a duty to seek a replacement tenant because contract law imposes on an injured party a duty to mitigate damages and a lease is "essentially a contract rather than a conveyance."[5] Furthermore, if a lease is a contract "like any other," then abandonment by the tenant can be treated as "anticipatory breach."[6]

It was not always so. Until the middle of the twentieth century, it could be authoritatively asserted that "the tenant is a purchaser of an estate in land," not a

---

1   *Javins* v. *First Nat'l Realty Corp.*, 428 F.2d 1071, 1075 (U.S. Ct. App., D.C. Cir.), cert. denied, 400 U.S. 925 (1970). The Court of Appeals decision was authored by Judge J. Skelly Wright, educated in Louisiana, who observed: "The civil law has always viewed the lease as a contract, and in our judgment that perspective has proved superior to that of the common law." Id n. 13 (citing La. Civ. Code Ann. art. 2669).

2   Uniform Commercial Code §§ 2-314, 2-315 (1968).

3   See, e.g., *Sargent* v. *Ross*, 308 A.2d 528 (N.H. 1973).

4   *Brown* v. *Southall Realty Co.*, 237 A.2d 834, 837 (D.C. Ct. App. 1968), cert. denied, 393 U.S. 1018 (1969).

5   *United States Nat'l Bank of Oregon* v. *Homeland*, 631 P.2d 761, 763 (Or. 1981). See also *Richard Barton Enterprises, Inc.* v. *Tsern*, 928 P.2d 368 (Utah 1996) (holding that "principles of contract law rather than property law" govern the computation of damages for a tenant's breach of a lease). No real "duty to mitigate" is involved; rather, the party suffering the breach is disabled to recover damages from the breaching party to the extent that action by the former could have reduced the loss caused by the latter.

6   See 1 *Am. L. Prop.* 203–204 (citing acceptance of contract theory of anticipatory breach as evidence of the trend toward treating the lease as a contract as well as a conveyance).

promisee in a contract.[7] Conveyances were traditionally understood to be without implied terms; therefore, "there is no implied covenant or warranty that at the time the term commences the premises are in a tenantable condition or that they are adapted to the purpose for which leased."[8] It was for the tenant to determine whether the premises were suitable or to demand an express warranty of fitness. For the duration of the lease, that is, so long as the leasehold estate continued, the landlord was not liable for injuries occurring on the leased premises. "The basic rationale for lessor immunity has been that the lease is a conveyance of property which ends the lessor's control over the premises, a prerequisite to the imposition of tort liability."[9]

Just as the new concept of a lease as a contract has generated the covenant of habitability, so the older view of a lease as a conveyance had generated the covenant of quiet enjoyment, the landlord's duty not to interfere with the tenant's possession of the premises. By this logic, a conveyance was not illegal, although the uses to which the tenant put the premises could be. And in the case of tenant abandonment, the landlord had no duty to do anything and could simply "let the premises lie idle and collect rent."[10] In fact, this would seem to be required by the covenant of quiet enjoyment, so long as the landlord did not take action to terminate the lease.

Because the lease was a transfer of control, the landlord had no duty to maintain the premises during the term of the lease. In fact, it was the tenant who had some (minimal) duty of repair, in order to keep leased structures wind and water tight, so that they could be returned to the landlord at the termination of the lease in the condition they were in at the beginning, "ordinary wear and tear excepted." Failure by the tenant was remedied by the ancient action of waste, providing in extreme cases for forfeiture of the tenancy and treble damages.[11] Indeed, so thoroughgoing was the concept of the lease as a conveyance that damage to leased structures, even their complete destruction, did not relieve the tenant of the duty to pay the full rent.[12] With the conveyance of the estate, the tenant took the risk of loss.

---

7   The principal forms of conveyance at common law were feoffment, lease, grant, and mortgage. 3 Id. 215. Lease and release became a means of conveying a fee simple without feoffment and livery of seisin. See Digby, *History of the Law of Real Property* 261–62, 366–67.

8   1 *Am. L. Prop.* 267.

9   Schoshinski, *Am. Law L. & T.* § 4:1, p. 186. "Immunity" is an inapt term. If one person owes no duty to another who was injured, then there is no liability in tort. Ordinarily, this is not described as an immunity.

10   1 *Am. L. Prop.* 392.

11   Statute of Gloucester, 6 Ed. 1, c. 5 (1278). Modern versions include N.C. Gen. Stat. § 1 534ff. (2007).

12   E.g., *Arbenz* v. *Exley, Watkins & Co.*, 50 S.E. 813 (W.Va. 1905). See also *Am. Law L. & T.* § 10:7, p. 660. In America, an exception was made in case of destruction of upper story apartments. *Stockwell* v. *Hunter*, 52 Mass. (11 Met.) 448 (1846). The exception is not allowed in England. 1 *Am. L. Prop.* 398.

Of course, there were almost always some contractual elements to a lease. Revealingly, promises in leases were known (and continue to be known) not as promises but as "covenants." Never true covenants, that is, promises under seal – the lease is not a sealed instrument – covenants in leases nonetheless resembled their sealed counterparts by being unilateral,[13] or (as it was said in the law of leases) "independent." The independency of covenants meant that breach of a covenant by one party did not relieve the other party of the duty to perform. If, for example, a landlord failed to perform an express covenant to provide some service, such as to keep the roof in a state of good repair, the tenant was not thereby relieved of the duty to perform other covenants, such as the covenant to pay rent, but could sue for damages.[14]

In time, the tenant's covenant to pay rent came to be thought of as an exception to the independency of covenants. It was dependent on the landlord's covenant to leave the tenant in quiet enjoyment of the premises: rent for possession.[15] Even a partial eviction by the landlord relieved the tenant's entire duty to pay rent.[16] But historically the payment of rent was not thought of as the performance of a promise by the tenant. It was rather a sort of interest the landlord retained in the land, reflecting the old common law's discomfort with contract and preference for property interests.[17] Describing the historic understanding of rent, the eminent legal historians, Pollock and Maitland, concluded: "We may almost go the length of saying that the land pays it through [the tenant's] hand."[18] The rent was "reserved"

---

13   Promises under seal, technically known as "specialties," were unilateral in the sense that they were enforceable without consideration. With the triumph of the concept of contract as a "bargained for exchange," the enforceability of specialties was explained by the fiction, "the seal imports consideration." John Maxcy Zane, *The Story of Law* 271 (1927). The common law action to recover under sealed promises was called the action of covenant.

14   The theory of the independency of covenants sometimes worked in favor of the tenant. See *Foundation Devel. Corp.* v. *Loehmann's, Inc.*, 788 P.2d 1189, 1193 (Ariz. 1990) ("at common law a landlord could not dispossess a tenant who failed to keep his promise to pay rent [in the absence of an express condition in the lease], and had to be satisfied with damages for the breach") – which is why most leases convey not an unqualified term of years but a term of years subject to condition subsequent (the condition being the timely payment of rent), and why states have adopted statutes allowing termination for nonpayment of rent. E.g., N.C. Gen. Stat. § 42-3 (2007).

15   See 1 *Am. L. Prop.* 278; Schoshinski, *Am. Law L. & T.* § 3:13, p. 113.

16   *Smith* v. *McEnany*, 48 N.E. 781 (Mass. 1897).

17   See 2 Frederick Pollock & Frederic William Maitland, *The History of English Law* 127 (2nd ed. 1898) ("The landlord who demands the rent that is in arrear is not seeking to enforce a contract, he is seeking to recover a thing."). For a more general argument concerning the substitution of contract for property as the organizing principle of the common law, see John v. Orth, Contract and the Common Law, in *The State and Freedom of Contract* 44–65 (ed. Harry N. Scheiber, 1999).

18   Pollock & Maitland, *History of English Law* 131.

in the lease in much the same way (and in the same *reddendum* clause) that a vendor reserved an easement in a deed.[19]

In only one situation did the earlier law seem to take the idea of a lease as a contract seriously: the tenant's assignment to a third party of all the remaining term. Property interests are presumed to be transferable, so since the tenant was a "purchaser of an estate in land" and the lease a "conveyance of property," the law naturally recognized that the tenant had an alienable interest. (Of course, the lease could include a covenant against transfer by the tenant, although as a restraint on alienation it was subject to heightened judicial scrutiny.)[20] If the tenant assigned the interest, the assignee became liable to pay the rent and to perform other duties imposed by covenants running with the land.[21] The assignee was said, for want of a better term, to be in "privity of estate" with the landlord: when the lease terminated, possession reverted immediately to the landlord, not *mediately* through the tenant.[22] But the tenant, even after the assignment, remained liable, as a surety, on all the covenants in the lease. In time this was rationalized by saying that the tenant remained in "privity of contract" with the landlord.[23]

Treating the lease as a conveyance – except in case of assignment by the tenant – had obvious benefits for the landlord, but at one time treating the lease as a conveyance actually favored the tenant. Centuries ago, when the common law was young with a "highly developed land law, but no theory of contract,"[24] it was to the tenant's advantage to be recognized as having an estate in land, even if it was not a freehold estate. So uncomfortable was the common law, or rather the common law lawyers, with interests that were not somehow property interests that leases were categorized as "chattels real," rights derived from land and therefore in some sense real property though passing as personal property on succession at death – in any event property, not contract. Likewise, agreements for the purchase of

---

19   An easement had to be reserved, not excepted, because "so long as there is unity of ownership, there can be no easement," 2 George Thompson, *Commentaries on the Modern Law of Real Property* § 352, p. 305 (1980), so it had to be created when the fee was transferred.

20   Recognizing covenants against transfer as restraints on alienation helps to explain the otherwise surprising Rule in Dumpor's Case, 4 Co. Rep. 119, 76 Eng. Rep. 1110 (K.B. 1603) – the rule that covenants against transfer without consent are presumed to be single and entire, that is, that consent to one transfer makes consent to further transfers unnecessary.

21   Covenants running with the land are an unusual type of contract, "the unique example of the possibility of one being sued as a promisor upon a promise he has not made." Restatement (3d) Prop.: Servitudes, part III, intro. note, p. 3158 (1944).

22   This was thought to be required by the venerable Statute Quia Emptores, 18 Ed. 1 (1290), which ended the feudal practice of subinfeudation by providing that transfer of an entire interest substituted the transferee for the transferor, eliminating intervening estates.

23   See *United States Nat'l Bank of Oregon* v. *Homeland*, 631 P.2d 761, 765 (Or. 1981) ("The tenant, by abandoning the leased premises, forfeits his *estate* in the real property, but remains liable for damages for breach of contract….") (italics in original).

24   2 *H.E.L.* 355.

land, while they remained executory, were treated as transferring to the purchaser an actual, if equitable, title from the moment of execution under the doctrine of "equitable conversion."[25] They still are, which is why contracts for the sale of land are recordable as transfers of interests in real property.[26]

Ironically, there arrived a time when the legal security of the tenant for a term was actually superior to that of the owner in fee simple. The action of ejectment, which protected the tenant's right to possession, was much more rational and expeditious (because relatively newer) than the ancient and cumbersome procedure initiated by the writ of right to determine ultimate ownership of land. So, a plaintiff suing for title to Blackacre took advantage of the tenant's remedy by alleging that he had leased the land to John Doe, who had been ejected by someone claiming authority from the defendant. The caption of the case – there were thousands like it – read "Doe on the Demise [lease] of *Plaintiff v. Defendant*," usually shortened to "Doe on the Dem. of...," or even "Doe d...."[27] The judges were cooperative and refused to hear the defendant's answer unless the fictitious lease and ejectment were first admitted.[28] To this day, ejectment is the common name for the action to try title to real property.

The fact of the matter, of course, is that the lease is both a conveyance and a contract; or, if one prefers, "A lease is a contract which contains both property rights and contractual rights."[29] – with all the complications and confusions the combination produces. That it remains a conveyance is most noticeable in the fact that it, like the contract for the sale of land, is recordable in the local registry of deeds.[30] Fairly typical is the California statute: "Every conveyance of real property, other than a lease for a term not exceeding one year, is void as against any subsequent purchaser or mortgagee of the same property, or any part thereof, in good faith and for a valuable consideration, whose conveyance is first duly recorded."[31] A lease, in other words, is a conveyance and if for a term of more than one year, eligible for the protections afforded by the recording act.

That a lease is (or has become) a contract is evident in the modern confusion surrounding the application of the Statute of Frauds. The drafter of the seventeenth-

---

25   An equitable title could not, of course, be recognized unless the contract was specifically enforceable. For a discussion of the logic (or "philosophy") involved in the doctrine of equitable conversion, see Cardozo, *Judicial Process* 38–39.

26   See, e.g., N.C. Gen. Stat. § 47 18(a) (2007) (providing for recording of contracts to convey, as well as options to convey and leases of land for more than three years).

27   In a few states such as New Jersey and North Carolina the name of the fictitious tenant mutated to Den, so the caption became "Den on the Dem. of...."

28   3 *Bl. Com.* 199–206. For more on the creative power of legal fiction, see Chapter 11, Fiction: Pious Fraud.

29   *Strader* v. *Sunstates Corp.*, 500 S.E.2d 752, 756 (N.C. App. 1998).

30   See *Chandler* v. *Cameron*, 47 S.E.2d 528, 531 (N.C. 1948) (recording a personal contract, even if included in a recordable contract for the sale of land, does not give constructive notice because a personal contract is not "of a class which is authorized... to be recorded") (quoting 45 Am. Jur., Records and Recording Laws, § 107).

31   Cal. Civ. Code § 1214 (2001).

century English original, the root of all modern American versions, obviously thought leases and contracts were different things and dealt with them in distinct clauses.[32] Although both were subject to the memorable requirement of a "writing signed by the party to be charged therewith," the English statute applied to leases for a term of more than three years "from the making thereof," while contracts were addressed in the so-called *infra annum* clause, covering agreements not performable within one year "from the making thereof." American versions continue to treat leases and contracts separately, although many shorten the lease term to one year and omit the phrase "from the making thereof."[33]

The modern problem arises because of the almost inevitable practice in leasing of executing a lease at one time to commence at a later date, *in futuro*. Must such a lease satisfy the *infra annum* clause? The traditional understanding, not recognizing the lease as a contract, was that the tenant acquired a property interest, an *interesse termini* or "interest in a term," on execution of the lease (somewhat like the equitable title acquired by a purchaser on the execution of a contract for the sale of land), and a non-freehold estate when the term eventually commenced. Some courts continue to adhere to this view and, particularly if the limiting phrase "from the making thereof" has been omitted from the section on leases in their state statute, hold that the one-year period refers only to the term of the lease.[34] Other courts, convinced that leases are contracts ("like any other") as well as conveyances, take the view that a lease must satisfy the *infra annum* clause as well as the lease provision and hold that an oral lease for one year to commence *in futuro* is an invalid contract, if not an invalid lease, under the Statute of Frauds.[35]

Whenever an oral lease is invalid, what is to be done when the parties nonetheless attempt to perform? The parties, for example, orally agree to a lease for a term of five years and the "tenant" takes possession. It seems obvious that the "lease" makes the entry permissive, not trespassory. Subsequent payment of rent and its acceptance by the landlord mean that some kind of tenancy is recognized by the parties, so must be recognized by the law. The historic solution was the periodic tenancy, a non-freehold estate measured by the period for which rent was reserved and terminable by either party with notice to the other measured by the rental period, but never more than one year.[36] While not achieving all that

---

32   29 Car. 2, c. 3, § 3 (leases), § 4 (contracts) (1677). See generally Causten Browne, *A Treatise on the Construction of the Statute of Frauds* (1857).

33   E.g., Va. Code Ann. § 11-2 (2006). Some statutes, while omitting the phrase "from the making thereof," preserve the three-year period for leases. E.g., N.C. Gen. Stat. § 22-2 (2007).

34   E.g., *Bell* v. *Vaughn*, 53 P.2d 61 (Ariz. 1935).

35   E.g., *Shaughnessy* v. *Eidsmo*, 23 N.W.2d 362, 366 (Minn. 1946) ("An oral lease of real estate for a term of one year, to commence in futuro, is within the statute of frauds.")

36   For America, see Restatement (2d) Prop.: Landlord & Tenant § 14.4 cmt. f ("a tenant who holds over becomes a periodic tenant, with the period determined by the way in which rent is computed." For England, see Geldart, *Introduction to English Law* 84 ("at common law a lease which ought to be made by a deed but is not, will not completely fail of

the parties intended to accomplish, this result at least gave both sides legal rights, and the tenant some security of tenure. Periodic tenancies are exempt from the Statute of Frauds; yet, ironically, unless timely notice is given, the tenancy may actually endure for as long as (or even longer than) the term of the unenforceable oral lease.

Latterly, as leases are increasingly re-conceptualized as contracts, it has been held that the contract theory of part performance may also be applicable to leases.[37] Pioneered in the case of contracts for the sale of goods[38] and extended to cover contracts for the sale of land,[39] part performance permits an exception to the Statute of Frauds if a significant change of position has occurred and if it is solely referable to the existence of an oral agreement. In such case, a court can enforce the oral contract despite the absence of a signed writing, consoling itself with the reflection that the spirit if not the letter of the statute is satisfied since there is reliable evidence of the parties' intention.

If leases are indeed contracts, then the covenants in leases ought to be "dependent," just as the promises in contracts are, and – rather predictably – the dependency of covenants has now been solemnly proclaimed by case and statute.[40] But despite the blithe assurance that leases are contracts "like any other," rules developed in the context of contracts for the sale of goods sometimes prove poor guides in the case of leases of real property. The covenant of habitability, the paradigm case of treating leases like contracts, is (more or less) easily implied in residential leases, particularly of urban apartments.[41] But what, if anything, is required beyond the standards imposed by the relevant housing code? And if the covenant to pay rent is just a promise, dependent on the landlord's (implied) promise to keep the premises "fit and habitable," then what happens to the rent if the landlord breaches (or is alleged to have breached) the promise? May the tenant simply cease paying rent while retaining possession – or abate

---

effect, if possession is taken and rent paid under it; the tenant will be treated as tenant from year to year upon the terms of the lease so far as they are applicable to such a tenancy.").

37   E.g., *Corder* v. *Idaho Farmway, Inc.*, 986 P.2d 1019 (Idaho App. 1999).

38   The original Statute of Frauds, 29 Car. 2, c. 3, § 17 (1677), expressly provided for a type of part performance in contracts for the sale of goods, but not for leases or contracts for the sale of land.

39   Actions such as a change in possession, payment, and the making of improvements are usually required. See Zechariah Chafee, Jr. & Edward D. Re, *Cases and Materials on Equity* 549–50 (5th ed. 1967).

40   E.g., *Richard Barton Enterprises, Inc.* v. *Tsern*, 928 P.2d 368, 378 (Utah 1996) ("the lessee's covenant to pay rent is dependent on the lessor's performance of covenants that were a significant inducement to the consummation of the lease"); N.C. Residential Rental Agreements Act, N.C. Gen. Stat. § 42 41 (2007) ("The tenant's obligation to pay rent under the rental agreement or assignment and to comply with [this Act] and the landlord's obligation to comply with [this Act] shall be mutually dependent.").

41   For more on the covenant of habitability, see Chapter 7, Covenants of Habitability: Making the Right Choice.

the rent to the extent of the breach, perhaps paying for the needed repairs out of the difference?[42]

If the covenant of habitability in residential leases is simply a specific instance of the more general contract rule concerning warranties of fitness for use, then it should be equally implied in commercial leases, which are (on that theory) equally contracts, yet here the courts have hesitated – for the very good reason that the parties are usually the best judges of whether the premises are suitable for the intended use.[43] In this case, the old idea of the lease as a conveyance seemingly still has some appeal.

That landlords should not be immune from liability in tort is an attractive enough proposition, particularly if the proximate cause of an injury was a condition of the premises known to (or knowable by) the landlord but not obvious to the tenant. Traditional property law handled the problem with the concept of "latent defect," an exception to the landlord's so-called "immunity." But whether "premises liability" should be extended to all injuries occurring on the leased premises is not so simple. After all, it is the tenant who has possession, and the landlord who is obligated under what is left of the covenant of quiet enjoyment to leave the tenant alone. Landlord liability for criminal acts of third parties resulting in injuries to the tenant or to licensees or invitees of the tenant has proven particularly problematic.[44]

Illegal leases – that is, leases of premises that for one reason or another may not legally be leased at all – should confer no rights, just as illegal contracts are not enforceable. But what if the tenant under an illegal "lease" takes possession and even pays "rent"? Is this simply the creation of another periodic tenancy, or would that too be illegal? Could a tenant under an illegal lease conceivably be a trespasser?[45] In property cases, unlike contract cases, one does not have the luxury of simply "leaving the parties where you found them" because in the case of an illegal lease they will have quite literally changed position, with the "tenant" in and the "landlord" out.

From contract law comes the duty of a non-breaching party to mitigate damages in case of breach by the other; as applied to leases, the duty of the landlord when

---

42   *Javins* at 1083 ("the trial court may require the tenant to make future rent payments into the registry of the court"); N.C. Residential Rental Agreements Act, N.C. Gen. Stat. § 42 44(c) (2007) ("The tenant may not unilaterally withhold rent prior to a judicial determination of a right to do so.").

43   Cribbet, *Property* 500 ("A significant majority of states has refused to extend the doctrine of implied covenants to commercial tenancies….").

44   Compare *Kline* v. *1500 Massachusetts Ave. Corp.*, 439 F.2d 477 (U.S. Ct. App., D.C. Cir. 1970) (holding landlord liable for failure to safeguard tenants from foreseeable criminal acts) with *Vera* v. *Five Crow Promotions, Inc.*, 503 S.E.2d 692 (N.C. App. 1998) (holding that lessor and sublessor have no duty to protect sublessee's invitees from the criminal acts of third parties).

45   See *William Davis, Inc.* v. *Slade*, 271 A.2d 412 (D.C. App. 1970) (holding that in the District of Columbia a tenant under an illegal lease is a tenant at sufferance rather than a trespasser and can remain in possession for at least 30 days following a proper notice to quit).

faced with an absconding tenant. But the duty raises difficult questions when the landlord has multiple vacancies to fill or when the lease to the replacement tenant is for a longer term.[46] Must the landlord reduce the rent if that is necessary in order to fill the space? Or, if the landlord is able to rent for more, must the landlord turn over the increment to the misbehaving tenant?[47] Is the duty the same for commercial as well as residential tenancies? If the contract theory of anticipatory breach is also carried over to leases, the calculation becomes immeasurably more difficult.[48]

In contract law, the duty to mitigate is not waivable, although contracts may include a provision for liquidated damages – so long, of course, as it is not simply a disguised penalty. But what about leases? In particular, what about commercial leases? Should a commercial landlord be allowed to enforce a lease provision waiving the duty to mitigate? Some cases have so held, ironically relying on a theory of "freedom of contract."[49]

In fact, leases are not "like any other contract" – or like anything else except themselves. The lease is a conveyance of a time-limited interest in real property that usually incorporates contractual elements. There is no reason to abandon the concept of a lease as a conveyance, just as there is no reason to deny that modern leases include a variety of promises in the form of covenants, or to pretend that the law always did a good job when dealing with these contractual elements. But simply to assimilate leases to contracts is to oversimplify, and – what's worse – to sow confusion. However helpful contract rules may be in resolving some landlord-tenant cases, rules made for contracts are an imperfect fit when applied to leases for the very simple reason, one known to the law for a very long time, that every parcel of land is unique. Land, even in the form of residential apartments or office or retail space, is unlike the proverbial widget or bushel of wheat for which contract rules were framed. The law of leases should remain true to itself and not be misled by a simile.

---

46   See Restatement (2d) Prop.: Landlord & Tenant § 12.1, cmt i ("A reletting may be for the benefit of the tenant even though it is for a term shorter or longer than the term in the original lease....").

47   Id. (answering Yes).

48   See, e.g., 16 *Cobalt LLC* v. *Harrison Career Institute*, 590 F.Supp.2d 44 (D.D.C. 2008).

49   *Sylva Shops Ltd. P'ship* v. *Hibbard*, 623 S.E.2d 785 (N.C. App. 2006) (holding that a clause in a commercial lease relieving the landlord of its duty to mitigate damages is not against public policy and is enforceable).

Chapter 6

The Burden of an Easement: Playing a Word Game[1]

Viola: They that dally nicely with words may quickly make them wanton....
Clown: ... words are grown so false, I am loathe to prove reason with them.

Shakespeare

The dictionary gives the primary meaning of the word "burden" as "something that is carried" with a secondary meaning stressing its onerousness – "something that weighs down, oppresses, or causes worry."[2] A synonym is "load."[3] Legal writers use burden metaphorically to mean a "duty or responsibility," as in the "burden of proof."[4] In the law of real property, "burden" has the specific meaning of a "restriction on the use or value of land" and is interchangeable with "encumbrance."[5]

Among the various interests that can encumber land, servitudes use the language of burden – and its correlative, benefit – most extensively. A real covenant or equitable servitude places a burden on one parcel of land, usually for the benefit of one or more other parcels.[6] Similarly with easements, the parcel subject to the easement is burdened by it, and if the easement is appurtenant to another parcel, that parcel is benefited. Using terms imported from Roman (civil) law, the

---

1 An earlier version of this chapter appeared under the title The Burden of an Easement in 40 *Real Property, Probate and Trust Journal* 639 (2006). © 2006 American Bar Association. This information or any portion thereof may not be copied or disseminated in any form or by any means or downloaded or stored in an electronic database or retrieval system without the express written consent of the American Bar Association.

2 *Webster's Third New International Dictionary* 298 (Philip Babcock Gove ed. 2002).

3 Id.

4 *Black's Law Dictionary* 208–9 (8th ed. 2004).

5 Id. at 208. See, e.g., *Brown v. Lober*, 389 N.E.2d 1188, 1191 (Ill. 1979) (defining encumbrance as "any right to, or interest in, land which may subsist in a third party to the diminution of the value of the estate, but consistent with the passing of the fee by conveyance").

6 If the burden does not benefit another parcel, it is said to be "in gross." "English law courts have consistently refused to recognize the validity of legal easements in gross against subsequent owners of the servient land...." 2 *Am. L. Prop.* 333, 429. "American decisions have split on the point, some allowing the burden side to run, and some not." William B. Stoebuck, Running Covenants: An Analytical Primer, 52 *Wash. L. Rev.* 861, 902 (1977) (footnotes omitted). The Restatement of the Law of Servitudes would allow the benefit of any easement to be held in gross. Restatement (3d) Prop.: Servitudes § 2.6 (2000).

burdened land is often described as servient and the benefited land as dominant.[7] In the law of easements, burden and its corresponding abuse, "overburden," are principally used to resolve two types of cases: (1) use of the burdened land by the easement owner other than the authorized use, and (2) use of the burdened land by the easement owner in connection with land other than the benefited land. In addition, the terms sometimes are invoked, less helpfully, in cases concerning use of the burdened land by the easement owner in excess of the authorized use.

An easement owner may not make an unauthorized use of the burdened land. A right-of-way easement, for example, may not be used for parking, or for any use except ingress and egress.[8] To make a use other than the authorized use overburdens the servient estate by adding the burden of another easement. The terms of the instrument creating an easement by express grant or express reservation define its scope. While problems of interpretation may well arise, the usual canons of construction address them. In the case of implied easements, the scope is determined by the use the parties might reasonably have contemplated (if the easement is implied from necessity) or the use as it existed at the time of conveyance (if the easement is implied from prior use). The scope of an easement acquired by prescription poses the greatest problem. The owner of the burdened land had no intention, express or implied, to create the easement in the first place,[9] but rather simply failed to object to an unauthorized use for the prescriptive period. The scope of the easement must therefore be defined by inferring what else would not have been objected to during the same period.[10]

The concept of burden (and overburden) is also critical for identifying the land benefited by an appurtenant easement. The owner of an appurtenant easement has no authority to use the easement to benefit any parcel other than the dominant parcel.[11] An attempt to use the easement in connection with other land represents

---

7   Roman law influenced the common law of easements. C.J. Gale, whose pioneering *Treatise on the Law of Easements* was first published in 1839, "had recourse to Roman law, continental writers, and American decisions" because of the scarcity of English decisions. 15 *H.E.L.* 295. Nonetheless, "though Roman rules have been used to develop the law as to easements, that law rests at bottom upon native foundations." 7 id. at 318.

8   See, e.g., *Loveman v. Lay*, 124 So. 2d 93 (Ala. 1960); Annotation, Right to Park Vehicles on Private Way, 37 A.L.R.2d 944 (1954).

9   This ignores the "lost-grant" theory of the creation of prescriptive easements, or rather treats it for what it is, a legal fiction. For literature on this exotic doctrine, see Jerome J. Curtis, Reviving the Lost Grant, 23 *Real Prop. Prob. & Tr. J.* 535 (1988); Mark A. Clawson, Note, Prescription Adrift in a Sea of Servitudes: Postmodernism and the Lost Grant, 43 *Duke L.J.* 845 (1994).

10   See Restatement (3d) Prop.: Servitudes § 4.1 cmt h (2000) ("The relevant inquiry is what a landowner in the position of the owner of the servient estate should reasonably have expected to lose by failing to interrupt the adverse use before the prescriptive period had run.").

11   See Bruce & Ely, *Easements* § 2:8 ("An easement appurtenant to one parcel cannot be used in connection with another parcel.").

another form of overburden, potentially subjecting the already burdened land to the additional burden of serving another dominant estate. In *S.S. Kresge Co. v. Winkelman Realty Co.*, for example, the court enjoined the use of a driveway as a conduit for the transfer of goods through the dominant land to nondominant land without regard to the amount of use:

> The owner of the servient estate is not required to wait until his property has been unreasonably burdened and thereby permit additional rights to be gained by prescription but he may proceed when any additional burden is placed upon his property and whenever the defendants improperly attempt to increase their rights under their easement.[12]

The latest Restatement of the Law of Servitudes simply restates the traditional rule: "Unless the terms of the servitude... provide otherwise, an appurtenant easement or profit may not be used for the benefit of property other than the dominant estate."[13]

When strictly applied, this rule renders *any* use of an appurtenant easement to serve a nondominant parcel an overburden of the easement. In *Penn Bowling Recreation Center, Inc. v. Hot Shoppes, Inc.*, for example, the court enjoined further use of an easement to serve nondominant land, even though "the area of the dominant and non-dominant land served by the easement [was] less than the original area of the dominant tenement" and the use made of the easement serving the lesser area was "not materially increased or excessive."[14] As the leading treatise on the law of easements explains, "An attempted extension of the easement to serve nondominant land represents an overburden of the servient tenement, *regardless of the amount of usage*."[15] In other words, for a right-of-way easement the issue is not how much traffic passes over the easement, but where the traffic is heading.

Although many courts have adhered to the traditional rule even in cases in which extension of the easement to a nondominant parcel would not substantially increase the use of the easement, other courts have avoided strict application of the rule. Courts avoiding strict application consider equitable factors such as acquiescence and clean hands or, more controversially, balance the burden imposed on the servient parcel if extension is allowed against the hardship to the easement owner if extension is denied. In *Ogle v. Trotter*, for example, the court refused to enjoin the use of a right-of-way easement for the benefit of a nondominant

---

12   50 N.W.2d 920, 922 (Wis. 1952).

13   Restatement (3d) Prop.: Servitudes § 4.11 (2000). "This section states the traditional rule." Id. Reporter's Note. The drafters explain their reluctance to alter the traditional rule by asserting that a "use to serve other property is not within the intended purpose of the servitude." Id. cmt b.

14   179 F.2d 64, 66 (D.C. Cir. 1949).

15   Bruce & Ely, *Easements* § 8:11 (emphasis added).

parcel, finding that "instead of increasing the burden" on the servient estate, the use "materially decreased such burden."[16]

The leading case adopting this approach is *Brown* v. *Voss*, in which the Washington Supreme Court agreed that the use of an easement to serve a house being constructed on both the dominant parcel and an adjacent nondominant parcel was an overburden, but nonetheless affirmed the trial court's denial of an injunction.[17] The court found that the easement owner had reasonably relied on the servient estate owner's silence during the easement owner's expenditure of a considerable sum of money, a rather conventional estoppel argument. More controversially, the court also held that "there was no increase in the volume of travel on the easement" and, therefore, "no increase in the burden on the servient estate."[18]

Unfortunately, the drafters of the latest Restatement contribute to the confusion. In justifying their adoption of the traditional rule concerning use in connection with land other than the benefited land, they explain that "the rule avoids otherwise difficult litigation over the question whether increased use unreasonably increases the burden on the servient estate" and add that the easement owner "is not entitled to use it to serve land that is subsequently acquired even if no additional use of the easement or burden on the servient estate would ensue."[19] While recognizing that an injunction is the ordinary remedy for use in connection with land other than the benefited land, the drafters acknowledge that in "exceptional situations" courts occasionally award damages instead, but caution that "ordinarily monetary relief should be substituted for coercive relief only if extension of the easement does not increase the burden on the servient estate, and if future use of the easement is restricted to limit the risk of future increases in the burden on the servient estate."[20]

What is involved here is an old-fashioned play on words. The additional use is an added burden (an overburden), but it is permissible because there is no additional burden (or at least not very much). The burden of an easement is a legal burden,[21] which exists regardless of the amount of actual use made of the easement

---

16   495 S.W.2d 558, 566 (Tenn. Ct. App. 1973). The opinion also quotes Corpus Juris Secundum for the proposition that "where the additional burden is relatively trifling, the user [i.e., the use] will not be enjoined." Id. (quoting 28 C.J.S. Easements § 92 (2005)) (emphasis omitted).

17   715 P.2d 514, 517 (Wash. 1986). Damages, albeit nominal, were awarded for the overburden of the easement. See id.

18   Id. at 518. See Pamela McClaran, Note, Extending the Benefit of an Easement: A Closer Look at a Classic Rule, 62 *Wash. L. Rev.* 295, 298–301 (1987).

19   Restatement (3d) Prop.: Servitudes § 4.11 cmt b (2000).

20   Id. at 620–21.

21   The Washington Supreme Court in *Brown v. Voss* acknowledged this fact, and quoted from *National Lead Co. v. Kanawha Block Co.*: "This classic rule of property law is directed to the rights of the respective parties rather than the actual burden on the servitude." Brown, 715 P.2d at 517 (quoting *National Lead Co. v. Kanawha Block Co.*, 288 F. Supp. 357, 364 (S.D.W. Va. 1968)).

or whether any use at all is made of it.[22] With an express easement in a recorded deed, the burden is an encumbrance of record, of which parties with an interest in the title have constructive notice. With an implied easement or an easement acquired by prescription, the burden is (usually) observable from inspection of the land. Because of its tangible connotations, however, the word burden can also refer to the load carried by the servient land, in the sense of actual use of the easement. When a court says there is an added burden but there is no added burden, it means that although the legal restriction on the use of the land increases, the increase in actual use is nonexistent, trivial, or reasonable.

Cases concerning the alleged use of the burdened land by the easement owner in excess of the authorized use may invoke burden and overburden even if there is no attempt to extend the benefit to a nondominant parcel. (This can arise as easily with an easement in gross as with an easement appurtenant.) Here the new Restatement, while supposedly stating commonly accepted principles, is not so clear:

> Except as limited by the terms of the servitude…, the holder of an easement… is entitled to use the servient estate in a manner that is reasonably necessary for the convenient enjoyment of the servitude. The manner, frequency, and intensity of the use may change over time to take advantage of developments in technology and to accommodate normal development of the dominant estate or enterprise benefited by the servitude. Unless authorized by the terms of the servitude, the holder is not entitled to cause unreasonable damage to the servient estate or interfere unreasonably with its enjoyment.[23]

What the Restatement apparently has in mind is a situation in which, for example, an infrequently used right-of-way easement begins to be used more intensively as patterns change on the dominant estate. At common law, this type of change would not have been understood as giving the easement owner anything extra because, as long as the easement was used as a right-of-way, no additional burden was imposed on the servient estate.[24] Unless the use changed, as from a right-

---

22　At common law, mere nonuse does not amount to abandonment of an easement. See Restatement (3d) Prop.: Servitudes § 7.4 cmt c (2000) ("Failure to take advantage of a servitude benefit, even for a lengthy period, is seldom sufficient to persuade a court that abandonment has occurred.") The civil law is to the contrary. See, e.g., La. Civ. Code Ann. art. 753 (1980) ("A predial servitude is extinguished by nonuse for ten years.").

23　Restatement (3d) Prop.: Servitudes § 4.10 (2000). According to the Reporter's Note, "The rules stated in [section 4.10] are generally accepted." Id. Reporter's Note. Elsewhere, the Reporter describes section 4.10 as restating "the traditional rule." Susan French, Relocating Easements: Restatement (Third), Servitudes § 4.8(3), 38 *Real Prop. Prob. & Tr. J.* 1, 11 (2003).

24　*City of Charlotte v. BMJ of Charlotte*, LLC, 675 S.E.2d 59 (N.C. App. 2009) (no overburden of railroad right-of-way although use increased from 10 freight trains a day to commuter trains passing every few minutes).

of-way easement to a parking easement, there was no overburden. "It was laid down in the nineteenth century that, if the dominant owner so used his rights as to cause a nuisance to the servient owner, he was liable."[25] And today courts treat an easement owner who exceeds the scope of the easement as a trespasser.[26]

By expressly allowing changes in the "manner, frequency, and intensity" of use,[27] the Restatement risks confusing the analysis. Changes in frequency and intensity seem to raise questions of excessive use, while changes in the manner of use could involve uses in addition to the authorized use – a true overburden. Setting the outermost limit as a use that does not "cause unreasonable damage to the servient estate or interfere unreasonably with its enjoyment,"[28] aside from inviting judicial reordering of private arrangements, goes beyond what the common law allowed, which was only to use the easement without damage to the burdened land. To think that "reasonable damage" to the servient estate or "reasonable interference with its enjoyment" is allowable is alarming.

The real question should be whether the use has passed beyond the scope of the easement and, if allowed to continue, would lead to the recognition of an additional (legal) burden on the servient estate. This would shift the inquiry back to its proper focus on whether the manner of use is reasonably within the contemplation of the parties that created the burden and benefit – not whether a later judge or jury would find the manner of use "reasonable."

Personally I prefer the traditional rules: no use other than the authorized use and no use in connection with land other than the benefited land. To allow more than this would overburden the servient estate. Change in the frequency or intensity of use, as long as it remains within the authorized use, is permissible – without the burden of proving its reasonableness to a judicial fact-finder. But whether others agree with me or not, I would hope that all would agree that if the traditional rules are to be departed from, it should be because of reasoned analysis, and not because of winning a word game involving the use of the word "burden."

---

25   7 *H.E.L.* 345.
26   See Bruce & Ely, *Easements* 10, § 7:05(5)(a).
27   Restatement (3d) Prop.: Servitudes § 4.10 (2000).
28   Id.

Chapter 7

Covenants of Habitability:
Doing the Right Thing

Suppose that an honest man wants to sell a house because of certain defects of which he alone is aware. The building is supposed to be quite healthy, but is in fact insanitary, and he is aware that it is; or the place is badly built and is falling down, but nobody knows this except the owner. Suppose he does not disclose these facts to purchasers, and sells the house for much more than he expected. Has he behaved unfairly and dishonestly?

Sound familiar? Questions like this are posed every year in the basic property course. After a discussion more or less Socratic, the usual picture that emerges is of an old rule in favor of sellers increasingly riddled with exceptions favoring buyers. The logical starting point turns out to be a common law position against implied warranties of quality in the sale of real estate, so in the absence of express warranties, prospective purchasers take the property as is. The rationale is said to be that since they are able to inspect the premises prior to purchase, "their eyes are their bargain."[1] The effect of the rule is captured by the Latin phrase: *Caveat emptor!* Let the buyer beware![2]

As disclosed in the usual course of discussion, the attack on the common law position did not begin with a frontal assault. Instead, using a common maneuver, the critics turned the rationale into a means to confine the rule. If their eyes were truly their bargain, then purchasers who were unable to see the property were not bound, if it turned out to be unfit. Purchasers operating at a distance were necessarily forced to rely on representations, implied if not express, concerning quality,[3] while a purchaser of an unfinished structure had only the builder's plans to look at.[4] Even in cases in which the premises were available for inspection,

---

1   See Cribbet, *Property* 1190.

2   See Broom, *Maxims* 768. See generally Walter H. Hamilton, The Ancient Maxim of Caveat Emptor, 40 *Yale L.J.* 1133 (1931).

3   Cf. *Ingalls v. Hobbs*, 31 N.E. 286 (Mass. 1892) (short term lease of furnished house at Swampscott); *Smith v. Marrable*, 11 M. & W. 5, 152 Eng. Rep. 693 (Exch. 1843) (short term lease of furnished house at Brighton). Because the common law regarded leases as conveyances, cases concerning claims of defective premises, whether leased or sold outright, are cited interchangeably in this article.

4   *Miller v. Cannon Hill Estates, Ltd.*, 2 K.B. 113 (Eng. 1931) (purchase of unfinished structure); *Vanderschrier v. Aaron*, 140 N.E.2d 819 (Ohio Ct. App. 1957) (purchase of unfinished structure) (on completion and occupancy, inadequate sewer system rendered house insanitary and unhealthy).

purchasers were bound to take only what they could see: latent or hidden defects were the vendors' responsibility.[5]

Eventually the attack centered on the rule itself. If manufacturers of consumer products are held to an implied warranty of fitness, then home-builders should be held to something similar. The purchasers' opportunity to inspect was no longer central; the complexity of the product made visual inspection, particularly by unskilled home-buyers, largely irrelevant. In a sense, this was merely a development of the rule concerning latent defects: even under the rule of *caveat emptor*, purchasers were not held to have accepted defects that could not reasonably have been discovered by "their eyes."[6] At last, purchasers of a completed house were allowed to recover against the builder-vendor because of an implied warranty of quality.[7]

Thereafter attention shifted to consolidating the new rule. Remaining questions concerned whether purchasers from the original buyer could also sue the builder: Was privity of contract required?[8] Whether purchasers could bargain away the protection provided by the implied warranty: Was waiver possible?[9] When did the statute of limitations begin to run: Did the cause of action accrue when construction was complete or when the defect first became apparent?[10]

The next stage is to determine what remains of the old rule of *caveat emptor*. It still holds apparently with respect to commercial, as opposed to residential, property. In the sale of land for development as a shopping center, where "the purchaser has full opportunity to make pertinent inquiries but fails to do so through no artifice or inducement of the seller, an action in fraud will not lie."[11]

---

5   *Barnes v. MacBrown & Co.*, 342 N.E.2d 619 (Ind.1976) (latent defect in pre-owned house).

6   Of course, purchasers could have been charged with the knowledge of what the eyes of a skilled inspector would have discovered, just as purchasers are charged with the knowledge concerning title that the eyes of a professional title-searcher would have discovered.

7   *Petersen v. Hubschman Constr. Co., Inc.*, 389 N.E.2d 1154 (Ill. 1979); *Hartley v. Ballou*, 209 S.E.2d 776 (N.C. 1974); *Cochran v. Keeton*, 252 So.2d 313 (Ala. 1971).

8   *Barnes v. MacBrown & Co.*, 342 N.E.2d 619 (Ind.1976) (privity not required); *Keyes v. Guy Bailey Homes, Inc.*, 439 So.2d 670 (Miss. 1983) (same); *Terlinde v. Neely*, 271 S.E.2d 768 (S.C. 1980) (same); *Real Estate Marketing, Inc. v. Frantz*, 885 S.W.2d 921 (Ky. 1994) (same).

9   *Petersen v. Hubschman Constr. Co., Inc.*, 389 N.E.2d 1154, 1159 (Ill. 1979) ("a knowing disclaimer of the implied warranty" is not contrary to public policy); *Crowder v. Vandendeale*, 564 S.W.2d 879 (Mo. 1977) (more than a "boilerplate" disclaimer is required).

10   Statutes of repose have in some instances determined the question by limiting actions to some gross period beginning with the completion of construction. See, e.g., N.C. Gen. Stat. § 1-50(a)(5)(a) (limiting cause of action to recover damages for defective improvement to real property to 6 years after "substantial completion of the improvement"); *Nolan v. Paramount Homes, Inc.*, 518 S.E.2d 789 (N.C. Ct. App. 1999) (construing the statute).

11   *C.F.R. Foods, Inc. v. Randolph Development Co.*, 421 S.E.2d 386, 389 (N.C. Ct. App. 1992) (citing *Libby Hill Seafood Restaurants, Inc. v. Owens*, 303 S.E.2d 565, 568 (N.C. Ct. App. 1983).

The rationale that purchasers could protect themselves through prior inspection still seemingly makes sense when businesspeople are involved on both sides of the transaction, special needs might be involved, and the public interest in housing is lacking. The old rule certainly remains with respect to titles, as opposed to physical defects. Concerning the state of the title, there still are no implied covenants, so express warranties of title continue to appear in almost every deed. Here "their eyes are their bargain" remains valid since the registry of deeds opens the chain of title to inspection.[12] The only remaining question concerns whether covenants contained in a prior contract of sale survived delivery of the deed or were terminated by merger, "an old but misleading concept," meaning that "any covenants in the contract merge into the deed on the execution of the deed and are no longer enforceable."[13]

Near the end of the usual classroom discussion come questions like those posed at the beginning of this chapter. The peculiar feature in these cases is that they involve the seller of "used" housing, not the original builder. The specific technical issue may now be fraudulent concealment of relevant facts rather than an implied covenant of fitness as such, but the general problem remains the same. Since the physical defects are known only to the seller, the buyer may not have assumed the risk. The question may be harder with respect to some "insanitary" conditions, perhaps best exemplified today by a stigmatizing feature such as a death on the premises by homicide, suicide, or AIDS.[14] The problem is not new. The depressing effect on the rental market of bad news connected with the premises was concisely illustrated in a century-old short story by O. Henry, "The Furnished Room," quoting an Irish-American landlady in New York: "There be many people will rayjict the rentin' of a room if they be tould a suicide has been after dyin' in the bed of it."[15] These may not, in fact, involve objective reasons to find fault with

---

12   Actually, as every title-searcher knows, examination of the record cannot disclose all possible defects of title. Forged or undelivered deeds, undisclosed spouses, and mistakes in indexing are only the most obvious sources of problems. Since buyers risk the loss of their investment, a special branch of the insurance industry has developed to offer policies of title insurance.

13   Cribbet, *Property* 1201. See *Tavares v. Horstman*, 542 P.2d 1275 (Wyo. 1975) (merger not applied); *Redarowicz v. Ohlendorf*, 441 N.E.2d 324 (Ill. 1982) (same).

14   See *Reed v. King*, 193 Cal. Rptr. 130 (Cal. Ct. App. 1983) (failure to disclose that premises were the site ten years earlier of a multiple murder); *Van Camp v. Bradford*, 623 N.E.2d 731 (Ohio Com. Pl. 1993) (failure to disclose recent rape on premises); *Stambovsky v. Ackley*, 572 N.Y.S.2d 672 (N.Y. App. Div. 1991) (failure to disclose that house was reputed to be haunted). Legislation in many states regulates the disclosure of stigmatizing features. See, e.g., Cal. Civ. Code § 1710.2(a) (no cause of action for failure to disclose AIDS-related death on premises more than three years previously); N.C. Gen. Stat. § 39–50 (death or illness of previous occupant not a material fact, but seller may not knowingly make a false statement regarding such past occupant).

15   O. Henry [William Sydney Porter], The Furnished Room, in *The Best of O. Henry* 47, 52 (1978).

the property, but prospective buyers may, for reasons of their own, consider them relevant.[16]

The course of legal development, the "progress of the law," as revealed by this discussion appears to be almost entirely driven by logic. The rule against implied warranties of quality in the sale of real property is posited, its rationale deduced; hypothetical cases are posed, designed to test whether the rule furthers the reason in specific instances. The old regime of *caveat emptor* swiftly crumbles; the only real question is whether any fragments of it survive. Considered as a matter of logic, the solution can be arrived at quickly, in no more than one or two class hours. After such a discussion, no student is particularly surprised to learn that in only a few years the common law position against implied warranties has been replaced by the routine implication of warranties of habitability in a majority of states.[17]

Before exploring further the reason for this sudden shift in legal rules, it may be helpful to return to the questions posed at the beginning of this article and to see them as they were originally phrased more than two thousand years ago:

> *Vendat aedas vir bonus propter aliqua vitia, quae ipse norit, ceteri ignorent, pestilentes sint et habeantur salubres, ignoretur in omnibus cubiculis apparere serpentes, male materiatae sint, ruinosae, sed hoc praeter dominum nemo sciat; quaero, si haec emptoribus venditor non dixerit aedesque vendiderit pluris multo, quam si venditurum putarit, num id iniuste aut improbe fecerit.*[18]

The questioner was Marcus Tullius Cicero (106–43 B.C.), Roman statesman and lawyer. The discussion, set out in Cicero's *De officiis* (On Duties) in 44 B.C., is remarkably like classroom dialogues today. Indeed, in strict accordance with Socratic precedent, Cicero records a dialogue between two Greek-named interlocutors. Antipater[19] argues that it is unfair and dishonest for a seller intentionally to mislead a buyer, drawing an analogy with the case of a person who refuses to help someone who is lost.[20] Diogenes[21] in reply denies that the seller is

---

16   Crime statistics on or near the premises may be relevant to estimates of future safety; in this case there would be an objective reason to reject the property.

17   Sean M. O'Brien, Caveat Venditor: A Case for Granting Subsequent Purchasers a Cause of Action Against Builder-Vendors for Latent Defects in the Home, 1995 *J. of Corp. Law* 525, 530 ("Although the theory of implied warranty of habitability, in a span of thirty years, became the rule in a majority of states, courts limited its application to the original purchaser of a new home from a builder-vendor.").

18   Cicero, *De officiis* 3:13:54 (Loeb ed. 1913). The translation used at the beginning of this article is from Cicero, *Selected Works* 179 (trans. Michael Grant 1960).

19   Antipater of Tarsus (2nd century B.C.), a Stoic philosopher, was the pupil of Diogenes of Babylonia, with whom the supposed dialogue is conducted.

20   The analogy is unpersuasive in the common law tradition in which there is in general no legal duty to render assistance to others.

21   Diogenes of Babylonia, also known as Diogenes of Seleucia, a Stoic philosopher, was the pupil of Chrysippus and the teacher of Antipater of Tarsus. He was part of a

duty-bound to disclose defects: people expect a seller to overpraise the product. Anticipating the maxim "their eyes are their bargain," Diogenes asks: "When the purchaser can exercise his own judgement, what fraud can there be on the part of the seller?"[22] Cicero himself views the problem as one of moral choice and in the end sides with the proponent of full disclosure, concluding "the man who was selling the house should not have withheld its defects from the purchaser."[23]

The point of rehearsing this ancient history is to demonstrate that the concerns still actively discussed today are as old as the hills of Rome. Indeed, they are older: Cicero relied on Greek sources. Which means that these arguments, at least standing alone, cannot possibly be what caused modern American law concerning the sale of defective houses to begin changing fairly suddenly only a few decades ago. Logic was not the cause; the logical arguments have been well understood not just for centuries but for millennia.[24] Like the mythical law school exam, the question has remained the same, only the answer has changed.

But if logic did not cause the change, what did? Aside from the logical arguments, the cases and commentators routinely allude to changes in the real estate market to explain the shifting legal rules. As one court put it:

> Because of the vast change that has taken place in the method of constructing and marketing new houses, we feel that it is appropriate to hold that in the sale of a new house by a builder-vendor, there is an implied warranty of habitability which will support an action against the builder-vendor by the vendee for latent

---

delegation of philosophers who visited Rome in 156 B.C. as ambassadors from Athens, seeking remission of a fine. While on their diplomatic mission, the philosophers gave public lectures, which were so well attended by young Romans that Cato the Elder persuaded the Senate to expel all philosophers from the city for fear they were diverting the young men from their military exercises. See Plutarch, *The Lives of the Noble Grecians and Romans* 428 (John Dryden trans., revised by Arthur Hugh Clough) (Modern Lib. ed., no date) (life of Marcus Cato).

22   Cicero, *Selected Works* 179 (trans. Michael Grant 1960).

23   Id. 180. Cicero did not limit his conclusion to cases of the sale of defective houses but extended it to sales of personal property as well, including sales of slaves. "If a man knows that a slave he is selling is unhealthy, or a runaway, or a thief, he must (unless the slave is one he has inherited) report accordingly." Id. 185–86. Similar problems arose in some American states prior to the adoption of the Thirteenth Amendment. See Ariela Gross, *Double Character: Slavery and Mastery in the Antebellum Southern Courtroom* 72 (2000) ("[The] 'sound price rule' operated to imply a warranty of soundness even into a contract for slave sale that did not contain any express language about the slave's health or fitness for labor.").

24   Cicero's *De officiis* was "used as their prime textbook by generations of university students in England and France and Germany." Moses Hadas, *A History of Latin Literature* 135 (1952). Studying Cicero was once also a prominent part of the education of American elites, particularly lawyers. See Stephen Botein, Cicero as Role Model for Early American Lawyers: A Case Study in Classical "Influence," 73 *Classical J.* 313 (1978).

defects and which will avoid the unjust results of *caveat emptor* and the doctrine of merger.[25]

Typical is the assertion that before 1945 the mass production of houses was unknown.[26] Statistics certainly show a post-World War II building boom, as productive capacity was redirected from the war effort to the task of making up for lost time and housing the newly demobilized military forces.[27] Something similar had, however, occurred before. Indeed, the birth of the suburbs is usually dated a generation earlier, in the period after World War I:

> In the 1920s the American population as a whole increased by 16%. Those living in the centers of cities increased by 22%. But those living in the satellite areas – the suburbs – increased by 44%. What does all this add up to? The United States took to wheels. This was quite truly the age of the mass automobile. With the automobile the United States began a vast inner migration into newly constructed, single-family houses in the suburbs; and these new houses were filled increasingly with radios, refrigerators, and the other household gadgetry of a society whose social mobility and productivity had all but wiped out personal service. Within these houses Americans shifted their food consumption to higher-grade foods, increasingly purchased in cans – or, later, frozen.[28]

Development of a new suburban housing pattern, no matter when exactly it emerged, seems hardly adequate as a complete explanation of the appearance of the modern implied covenant of fitness in the sale of residential real estate because the new legal rule concerning houses was closely linked with a simultaneous development in urban real estate law. In the law of landlord and tenant, predominantly a concern of city-dwellers, an implied covenant of habitability in residential leases was recognized.[29] Leases had traditionally been viewed as a form of conveyance

---

25   *Petersen v. Hubschman Constr. Co., Inc.*, 389 N.E.2d 1154, 1157–58 (Ill. 1979). Introduction of the phrase "latent defects" in the holding raises a question about how new the rule really is: purchasers even under a strict regime of *caveat emptor* were not required to accept defective property when the defect was latent and not discoverable by inspection.

26   Leo Bearman, Jr., Caveat Emptor in Sales of Realty – Recent Assaults Upon the Rule, 14 *Vand. L. Rev.* 541, 542 (1961) ("A changing law for sales of personalty, stimulated perhaps by early mass production and accompanying mass buying and consequent mass expectation of quality, had little effect upon the rules governing sales of realty, since before 1945 no similar mass production methods had so totally invaded the building industry.").

27   Id. 542 n. 6 ("Statistics reveal that the value of annual new construction of private residential buildings rose from less than $2,000,000,000 annually in 1945 to about $15,000,000,000 annually in 1950 and about $18,000,000,000 annually by September 1959.").

28   Walt Rostow, *The Stages of Economic Growth* 77 (2nd ed. 1971).

29   See, e.g., *Javins v. First Nat'l Realty Co.*, 428 F.2d 1071, 1076 (D.C. Cir. 1970) (finding an implied covenant of habitability in residential leases and noting that "courts

with, perhaps, a few promises known as "covenants" attached. As a conveyance, the lease fell under the common-law rule against implied warranties, so unless an express covenant of fitness was included in the lease, none was implied.[30] Then, again fairly suddenly, an implied covenant or warranty of habitability was recognized in residential leases.[31]

In the law both of leasing and selling residential real property the shift toward implied covenants was associated with a renewed emphasis on the contractual aspect of the transaction.[32] So long as leasing and selling real estate were viewed primarily as conveyancing, that is, transferring an interest in real property, the legal emphasis remained on the effectiveness of the transfer as such, rather than on the characteristics of the property transferred. The common law presumed that title to land was of paramount concern to the transferee and restricted the legal inquiry to whether and when title passed and to the quality of title involved. Once the transactions were reconceptualized in terms of contract, the seller's performance could be seen as essentially the performance of a set of promises, rather than as simply the delivery of title. The property itself, as opposed to the title to it, emerged as a focus of legal interest.

Although the changes in the law of leasing and selling residential real property advanced in tandem, differences in the legal structure of the two transactions produced different doctrinal emphases. The lease was increasingly assimilated to a contract, while in sales of real property the emphasis shifted from the deed that conveyed title to the preceding contract for the sale of land that promised to transfer the property. Leases and deeds were now treated as conceptually distinct. In the law of landlord and tenant, the covenant of habitability was simply implied in the lease; in the law of conveyancing, on the other hand, it was usually implied in the contract of sale. Emphasis on the contract of sale in conveyancing may

---

have begun to hold sellers and developers of real property responsible for the quality of their product"), cert. denied, 400 U.S. 925 (1970); *Petersen v. Hubschman Constr. Co.,* Inc., 389 N.E.2d 1154 (Ill. 1979) (finding an implied warranty of fitness in a contract for the sale of a house and noting that same court had already recognized an implied warranty of habitability in a residential lease).

30 1 *Am. L. Prop.* 267 ("There is no implied covenant or warranty that at the time the term commences the premises are in a tenantable condition or that they are adapted to the purpose for which leased…. The reason assigned for this rule is that the tenant is a purchaser of an estate in land, subject to the doctrine of *caveat emptor*. He may inspect the premises and determine for himself their suitability or he may secure an express warranty.").

31 The law of landlord and tenant is today increasingly divided into residential and commercial components. This, in turn, has placed a hitherto unknown emphasis on the definition of "residential tenant." See, e.g., *Brigdon v. Lamb,* 929 P.2d 1274 (Alaska 1997) (distinguishing "possession prior to sale" from tenancy). See also John *v.* Orth, Who Is a Tenant? The Correct Definition of the Status in North Carolina, 21 *N.C. Cent. L.J.* 79, 81 (1995); John *v.* Orth, Confusion Worse Confounded: The North Carolina Residential Rental Agreements Act, 78 *N.C. L. Rev.* 783 (2000).

32 See Chapter 5, Leases: Misled by a Simile.

be attributed to the continuing strength of the rule against implied covenants in deeds,[33] as well as to the greater flexibility of contract doctrine. Whatever its cause, the new emphasis led in turn to pressure in the law of deeds to relax the old doctrine of merger in order to preserve elements of the contract after the effectiveness of the conveyance.

Again, logical arguments in favor of changing the law of landlord and tenant are routinely supplemented with a recital of facts concerning developments in the rental housing market; this time the emphasis is on the circumstances of urban dwellers rather than suburbanites. In 1970, in *Javins* v. *First National Realty Corp.*, the landmark case concerning the implied warranty of habitability in leases, Judge J. Skelly Wright wrote on behalf of the United States Court of Appeals for the District of Columbia:

> The assumption of landlord-tenant law, derived from feudal property law, that a lease primarily conveyed to the tenant an interest in land may have been reasonable in a rural, agrarian society; it may continue to be reasonable in some leases involving farming or commercial land. In these cases, the value of the lease to the tenant is the land itself. But in the case of the modern apartment dweller, the value of the lease is that it gives him a place to live.... When American city dwellers, both rich and poor, seek "shelter" today, they seek a well known package of goods and services – a package which includes not merely walls and ceilings, but also adequate heat, light, and ventilation, serviceable plumbing facilities, secure windows and doors, proper sanitation, and proper maintenance.[34]

While this catalog of wants of modern urban apartment dwellers may be readily accepted as accurate, it is hardly the case that these wants arose for the first time in the last half of the twentieth century. Apartment-dwelling has been a perennial feature of urban life. Nor is it plausible to attribute the modern revaluation of tenants' rights to the decline of the agrarian tenant or the demise of feudalism – both of which preceded the doctrinal development by years, if not by centuries.[35]

Emphasis on the contractual aspect of the lease made it fairly easy to draw an analogy to concurrent developments in the general law of contracts. The

---

33   The rule against implied covenants in deeds is related to the use of covenants for title: where express covenants are involved, and presumably bargained for, it is reasonable to exclude implied covenants. It would, of course, also be possible to limit the rule against implied covenants in deeds to implied covenants concerning title, the subject of the express covenants.

34   *Javins* at 1074.

35   If American property law did indeed maintain a legal rule suitable to feudalism, the question remains why the rule so long outlived its historical context, and why it was abandoned when it was. See *Am. L. Prop.* § 3.45 n. 12 (Supp. 1977) (suggesting that the provision in the 1960s of federally funded legal services for the poor was a major factor motivating the change).

ubiquitous Uniform Commercial Code (UCC) popularized in the law of sales of personal property a general warranty of merchantability or fitness for a particular purpose.[36] Consumer products such as the automobile and assorted household gadgets now came with implied warranties of quality. Courts inclined to extend the rights of purchasers and lessees of residential real property routinely cited the related concepts of the UCC.[37] As one commentator sharply expressed it in 1965, "As far as assurances of quality are concerned, our law offers greater protection to the purchaser of a seventy-nine cent dog leash than it does to the purchaser of a 40,000-dollar house."[38] The point became even more telling as the prices of houses and even of dog leashes escalated.

Seemingly minor terminological problems incident to importing concepts from the law of sales of personal property reveal the imperfect join of modern contract law and traditional real property law. While the UCC speaks in terms of merchantability, the word has not caught on in describing the new implied warranty in the sale and lease of residential real property. The common law long recognized an implied "warranty of merchantability" in contracts for the sale of land, but here again it was the state of the title that was impliedly warranted to be merchantable, not the condition of the premises.[39] Hence the search for a more descriptive term. "Warranty of habitability" is often used, but "habitability," too, hardly describes the scope of the new warranty. As one court has phrased it in a case involving the sale of residential real property, "the mere fact that the house is capable of being inhabited does not satisfy the implied warranty."[40] Construing the warranty of habitability in leases, another court read it expansively to include, in addition to the physical condition of the premises, "reasonable safeguards to protect tenants from foreseeable criminal activity."[41] An implied warranty of fitness or quality seems, therefore, a more descriptive label.

Invocation of the UCC and the law of sales of personal property suggest that the principal driving force in changing the law of sales and leases of residential real property has not been either newly discovered flaws in real property doctrine

---

36   Unif. Commercial Code § 2-314 (implied warranty of merchantability); id. § 2-315 (implied warranty: fitness for particular purpose).

37   See, e.g., *Javins* at 1075; *Petersen v. Hubschman Constr. Co., Inc.*, 389 N.E.2d 1154, 1158 (Ill. 1979).

38   Paul G. Haskell, The Case for an Implied Warranty of Quality in Sales of Real Property, 53 *Geo. L. J.* 633, 633 (1965). It could, of course, be argued that the purchaser of the more expensive item should be held to a higher standard of care before purchase.

39   See *Wallach v. Riverside Bank*, 100 N.E. 50 (N.Y. 1912) (holding that an executory contract for the sale of land includes an implied covenant that vendor must deliver a merchantable title at the closing). See also Unif. Land Transfer Act § 2-304(d) (adopting "the rule of *Wallach*").

40   *Petersen v. Hubschman Constr. Co., Inc.*, 389 N.E.2d 1154, 1158 (Ill. 1979).

41   *Trentacost v. Brussel*, 412 A.2d 436 (N.J. 1980). See also *Javins* at 1074 (referring to habitable premises as having "secure windows and doors," which may imply more than apertures that are wind and waterproof).

or recent changes in the real estate market. Such local causes are inadequate to explain a global change. What developments in the law of sales of personal property, residential leases, and conveyancing of residential real estate have in common is, to put it bluntly, a preference for purchasers – whether of chattels, residential leaseholds, or fee interests in residential real estate – over sellers of consumer products, landlords, and builders. The preference for purchasers began with purchasers of consumer goods, particularly automobiles,[42] but then spread fairly rapidly to tenants and home-buyers. The underlying premise seems to be that buyers need legal protection against sellers. In a democracy, of course, it is not irrelevant that purchasers outnumber sellers.

Ambient factors that eased the change in policy in these areas of the law include a generalized preference for plaintiffs: buyers are more likely to sue than sellers, and plaintiffs are more likely to win today. Increased social tolerance for litigation may also have played a role: the old rule of *caveat emptor*, rigorously applied, served to reduce the number of lawsuits. Increased judicial activism obviously contributed to the development: unless the pull of precedent was reduced, such wholesale legal change by judicial decision would have been impossible.

Concern for efficiency may have been another factor that influenced the change of policy. If purchasers knew and understood the rule of *caveat emptor*, it may have retarded transactions, particularly in the consumer product market. A rule encouraging inspection prior to purchase is less likely to retard real estate transactions, whether sale or lease, because delay and some sort of inspection are already standard procedure. Whether because of concern that the legal message concerning the peril of not inspecting products before purchase did not get through or because of the increased transaction costs imposed by the rule if it did, law makers (whether legislators or judges) may have chosen to shift the risk of loss from buyers to sellers. In practical terms, legal allocation of the risk means, in cases involving knowledgeable parties, the assignment of the cost of inspection and the implementation of some method of spreading the cost of failure to discover defects, such as through pricing or insurance. Despite the demise of *caveat emptor* in sales of residential real estate, purchasers routinely seek professional inspections, as evidenced by the thriving business of private building inspectors. The practical question, then, is whether the buyer or the seller should bear the cost of inspection and the risk of mistake.

Here again, doctrine did not lead the change, but followed it. The role of doctrine was to implement a policy choice not to dictate one. Doctrine's principal purpose in the decision of individual cases is to direct the attention of the judge away from the particularities of the parties and the specifics of the given dispute. Its broader social purpose is to secure the first rule of justice, that like cases be decided alike. But the new policy preference in favor of purchasers inspired further doctrinal development. The age-old common law distinction between real and personal

---

42   See, e.g., *MacPherson v. Buick Motor Co.*, 111 N.E. 1050 (N.Y. 1916) (eliminating requirement of privity and permitting ultimate consumer to sue manufacturer).

property, already weakened, was eroded further as sales and leases of residential real property were assimilated to purchases of personal property.[43] Leases, once a form of conveyance, became a contract "like any other," and the contract for the sale of land gained a new significance. The implication of a warranty of habitability in leases meant expanded scope for the doctrine of constructive eviction,[44] and quickly translated into increased tort liability for landlords.[45] Expanding tort liability for sellers of residential real estate seems likely.

The recognition of an implied warranty of habitability in leases and sales of residential real estate raised serious questions about whether an implied warranty of fitness should be recognized in the lease and sale of commercial real estate as well. The appeal of the argument was more logical than practical because of the diversity of commercial uses, and the urge has generally been resisted, despite the fact that the UCC protects merchant as well as non-merchant buyers. In this case, the differences between real and personal property are still salient.

It is noteworthy that Cicero, long ago, seemed to think that he could discuss the issue of the sale of a defective house without reference to market conditions in the Roman Empire. Has the "honest man" who failed to disclose the facts to the unsuspecting purchaser, he asked, "behaved fairly"? This was the question, of course, because Cicero viewed the issue as one primarily of moral choice, in the sense of rule-making that reflected and created good mores or customary patterns of behavior. Moral discourse is today discouraged in legal decision-making in favor of utilitarian arguments,[46] but moral choices continue to be made. It may, in fact, be far more explanatory to begin a discussion of the changing law concerning

---

43   The common law routinely distinguished real property (loosely defined as land and everything growing out of it or affixed to it) from personal property (everything else). Many different rules applied to the two species of property, particularly in case of inheritance. In many states and in England succession to land and to personalty have today been completely assimilated. See Dukeminier, *Wills, Trusts, and Estates* 33. But see N.C. Gen. Stat. § 29-14 (2007) (continuing distinction between real and personal property where decedent is survived by a spouse and one or more descendants).

44   See Schoshinski, *Am. Law L. & T.* § 3: 6, pp. 103–04 ("the interrelationship between the doctrine of constructive eviction and the recently fashioned implied covenant of habitability is clear: where recognized, the implied warranty allows the tenant, in addition to whatever other remedies may flow from recognition of the covenant, to abandon the premises and be absolved of all responsibility for future rental payments").

45   See *Sargent v. Ross*, 308 A.2d 528, 534 (N.H. 1973) (adoption of an implied warranty of habitability destroys "the very legal foundation and justification for the landlord's immunity in tort for injuries to the tenant or third persons"); *Trentacost v. Brussel*, 412 A.2d 436, 443 (N.J. 1980) ("By failing to provide adequate security, the landlord has… breached his implied warranty of habitability and is liable to the tenant for the injuries attributable to that breach.").

46   See John v. Orth, Casting the Priests out of the Temple: John Austin and the Relation Between Law and Religion, in *The Weightier Matters of the Law: Essays on Law and Religion* 229–49 (John Witte & Frank S. Alexander eds, 1988).

the sale of defective houses by focusing on the moral choice between favoring consumers, on the one hand, and producers, on the other, without regard to the particular product consumed.

Legal discourse that emphasizes objective, external factors that influence the development of legal rules seems designed to conceal the extent to which legal development is the product of conscious choice. Emphasis on changing market conditions, such as the increasing prevalence of mass produced goods, whether consumer products, urban apartments, or suburban houses, suggests a sort of economic determinism: the implication is that legal rules respond, sometimes belatedly, to market forces. Equally deterministic, if less obviously so, is emphasis on the need for legal rules to conform to patterns of behavior, for example, the supposed fact that consumers do not or cannot protect themselves by inspection prior to purchase. That legal rules follow public opinion or practice also implies that external factors drive judicial choice.[47]

A more sophisticated version of this sort of non-economic determinism is the argument that the need for consistency with other legal developments constrains legal choice, for example, the argument that the same rule must apply to all consumer purchases, whether of chattels or real estate (except as to the state of the title). That modern American judges should seek to emphasize factors that seem to reduce their policy-making role is perhaps partly to be explained by considerations of separation of powers. Judges, after all, are not explicitly vested with legislative power. Cicero obviously had no experience with modern constitutional democracy, so was unembarrassed about his rule-making.

Emphasis on the moral choice in legal development does not, however, necessarily equate the judicial and legislative roles. While not a denial of practical factors, neither is it a simple abdication to the market or popular practice. It can be, instead, a principled attempt to formulate a workable rule that will shape the market and lead to popular practice. Good social customs exist in a reciprocal relation with good legal rules: custom reflects popular understanding, but it also responds to legal rules, at least to known legal rules that embody enlightened moral choices.

---

47   The most prominent proponent of the idea that legal development follows the demands of "public opinion" was the English legal scholar, Albert Venn Dicey. See A.V. Dicey, *Lectures on the Relation Between Law and Public Opinion in England During the Nineteenth Century* (1905).

Chapter 8
Escheat: Picking Up the Pieces

In personal estates, which are allodial by law, the king is last heir where no kin.

Lord Mansfield

Strictly speaking, escheat applies only to real property. If a landowner dies without a valid will or known heir,[1] the property escheats to the state. Nowadays escheat can also refer to personal property.[2] If the same person dies owning chattels as well as land, the now unowned personal property also passes to the state. And, because the state takes possession of certain items of unclaimed personal property, such as inactive bank accounts, these too are loosely said to escheat.

There is, obviously, a practical reason to treat all these cases – real and personal property left by an owner who dies without a will or legal heir as well as personal property that is unclaimed – as instances of escheat. In each case, the result is the same: the state takes possession. But although the property ends up in the same place, the historical and theoretical routes that lead to that destination are quite different. And the titles by which the state holds the various types of escheated property are also different – which may have practical implications even today.

Escheat was an incident of feudal tenure. The legal theory of the effect of the Conquest of England in 1066 by Duke William of Normandy, which made him King William I ("the Conqueror"), was that all land belonged to the king by right of conquest. When William granted out estates to his vassals, he retained his overlordship, which entitled him and his successors to the land when those estates came to an end. In the case of life estates, the death of the life tenant obviously ended the estate. In the case of estates in fee simple, which can endure forever,[3] the estate ended if the owner died without a valid will or known heir.[4]

Under feudalism it was essential that the person possessed of the right to the land – the one seized of the estate – could be identified at all times. There could

---

1   The emphasis is on *known* heir. If the state's inheritance law admits kindred of any degree, then no one actually dies without an heir. More than two hundred years ago, Sir William Blackstone stated the obvious: "All men are in some degree related to each other." 2 *Bl. Com.* 205. The problem is establishing the exact degree of kinship.

2   *Black's Law Dictionary* 584 (8th ed. 2004) defines escheat as "reversion of property (esp. real property) to the state upon the death of an owner who has neither a will nor any legal heirs."

3   See, e.g., 4 *Kent Com.* *4 ("No estate is deemed a fee, unless it may continue forever.").

4   Prior to the adoption of the first Statute of Wills in 1540, 32 Hen. 8, c. 1, real property could not be devised. Also in pre-modern times, estates escheated if the owner (tenant) committed a felony (*propter delictum tenentis*). 3 *Bl. Com.* 258.

be "no gap in seisin."[5] This was because the feudal estate owed duties to the lord that had to be discharged by the person with seisin. On the death of a person seised in fee simple, seisin passed immediately to the decedent's heir.[6] To this day, that remains the theory of inheritance of land.[7] If no heir was immediately identifiable, a legal officer held a proceeding known as an inquest of office to determine if the property had escheated, that is, reverted to the Crown "from defect of heirs" (*propter defectum sanguinis*).[8]

When the American colonies of Great Britain became independent states in 1776, they succeeded to the Crown's right of escheat. After the formation of the federal union, the national government did not assert a claim to escheated property, presumably on the view that, as a government of delegated powers, it had not been granted that aspect of sovereignty. Even in states formed out of after-acquired territories, such as those in the Old Northwest and those acquired by the Louisiana Purchase, the federal government never claimed a right to escheats, presumably on the ground that new states entered the union with the same legal rights as earlier ones.[9]

In the common-law canons of descent, listing the order in which heirs succeeded to land, the Crown (or, in America, the state) did not appear.[10] Instead, escheat was understood as the recognition of an underlying – or, perhaps better, an overlying – title. As the Supreme Court of Nebraska once explained:

> Clearly the theory of the law in the United States… is that first and originally the state was the proprietor of all real property and last and ultimately will be its proprietor, and what is commonly termed ownership is in fact but tenancy…. When this tenancy expires or is exhausted by reason of the failure of the state or the law to recognize any person or persons in whom such tenancy can be continued, then the real estate reverts to and falls back upon its original and ultimate proprietor, or, in other words, escheats to the state.[11]

---

5   See Cornelius J. Moynihan & Sheldon F. Kurtz, *Introduction to the Law of Real Property* 30 (3rd ed. 2002).

6   2 *Bl. Com.* 201.

7   Atkinson, *Wills* § 103, pp. 563–64 (noting that the theory of the heir's "immediate title" has been reduced by modern statutes to a "hollow shell").

8   3 *Bl. Com.* 258.

9   The principle had been established by the Northwest Ordinance of 1787, originally adopted under the Articles of Confederation on July 13, 1787, confirmed and adapted to the United States Constitution on August 7, 1789 (1 U.S. Stats. 50) (new states to be admitted "on an equal footing with the original States").

10   For England, see 2 *Bl. Com.* 208–36; for America, see 4 *Kent Com.* *375–*412.

11   *In re O'Connor's Estate*, 252 N.W. 826, 827 (Neb. 1934). Two state constitutions have something similar: S.C. Const. art. XIV, § 3 ("The people of the State are declared to possess the ultimate property in and to all lands within the jurisdiction of the State; and all lands the title to which shall fail from defect of heirs shall revert or escheat to the people."); Wis. Const. art. IX, § 3 ("The people of the state, in their right of sovereignty, are declared to

As the law concerning intestate succession became codified, the practice arose for simplicity's sake of listing the state as the ultimate taker, and as heirs came to be defined as "those who take the property under the relevant statutes of descent,"[12] the state became in that sense – and in that sense only – the "last heir." But the state was never a true heir. Notoriously, an heir has no rights in the property while the ancestor lives, only a "mere expectancy."[13] The state has a right all along, a paramount title – at least, as to real property.

Feudal incidents, including escheat from defect of heirs, applied only to land, not to chattels. The explanation is historical. When feudalism emerged, land was essentially the only source of wealth. The land was what King William had taken by conquest, and it was the land that he apportioned among his loyal retainers. Chattels were not held of any overlord; they were – in a word borrowed from Roman law – "allodial," subject to absolute ownership, not feudal. When, over time, personal property assumed more importance, the question arose of succession on the death of an owner of personal property without a valid will or known heir. Escheat, or rather its practical effect, crossed the artificial barrier that separated land and chattels. For want of any other label, ownerless personal property was styled *bona vacantia* – vacant, that is, unowned goods[14] – and was taken by the Crown, probably for no better reason than that it was the royal courts that decided the matter. By the mid-eighteenth century, Lord Mansfield could lay it down that "in personal estates, which are allodial by law, the king is last heir where no kin."[15]

Ironically, in England, where it all began, escheat has been abolished, replaced by a right in the Crown to take land as *bona vacantia* in the same way that it takes goods.[16] In America, the situation was not so simple. A few states, in a burst of republican ardor, constitutionalized the rule that estates in land are allodial and that feudal incidents are not allowed, without however abandoning their claim to escheats.[17] Further confounding the old distinction between real and personal property, the intestate succession acts in most states now treat both real and

---

possess the ultimate property in and to all lands within the jurisdiction of the state; and all lands the title to which shall fail from a defect of heirs shall revert or escheat to the people.").

12   Cribbet, *Property* 258.

13   See Herbert Thorndike Tiffany, *The Law of Real Property and Other Interests in Land* § 172 (Renard Berman ed., abr. 3rd ed. 1970). Technically while the ancestor lives, there are no heirs. *Nemo est haeres viventis*. 3 *Bl. Com.* 224.

14   Although *bona vacantia* as used in this chapter refers only to personal property left unowned at the death of an owner without heirs or valid will, historically it could be used to refer to any personal property for which no owner could be identified. See, e.g., 1 *Bl. Com.* 288 (listing "royal fish, shipwrecks, treasure trove, waifs, and estrays").

15   *Burgess* v. *Wheate*, 1 Eden 177, 229, 28 Eng. Rep. 652, 672 (Ch. 1759).

16   15 Geo. 5, c. 3, § 41(1) & 46 (1925). Other common law jurisdictions followed the English lead. See, e.g., Administration of Estates Act 1954 (NSW).

17   Ark. Const. art. 2, § 28 ("All lands in this State are declared to be allodial; and feudal tenures of every description, with all their incidents, are prohibited."); Minn. Const. art. I, § 15 ("All lands within the state are allodial and feudal tenures of every description

personal property identically.[18] So it appears that indeed the state is the last heir with respect both to land and to chattels.

Much personal property also passes to the state today other than by intestate succession. Under the circumstances of modern economic life, large amounts of property are held by corporations or similar entities on behalf of individuals: deposit accounts, amounts due for interest or dividends, customers' overpayments, employees' unpaid wages, tenants' security deposits, stocks, bonds, proceeds of insurance policies, the contents of safe deposit boxes, and many more.[19] Pursuant to legislation, states take possession of such property if its owner initiates no action with respect to it for a specified number of years[20] and provide publication notice to the owner.[21] The practical reason behind the states' action is to prevent unclaimed personal property from being appropriated by the present holder.[22] The states are better able to provide long-term (perpetual) custody. In addition, it is sometimes admitted that the statutes are also a means of raising revenue.[23] The revenue-raising aspect is not new. In the eighteenth century Blackstone listed *bona vacantia* as one of the sources of royal revenue.[24] The sums involved today are enormous.[25] Many states dedicate unclaimed personal property, along with escheats, to the support of education.[26]

---

with all their incidents are prohibited."); Wis. Const. art. I, § 14 ("All lands within the state are declared to be allodial, and feudal tenures are prohibited.").

18   See Dukeminier, *Wills, Trusts, and Estates* 33.

19   For an even longer list, see Uniform Unclaimed Property Act § 1(13) (1995). See also *Rose's Stores, Inc.* v. *Boyles*, 416 S.E.2d 200 (N.C. Ct. App. 1992) ("escheat" of abandoned layaway payments).

20   See Uniform Unclaimed Property Act § 2(a) (1995) (period of inactivity varies from one to fifteen years, depending on the type of property).

21   Id. § 9 (notice in "a newspaper of general circulation in the [county] of this State in which is located the last known address of any person named in the notice").

22   Many retailers shift unused gift card credits from a liability account to an income account. Erica Alini, Governments Grab Unused Gift Cards, *Wall St. J.*, June 30, 2009, at A3 (citing filings with the Securities and Exchange Commission and annual financial statements.). It is reported that "many companies" assign gift card credits to subsidiaries in states that make no effort to claim those that are unused. Ron Lieber, Redeem All of Gift Card, or Give Store a Present, *New York Times*, Dec. 12, 2009, at B1.

23   See, e.g., *Louisiana Health Service & Indemnity Co.* v. *McNamara*, 561 So.2d 712, 716 (La. 1990) ("Although one purpose of such acts is to protect the missing owners, the primary rationale behind this legislation is its use as a revenue raising device."). See also 1 David J. Epstein, *Unclaimed Property Law & Reporting Forms* § 1.07 (2008).

24   1 *Bl. Com.* 288.

25   *The Wall Street Journal*, citing data from the National Association of Unclaimed Property Administrators and the state of Delaware, reported that as of June 2006 the states collectively held almost $35 billion in unclaimed property. Scott Thurm & Pui-Wing Tam, States Scooping Up Assets From Millions of Americans, *Wall St. J.*, Feb. 4, 2008, at A1.

26   E.g., N.C. Const. art. IX, § 10(2) ("All property that, after June 30, 1971, shall accrue to the State from escheats, unclaimed dividends, or distributive shares of the estates

Property that is equivalent to cash, such as the balance of an inactive bank account, is immediately deposited in a designated state fund, while marketable property, such as stock in a publicly traded corporation, is sold by a state officer – according to a common statutory provision, within three years of receipt[27] – and the proceeds of sale added to the fund. All statutes require the return of the property (or its value, if it was sold) to the owner on demand, regardless of how much time has elapsed.[28] Under some acts, the owner is entitled only to the original value of the property,[29] while other statutes allow the owner of saleable property in addition any increments that accrued at or prior to sale.[30] Still other statutes

---

of deceased persons shall be used to aid worthy and needy students who are residents of this State and are enrolled in public institutions of higher education in this state."); N.C. Gen. Stat. § 116B-7(a) (2007) (limiting expenditure to income derived from Escheat Fund). Prior to June 30, 1971, such property was appropriated by the constitution "to the use of The University of North Carolina." N.C. Const. art. IX, § 10(1). See John v. Orth, *The North Carolina State Constitution: A Reference Guide* 6, 7, 21, 148–49 (1993). Many state constitutions devote the money more generally to educational purposes. Ala. Const. art. XIV, § 258 ("the furtherance of education"); Ariz. Const. art. XI, § 8 ("the permanent State school fund"); Colo. Const. art. IX, § 5 ("the public school fund"); Idaho Const. art. IX, § 4 ("the public school permanent endowment fund"); Ind. Const. art. 8, § 2 ("the Common School fund"); Mo. Const. art. IX, § 5 ("the state school fund"); Mont. Const. art. X, § 2 ("the public school fund"); Neb. Const. art. VII, § 7 ("perpetual funds for common school purposes, including early childhood educational purposes operated by or distributed through the common schools"); Nev. Const. art. 11, § 3 ("for educational purposes"); N.M. Const. art. XII, § 4 ("the current school fund"); N.D. Const. art. IX, § 1 ("a perpetual trust fund for the maintenance of the common schools of the state"); Okla. Const. art. X, § 32 ("a State Public Common School Building Equalization Fund"); Or. Const. art. VIII, § 2 ("the Common School Fund"); S.D. Const. art. VIII, § 2 ("a perpetual fund for the maintenance of public schools in the state"); Wash. Const. art. IX, § 3 ("the common school fund"); Wis. Const. art. X, § 2 ("the school fund"); Wyo. Const. art. 7, § 2 ("perpetual funds for school purposes").

27   Uniform Unclaimed Property Act (1995) § 12.

28   Id. § 16. According to the official comment on this section, "The owner's rights are never cut off; under this Act, the owner's rights exist in perpetuity." 8C U.L.A. 132 (2001).

29   E.g., N.C. Gen. Stat. § 116B-64 (2007) (unclaimed personal property is held "without liability for income or gain"); Ind. Code Ann. § 32-34-1-30(b) (2002) (owner not entitled to receive dividends, interest, or other increments accruing after the state takes possession); 765 Ill. Comp. Stat. 1025/15 (2001) (owner not entitled to receive income or other increment accruing after state takes possession); Ohio Rev. Code 169.08(D) (2007) ("Interest is not payable to claimants of unclaimed funds held by the state."), declared unconstitutional in Sogg v. Zurz, 905 N.E.2d 187 (Ohio 2009).

30   See state statutes modeled on the Uniform Unclaimed Property Act § 21 (1981). E.g., Haw. Rev. Stat. § 523A-21(2006); S.D. Codified Laws Ann. § 43-41B-22 (1997). Prior versions of the uniform act did not provide for payment to the owner of any income or other increment accrued after delivery to the state officer. Id. Comment. 8C U.L.A. 239 (2001).

add accumulated interest on the amount taken from interest-bearing accounts for a certain number of years while in the state's custody.[31]

The theory by which the states take possession of unclaimed personal property is unclear. The Uniform Unclaimed Property Act, which in one version or another (1954, 1966, 1981, 1995) forms the basis for much state legislation, describes the property as "presumed abandoned,"[32] although it emphasizes that the state "does not take title to unclaimed property, but takes custody only, and holds the property in perpetuity for the owner."[33] The theoretical difficulties are significant. As one appellate court recognized: "While it is true that the Act is not a true escheat act, it is also true that it is not purely custodial in nature."[34] The right acquired by the state is anomalous, sometimes described as "custodial escheat."[35]

Abandoned property is unowned, not unclaimed, and ordinarily belongs to the first person to take possession of it.[36] Strictly speaking, personal property is abandoned the moment an owner surrenders dominion and control with the intention never to reclaim the item.[37] A common example is an item intentionally deposited in a wastebasket. Most instances of abandoned personal property involve a tangible item (*chose in possession*), not an intangible interest such as the ownership of the balance of a bank account or the share of ownership in a corporation represented by a stock certificate (*chose in action*). Almost all the personal property taken by the state as unclaimed is of the latter type.[38] The presumption of abandonment raised by the statute is rebuttable at any time since the state never claims title, but only perpetual custody. Ordinarily, non-use of property, even long-continued

---

31   See state statutes modeled on the Uniform Unclaimed Property Act § 11 (1995) (interest for up to 10 years at lesser of legal rate or rate paid while held by private depository). La. Rev. Stat. 9:164 (2004); Me. Rev. Stat. Ann. tit. 33, § 1962 (2004).

32   Uniform Unclaimed Property Act § 2.

33   Prefatory Note to the Uniform Unclaimed Property Act (1995), 8C U.L.A. 89 (2001). Similar language appeared in the earlier versions of the Act. Id. Any legally protected interest in property is in some sense a "title," but the distinction drawn here is the commonly encountered one between an interest good "against all the world" and an interest that is inferior to some other (or others).

34   *Smyth* v. *Carter*, 845 N.E.2d 219, 223 (Ind. Ct. App. 2006).

35   *Louisiana Health Serv. & Indem. Co.* v. *McNamara*, 561 So.2d 712, 717 (La. 1990).

36   See e.g., La. Civ. Code Ann. art. 3412 (2004) ("Occupancy is the taking of possession of a corporeal movable that does not belong to anyone. The occupant acquires ownership the moment he takes possession.").

37   1 *Am. Jur.* 2d, Abandoned, Lost, and Unclaimed Property, § 10 (2005). Title to real property cannot be abandoned, although some interests in real property, such as easements, can be. See *Powell on Real Property* § 423, p. 574 (one-vol. ed. by Richard R. Powell & Patrick J. Rohan 1968).

38   Tangible personal property, such as jewelry or even cash, may be included among the contents of an unclaimed safe deposit box. See Uniform Unclaimed Property Act § 3 (1995) (concerning "tangible property held in a safe deposit box").

nonuse, is not conclusive of an intent to abandon.[39] Once rebutted, the presumption of abandonment disappears and the owner's interest is recognized as uninterrupted – relating back to the state's first taking of possession.

Custody also seems an awkward description of the state's right to unclaimed personal property. Traditionally distinguished from bailment by reference to the owner's intent, custody is transferred when the owner places goods in the physical control of another but does not intend to surrender dominion over them. The handing of goods to a customer in a store to examine under supervision is a common example.[40] A custodian has physical control and some duty to protect and preserve the property, but state officers with custody of unclaimed personal property are regularly empowered to commingle the property with other state property and use it for state purposes, as well as to sell marketable property, conferring good title on the purchaser.[41] Even in the case of statutes that provide for accounting to the owner for increments in the value of saleable property or for interest on funds taken from interest-bearing accounts, the accumulation ceases after a period of time. Despite the assertion that the state is a "perpetual custodian," no statute provides for the compounding of interest for the entire period of the state's potential custody: in perpetuity. If it did, it would implicate the concerns reflected in the common-law Rule Against Accumulations of Income.[42]

The practical significance of the difficulty in identifying the state's right to unclaimed personal property is demonstrated by suits brought by owners seeking not just the return of their property – which is readily conceded by the state – but also an accounting for interest accrued while in the state's possession. Although recent suits have been against states that deny all interest, the same claim could eventually be made against states that limit the accumulation of interest or terminate it altogether after a certain number of years.[43] Some courts have upheld the state's refusal to account for interest on the ground that the proximate cause

---

39 1 Am. Jur.2d, Abandoned, Lost, and Unclaimed Property, §§ 9, 13, 14 (2005). See, e.g., *Sea Hunt, Inc.* v. *Unidentified Shipwrecked Vessel*, 221 F.3d 634 (4th Cir. 2000) (Spain had not abandoned ship wrecked hundreds of years ago); *State* v. *West*, 235 S.E.2d 150 (N.C. 1977) (state had not abandoned 200 year-old documents that had been lost).

40 Brown, *Personal Property* § 76, p. 269.

41 Uniform Unclaimed Property Act § 12(c) (1995) ("A purchaser of property at a sale conducted by the administrator pursuant to this [Act] takes the property free of all claims of the owner or previous holder and of all persons claiming through or under them."). In this section the property is referred to simply as "abandoned," not "presumed abandoned."

42 See *Thellusson* v. *Woodford*, 11 Ves. Jun. 112, 32 Eng. Rep. 1030 (Ch. 1805).

43 With respect to saleable unclaimed personal property, statutes limit the owner's accumulation to increments that accrued at or prior to its sale. Uniform Unclaimed Property Act § 21 (1981). Statutes that provide for interest on balances taken from interest-bearing accounts limit the amount (lesser of legal rate or rate paid while held by private depository) and the period of accumulation (no more than 10 years). Uniform Unclaimed Property Act § 11 (1995).

of the owners' loss was not the state's action but the owners' failure to act,[44] while others have held the state's retention of interest an unconstitutional taking.[45] Even in the latter case, a statute of limitation will eventually bar the owner's claim.[46] Although it is a maxim of law as well as of economics that "interest follows principal,"[47] interest is nonetheless distinct from principal and may be converted even when the principal is not.[48]

Is the state the last heir? If a person owning real and personal property dies without a valid will or known heir, the property passes to the state. In the case of escheat of land, the state has title; with respect to *bona vacantia*, it takes title.[49] By contrast, unclaimed personal property passes only into the state's "perpetual custody." The state never claims title. Interest earned by unclaimed personal property is another matter. Whether denied outright by the statute or limited by it in certain ways, title to the interest on unclaimed personal property sooner or later belongs to the state either as adverse possessor or as "last heir."

---

44   *Smyth* v. *Carter*, 845 N.E.2d 219 (Ind. Ct. App. 2006); *Rowlette* v. *North Carolina*, 656 S.E.2d 619 (N.C. Ct. App.), appeal dismissed, 666 S.E.2d 487 (N.C. 2008); *Smolow* v. *Hafer*, 867 A.2d 767 (Pa. Commw. Ct. 2005).

45   *Sogg* v. *Zurz*, 905 N.E.2d 187 (Ohio 2009); *Canel* v. *Topinka*, 818 N.E.2d 311 (Ill. 2004).

46   See *Sogg*, 905 N.E.2d 187 (applying four-year statute of limitation for conversion).

47   Broom, *Maxims* 497.

48   In similar manner, the state may acquire easements by prescription (adverse use), while leaving title to the underlying fee simple unaffected.

49   Ordinarily, final probate court decisions bar claims by "lost heirs" or devisees under previously undiscovered wills. See, e.g., Uniform Probate Code §§ 3-108 (three years after death of decedent) and 3-412 (sooner of 6 months after filing of closing statement by personal representative or 12 months after entry of any order). In similar fashion, nonclaim statutes bar creditors' rights. Id. § 3-803 (one year).

PART II
Driving Forces

Chapter 9
Intention: The Law of Unintended Consequences

In world history something else results from the actions of men than that which they intend and achieve, something else than they know or want.

Friedrich Hegel

Intention is a pervasive concept in the law. Torts are traditionally divided into intentional and unintentional torts, although the meaning of the distinguishing characteristic requires some explanation. Beginning law students are routinely baffled to discover that they can commit the "intentional" tort of trespass by entering land in the innocent but mistaken belief that they have a right to be there. Intention is also an essential element of criminal law, although it too requires some explanation. "Malice aforethought" does not demand quite the amount of time or mental effort that one might think. Contract is probably the legal discipline in which intention is most prominent. Agreement is of the essence of contract, but the "meeting of the minds" is a legal, not a psychological, concept. "The law has nothing to do with the actual state of the parties' minds," Oliver Wendell Holmes reminded his audience: "In contract, as elsewhere, it must go by externals, and judge parties by their conduct."[1]

Property law, too, must concern itself with intention, although it is generally more involved with the rights and responsibilities of ownership. Intention enters the law of property primarily when transfers of title are contemplated, particularly sales or gifts. Intention is also an element in the acquisition of personal property by finding and of real property by adverse possession, but these involve relatively small amounts of property.[2] The sale of property is a matter of agreement and would properly be treated as part of contract law except that, as to real property, special doctrines are involved and a deed is required to consummate the transaction.[3]

---

1   Holmes, *Common Law* 242.

2   Unintentional deprivations of title occur in cases of forfeiture and loss of title to adverse possessors; inheritance and escheat operate as unintentional gratuitous transfers. Condemnation, or the taking of property by the power of eminent domain, is an unintentional transfer for value (a forced sale) to the sovereign.

3   The lease of real property, historically characterized as the conveyance of a non-freehold estate, is also dependent on intention, but the requisite intention is stereotypically

Intention is a necessary element of the law of gifts. Every law student learns that the requisites of an *inter vivos* gift are intention, delivery, and acceptance.[4] Testamentary gifts are more complicated: the requisite intention, the *animus testandi*, must be expressed in certain stereotyped ways, usually in a writing, signed by the testator and attested by two witnesses.[5]

Intention was not always the lodestar in the law that it is today. As Professor Patrick Atiyah reminded us, for much of the long history of the common law, "giving effect to intentions" was not "the primary objective of the social order or of the law,"[6] but since the time of Lord Mansfield at the end of the eighteenth century, the steady advance of individualism has reoriented many legal doctrines. In the modern world the biblical question, "Is it not lawful for me to do what I will with mine own?"[7] is generally considered to be unanswerable. So obviously desirable has the effectuation of intention become that it requires some effort to recall that there are still legal rules, other than the criminal law, that are designed to frustrate it. Property law, in a sense the oldest part of the common law, remains the province of archaic and often intention-defeating rules.[8]

"We sit here," explained an influential English judge in an important wills case, "not to try what the Testator may have intended, but to ascertain, on legal principles, what testamentary instruments he has made."[9] The idea is still current in the twenty-first century: "The dispositive issue when construing a will is the expression of the words of it and not the attempt to divine the mind of the testator."[10] The Rule in Shelley's Case, where it still exists, means that a grant of a life estate to A followed by a remainder in fee simple to A's heirs will be construed to convey

---

indicated by the delivery of a signed document. See 219 *Broadway Corp. v. Alexander's, Inc.*, 387 N.E. 2d 1205 (N.Y. 1979).

4   Brown, *Personal Property* § 38, p. 84.

5   Atkinson, *Wills* § 62, p. 293 ("no will is valid unless there is compliance with all of the statutory requirements. The fact that the testator intended to comply… is not ground for relaxing the rules."). Many states recognize holographic (handwritten) wills and a few, nuncupative (oral) wills. Traditionally, the statutory requirements had to be complied with, although recently an effort has been made to relax the requirements. See John v. Orth, Wills Act Formalities: How Much Compliance is Enough? 43 *Real Prop., Tr. & Est. L. J.* 73 (2008).

6   P.S. Atiyah, *The Rise and Fall of Freedom of Contract* 122 (1979).

7   Matt. 20:15 (KJ).

8   The early common law has been described as "a primitive legal system which has a highly developed land law, but no theory of contract." 2 *H.E.L.* 355. See also John v. Orth, Contract and the Common Law, in *The State and Freedom of Contract* 44, 45–49 (Harry N. Scheiber ed. 1998). Without attention to contract with its insistence on intention, it was easier to focus on hard-and-fast rules and ignore expectations.

9   *Croker v. Marquis of Hertford*, 4 Moo. P.C. 339, 369, 13 Eng. Rep. 334, 344–45 (P.C. 1844) (Lushington, Dr.). See S.M. Waddams, *Law, Politics and the Church of England: The Career of Stephen Lushington, 1782–1873*, at 190–93 (1992).

10   *Hammer v. Hammer*, 633 S.E.2d 878, 882 (N.C. Ct. App. 2006) (citing *Faison v. Middleton*, 88 S.E. 141, 143 (N.C. 1916)).

the entire estate to A without regard to the grantor's intention, making it possible for A to alienate or devise the property away from his or her heirs.[11]

The rule that the four unities of time, title, interest, and possession are essential for the creation and preservation of a joint tenancy can defeat obvious intention, and a joint tenant has nothing to devise in the jointly owned property, no matter how clearly expressed the intention.[12] Nor are intentional restraints on alienation valid except in certain trusts[13] – which helps to explain the otherwise inexplicable Rule in Dumpor's Case,[14] the rule that covenants in a lease against transfer without the landlord's consent are presumed to be single and entire rather than multiple and several; that is, that consent to one transfer makes consent to further transfers unnecessary.

At one time, mortmain statutes empowered surviving spouses and children to set aside gifts to charity in death-bed wills,[15] and purging statutes, voiding the interests of an attesting witness, make no reference to the testator's intent.[16] The ubiquitous statutes that today grant a surviving spouse an elective share in the estate of the deceased partner are obviously intended to defeat an intention to reduce or eliminate the survivor's share.[17] The Rule Against Perpetuities, of course, is the most celebrated check on intention, and its chief expounder, John Chipman Gray, seemed to glory in the Rule's intention-defeating potential:

> The Rule against Perpetuities is not a rule of construction, but a peremptory command of law. It is not, like a rule of construction, a test, more or less artificial, to determine intention. Its object is to defeat intention. Therefore every provision in a will or settlement is to be construed as if the Rule did not exist, and then to the provision so construed the Rule is to be remorselessly applied.[18]

---

11   See Chapter 2, The Rule in Shelley's Case: Staying Too Long.

12   See Chapter3, Joint Tenancy: Accounting for Continuity.

13   See Simes, *Future Interests* § 113, p. 238 ("all disabling restraints are void" except "restraints on alienation incident to beneficial interests in spendthrift trusts").

14   4 Co. Rep. 119, 76 Eng. Rep. 1110 (K.B. 1603).

15   For what appears to be the last remaining American mortmain statute, see Ga. Code § 53-2-10 (1998). For what may have been the next-to-last, see New York Est., Powers & Trusts Law § 5-3.3 (repealed 1981). The earliest mortmain statutes required the donor to seek permission by statute or royal license before land could be transferred to a corporation, usually at that time some arm of the Church. For an historical survey, see Sandra Rabban, *Mortmain Legislation and the English Church, 1279–1500* (1982).

16   See, e.g., *Estate of Parsons*, 163 Cal. Rptr. 70 (Cal. Ct. App. 1980).

17   See, e.g., Conn. Gen. Stat. § 45a-436 (1998); N.C. Gen. Stat. § 30-3.1ff. (2000). Elective share statutes are found in all separate property states except Georgia. Dukeminier, *Wills, Trusts, and Estates* 425 & n. 1. In community property states the spouses own all acquisitions from earnings after marriage in equal undivided shares. The Uniform Probate Code tries to reconcile the spouse's elective share with intention by invoking an "unspoken marital bargain under which the partners agree that each is to enjoy a half interest in the fruits of the marriage." Unif. Probate Code, art. II, pt. 2, gen'l cmt (1990).

18   Gray, *Rule Against Perpetuities* § 629, p. 599. In the interest of unfettered intention, the Rule Against Perpetuities seems to be in process of disappearing. See Va. Code Ann.

Rules of construction, unlike rules of law, are supposed to effectuate intention. By raising a rebuttable presumption that specific words and phrases have certain meanings, they reduce the likelihood of disputes and increase the speed and efficiency of property transactions. The Doctrine of Worthier Title, where it still exists, raises a presumption that a limitation in a deed, including a deed of trust, creating a remainder in the grantor's heirs is actually intended to leave a reversion in the grantor, giving the grantor power to alienate or devise the property away from his or her heirs.[19] Ambiguous terms in conveyances are construed to avoid the possibility of forfeiture; in consequence, restrictive covenants are preferred to conditions subsequent, and fees subject to conditions subsequent are preferred to determinable fees.[20]

Pretermission statutes are designed to carry out the testator's presumed intention by providing for a neglected spouse or child.[21] The same may be said of so-called anti-lapse statutes, substituting gifts to issue for gifts to deceased family members,[22] and statutes revoking testamentary gifts in favor of divorced spouses.[23] Ademption (by extinction) means that when a testator has during life disposed of the subject of a devise, "whatever may have been the intent or motive of the testator," the gift fails, although modern courts attempt to salve their conscience with the observation that "the doctrine seeks to give effect to a testator's probable intent by presuming he intended to extinguish a specific gift of property when he disposed of that property prior to his death."[24]

While rules of construction are intended to effectuate intention, they may in some cases actually defeat it. Not only are mistakes in application possible, but the presumption in favor of one construction over another will resolve or preclude disputes in cases in which evidence is lacking or inconclusive. There are, in addition, rules of construction that, under the guise of effectuating intention, are in fact designed to make it more difficult to accomplish certain ends, permissible in themselves but viewed as undesirable or unlikely to be the product of informed

---

§ 15-15.3 (Rule applies only in absence of expression to the contrary); N.C. Gen. Stat. § 41-15, -23 (all restraints on perpetuities repealed as to beneficial interests in trust where trustee has a power of sale). For an article questioning the constitutionality under the state constitution of the statute, see John v. Orth, Allowing Perpetuities in North Carolina, 31 *Campbell L. Rev.* 399 (2009).

19   Although it began as a rule of law, *Co. Litt.* § 19, p. 22b, the Doctrine of Worthier Title has, at least since Judge Benjamin Cardozo's landmark opinion in *Doctor v. Hughes*, 122 N.E. 221 (N.Y. 1919), been generally regarded as a rule of construction, therefore rebuttable by evidence to the contrary.

20   Restatement of Property § 45, cmt m.

21   See, e.g., Fla. Stat. § 732.301 (1993) (pretermitted spouse); N.H. Rev. Stat. Ann. § 551:10 (1974) (pretermitted child).

22   See, e.g., Tex. Probate Code § 68 (1997). So-called anti-lapse statutes do not actually prevent lapse; rather, they substitute one gift for another under certain circumstances.

23   See, e.g., Mass. Gen. Laws Ann. ch. 191, § 9 (1997).

24   See, e.g., *Wasserman v. Cohen*, 606 N.E.2d 901, 902-03 (Mass. 1993).

choice. The butcher's (or, rather, the judge's) thumb weighs more heavily in some determinations of intention than in others.

The strong presumption in favor of marketable title in contracts for the sale of land means that an agreement to convey land that is silent as to the title to be conveyed, even an agreement to convey by means of a quitclaim deed, is construed to be an agreement to convey a full marketable fee simple.[25] Public policy in favor of an implied warranty of habitability in the sale of residential real estate is so strong that, for a waiver to be effective, the contract of sale must explicitly refer to the "warranty of habitability" *in ipsissima verba*.[26] The class-closing rule in the law of trusts creates so powerful a presumption that the settlor would prefer a class to close as soon as any member thereof can demand distribution that it has been confused with a rule of law.[27] The presumption against agreements among cotenants not to partition means that an agreement to do "nothing to defeat the common tenancy" might not be interpreted as intended to prohibit partition.[28] The rule (usually statutory) in favor of tenancy in common means that a grant to two or more to hold "jointly" will not be construed to create a joint tenancy.[29] If two grantees are in fact married to one another, even if not so described in a conveyance, there may be a presumption that they are to hold as tenants by the entirety.[30]

Legal words are presumed to be used with their legal meanings, which is just a specific application of the general rule that where written words have what appears to be a plain meaning, that meaning is to be preferred above all others.[31] This

---

25   See *Wallach v. Riverside Bank*, 100 N.E. 50 (N.Y. 1912). See also Unif. Land Transfer Act § 2-304(d) (adopting "the rule of *Wallach*").

26   See *Board of Managers v. Wilmette Partners*, 760 N.E.2d 976 (Ill. 2001) (holding waiver of "warranties of fitness for particular purpose and merchantability" insufficient to waive implied warranty of habitability); Va. Code Ann. § 55-70.1 (permitting waiver of warranties in the sale of new homes "only if the words used to waive, modify or exclude such warranties are conspicuously... set forth on the face of the contract...."). In leases the implied warranty can often not be waived at all. See *Javins, Saunders, and Gross v. First Nat'l Realty Corp.*, 428 F.2d 1071, 1082 (D.C. Cir. 1970); N.C. Gen. Stat. § 42-42(b).

27   See *Re Wernher's Settlement Trusts*, [1961] 1 All Eng. Rep. 184. Expert observers have conceded that the class closing rule is "adhered to more closely than any other rule of construction." Dukeminier, *Wills, Trusts, and Estates* 663.

28   See *Michalski v. Michalski*, 142 A.2d 645 (N.J. 1958) (reversing trial court's finding that the agreement did not prohibit partition but refusing to enforce it anyway because of "changed circumstances").

29   See *Mustain v. Gardner*, 67 N.E. 779 (Ill. 1903); *In re Estate of Hillyer*, 664 So.2d 361 (Fla. 1995). But see 4 *Thompson on Real Property* § 31.06(d), p. 24, noting that in a few states the opposite rule applies.

30   This was the common law rule, see Id. § 33.06(a), p. 129, and it has been adopted by statute in some states. See, e.g., Alaska Stat. § 34.15.110(b); N.C. Gen. Stat. § 39-13.6(b).

31   *Suffolk Business Ctr. v. Applied Digital Data*, 581 N.E.2d 1320, 1322 (N.Y. 1991) (construing a deed). See also Atkinson, *Wills* § 146, p. 811 ("If the testator employed a draftsman skilled in the use of technical words these must be given their technical

seemingly simple rule may have unintended consequences. A scrivener might not translate the grantor's intention into the right legal words. Instructed to draft a deed conveying title in joint tenancy with right of survivorship, the drafter might neglect, out of ignorance or inadvertence, to use the form of words necessary in the jurisdiction.[32] Legal words may be used in a will, but the testator, if not the lawyer, may have understood them in another, less specific sense. The word "heirs," for example, may be thought to include relatives such as in-laws and stepchildren not provided for in the relevant statute of descent.[33]

Rules concerning the manifestation of legal intention have the effect of making some manifestations final, "privileging," to use a modern expression, the intention of one time over another or of one form of expression (usually certain types of writing) over others. *Inter vivos* gifts are irrevocable once "completed," and oral revocations of wills are not allowed. But the intention that originally supported the gift may have changed. In such cases there is ordinarily no remedy – unless the donor reserved a power of revocation, as in a conditional gift or revocable trust, or unless the law treats the act as inherently revocable as, for example, a gift *causa mortis*. Nor is the discernment of intention simple. Fact-finders, both judges and juries, are notoriously capable of manipulating rules concerning mental capacity, undue influence, and fraud to upset unpopular or unconventional dispositions in wills, so much so that one scholar has dismissed freedom of testation as no more than a "myth."[34]

Formal requirements are meant to ensure that intention properly expressed is given effect,[35] but they may operate in some cases to defeat intention. Although

---

meaning."). The practical effect of the plain meaning rule is to exclude evidence of other possible meanings.

32   The Pennsylvania Supreme Court has observed that in that state "to create a right of survivorship the *normal* procedure is to employ the phrase 'joint tenants, with a right of survivorship, and not as tenants in common.'" *In re Estate of Michael*, 218 A.2d 338, 342 (Pa. 1966) (italics in original). In Michigan the same form of words has been held to create an estate for joint lives with alternative contingent remainders in the survivor. *Jones v. Green*, 337 N.W.2d 85 (Mich. App. 1983). See Byron D. Cooper, Continuing Problems With Michigan's Joint Tenancy "With Right of Survivorship," 78 *Mich. B.J.* 966 (1999).

33   See *Mahoney v. Grainger*, 186 N.E. 86 (Mass. 1933) (rejecting proffer of evidence that testatrix understood "heirs" to mean her first cousins, when she had a surviving aunt who was her actual heir under the relevant intestate succession act).

34   Melanie B. Leslie, The Myth of Testamentary Freedom, 38 *Ariz. L. Rev.* 235 (1996) (examining cases on undue influence and will formalities). There is a distinction between the intention that a transaction be effective and intention with respect to the meaning of some of its terms, but in practice a fact-finder can negate the substantive intent by failing to find the operative intent.

35   In their classic analysis of the role of formal requirements in the law of testation, Gulliver and Tilson identified ritual, evidentiary, and protective functions, while insisting that the forms "should not be revered as ends in themselves, enthroning formality over frustrated intention." Ashbel G. Gulliver & Catherine J. Tilson, Classification of Gratuitous

donative intent may be established, a gift may nonetheless fail for want of delivery.[36] Perhaps the most troubling cases concern attempted testamentary gifts. Failure to satisfy certain formal requirements, typically involving a writing, signature, and witnesses, may result in the frustration of the obvious intention of a person now deprived by death of the ability to cure the defect. The remedy most commonly proposed for the frustration of testamentary intent by failure to comply with the proper forms is simply to devolve upon legal decision-makers discretion to accept as wills documents that do not in fact comply with the statute.

As amended in 1990, the Uniform Probate Code (UPC), in a section adopted in half a dozen states, provides:

> Although a document… was not executed in compliance with [the formalities required of wills], the document… is treated as if it had been executed in compliance… if the proponent of the document… establishes by clear and convincing evidence that the decedent intended the document… to constitute… the decedent's will….[37]

There exists some confusion about the exact nature of this provision. The UPC itself treats the section as if it merely excused "harmless error," but at least one court has described it as adopting a "doctrine of substantial compliance,"[38] while commentators generally admit that it confers on the courts a plenary "dispensing power," that is, the power to dispense with the statutory requirements altogether if necessary to effectuate intention.[39] Thus does intention trump form; or, more precisely, thus does the judicial determination of intention trump the legislative prescription of form.

A troubling illustration of the problem is provided in *Johnson v. Johnson*, a 1954 wills case from Oklahoma.[40] Dexter Johnson, himself a lawyer who had prepared many wills in proper form for his clients, left at his death a typed document appearing to be his own will but neither signed nor witnessed as required.[41] At its foot appeared a handwritten and signed statement leaving a nominal gift to his

---

Transfers, 51 *Yale L. J.* 1, 3, 5–13 (1941). Frequent failure to comply with formal requirements may indicate that the requirements are not congruent with common expectations.

36 *Foster v. Reiss*, 112 A.2d 553, 560 (N.J. 1955) (gift *causa mortis*) ("Although the writing establishes her donative intent at the time it was written, it does not fulfill the requirement of delivery of the property, which is a separate and distinct requirement ….").

37 Unif. Probate Code § 2-503 (harmless error).

38 *In re Will of Ranney*, 589 A.2d 1339, 1343 (N.J. 1991). Substantial compliance seems to require at least some compliance or attempted compliance.

39 Dukeminier, *Wills, Trusts, and Estates* 233–35. Harmless error, as its name implies, seems to admit some error, however minor, in compliance. A dispensing power, on the other hand, suggests no need to comply (or attempt to comply) at all.

40 279 P.2d 928 (Okla. 1954).

41 No lawyer who has ever supervised the elaborate ceremony of executing a written attested will could possibly think that he had executed his own will without signature or

brother and reciting the seemingly obvious fact that "this will shall be complete unless hereafter altered, changed or rewritten."[42] *Devisavit vel non?* Local law permitted holographic wills and codicils, so the handwritten part could be probated, assuming testamentary intent was found. But what of the typewritten part? The lower courts rejected the entire document as lacking testamentary intent, but the Oklahoma Supreme Court reversed. In a confused opinion relying largely on the argument that the typewritten "will" had been "republished" by the handwritten "codicil," the Court ordered the probate of the entire document.[43]

Associate Justice Nelson S. Corn concurred in the result and authored a precocious statement of the doctrine of substantial compliance: "It was not the intent of our law-makers, in enacting these statutes, if substantially complied with, to ever allow a miscarriage of justice by a wrongful disposition of the testator's property contrary to his intent."[44] Not interested in technical subtleties, Justice Corn would have held simply that "in the instant case, the intent expressed by the testator... is clear and beyond any question."[45] One might applaud the justice's opinion as the triumph of substance over form and a premonition of the "substantial compliance" or "harmless error" standard if the evidence was as unequivocal as he said it was – and if the justice himself had not been one of America's most corrupt judges![46]

Students and commentators alike too often assume that the choice is between a regime of rules with the potential to defeat intention and the simple effectuation of intention without regard to rules. In fact, the choice is between prescribing rules to guide decision-makers and entrusting them with still more discretion. Granting judges the authority to accept less than the prescribed formalities in the law of wills, while perhaps reducing the likelihood of intention-defeating decisions, will also have the necessary consequence of requiring extensive fact-finding in many cases that do not eventually result in the "clear and convincing" establishment of the decedent's intention.[47] And – in light of the evidence that fact-finders already

---

witnesses. For the recommended method of executing a will, see 1 A. James Casner, *Estate Planning* § 3.1.1 (6th ed. 1998 with Jeffrey N. Pennell).

42   279 P.2d at 933 (photocopy of original document). As every lawyer knows, wills are inherently revocable and ambulatory. Atkinson, *Wills* § 1, p. 2.

43   "Publication" of a will is defined as "the signification by the testator to the witnesses that the instrument is his will." Atkinson, *Wills* § 68, p. 327. Since the typewritten part had never been "published" in the first place, it necessarily follows that it cannot have been "republished." It is at least arguable that the handwritten part was not a holographic codicil but a holographic will that incorporated the typewritten part by reference.

44   279 P.2d at 932 (Corn, J., concurring).

45   Id. The evidence did not seem so clear to the judges of the district and county courts or to the three Supreme Court justices who dissented in the case.

46   See *Johnson v. Johnson*, 424 P.2d 414, 416 (Okla. 1967) (describing bribe-taking by Justice Corn over more than twenty years but finding no evidence that bribery influenced the decision in this particular case).

47   Judges actually prefer to work with rules, both to ensure fairness and to economize their time and effort, and in the absence of rules generate them spontaneously. In certain

manipulate the rules in order to defeat substantive dispositions – it will only increase the opportunity for abuse. Without fidelity to rules as a standard by which to review judicial performance, judges may escape effective oversight. Faulting "judgment calls" is far more difficult than detecting lapses in the application of rules. In the end, the commendable intention to effectuate intention may instead lead only to consequences that are as unfortunate as they are unintended.

Australian states that have given judges a dispensing power, the cases have "produced a ranking of the Wills Act formalities..., devaluing attestation while insisting on signature and writing." John H. Langbein, Excusing Harmless Errors in the Execution of Wills: A Report on Australia's Tranquil Revolution in Probate Law, 87 *Colum. L. Rev.* 1, 52–54 (1987). In other words, the judges have effectively amended the Wills Act.

Chapter 10
Competition: The Race to the Bottom

> The life of the law has not been logic and it has not been experience. It has been borrowing.... In the Western world..., borrowing is the name of the legal game.
>
> Alan Watson

"The race to the bottom" is a phrase made famous in the history of the law of business associations.[1] Starting in the 1890s, New Jersey and Delaware competed for the privilege of chartering corporations (and reaping the associated economic benefits). The states engaged in a sort of Dutch auction, progressively offering better and better, that is, lower and lower, terms in their standard-form corporate charters. Eventually, New Jersey dropped out of the running, and Delaware won the race – which, of course, is why today one of the nation's smallest states hosts the "headquarters" of so many large corporations and why the Delaware Chancery Court is one of the world's most important business courts.

Competition between American states is not surprising. The single economic and social union that is the United States, legally bound up by the Federal Constitution, makes it almost inevitable. The state of Nevada provides an obvious example. Permissive divorce laws made it an early destination for unhappy couples, just as relaxed marriage requirements still make it popular with hopeful young people.[2] Legalized gambling attracts millions of visitors annually, even as

---

1   See, e.g., 2 Jerry W. Markham, *A Financial History of the United States* 58 (2002). The classic statement of the race-to-the-bottom thesis is William L. Cary, Federalism and Corporate Law: Reflections Upon Delaware, 83 *Yale L.J.* 663 (1974). Whether the race was truly to the "bottom" is debated; whether there was even a race at all is denied. See, e.g., Marcel Kahan & Ehud Kamar, The Myth of State Competition in Corporate Law, 55 *Stan. L. Rev.* 679 (2002). Extending the argument to property law, see Abraham Bell & Gideon Parchomovsky, Of Property & Federalism, 115 *Yale L. J.* 72 (2005) (arguing that state laws governing property, including adverse possession, easements, and same-sex marriage, permit individuals to push property law in innovative and efficient directions).

2   The Clark County, Nevada, Marriage License Bureau is open seven days a week 8am to midnight and 24 hours on legal holidays. No blood test is required and there is no waiting period; the fee is about $35. *Frommer's Las Vegas 2001* at 184–85 (2001). Nevadans seem to have lost their nerve when it came to toleration of same-sex marriage. Not only did Massachusetts win that race by legalizing such unions before any other state, see *Goodridge* v. *Dept. of Public Health*, 798 N.E.2d 941 (Mass. 2003), but Nevadans even amended their state constitution to prohibit their state from competing for the business. Nev. Const. art. I, § 21 ("Only a marriage between a male and female person shall be recognized and given effect in this state.").

other states (and Indian reservations) have entered the field.[3] Still the only state to allow betting on collegiate athletics and to give most of its counties the option to legalize prostitution, Nevada continues to exploit its law-making, or rather its law-repealing, advantages. It is ironic that a state so closely associated in the public mind with lawlessness and the Mob is the supreme example of the law's power to influence behavior.

Whether this competition is good or bad depends on one's point of view. The phrase "race to the bottom" obviously encodes a negative judgment, but a different label suggests a different assessment. In a celebrated dissent, U.S. Supreme Court Justice Louis Brandeis described as "one of the happy incidents of the federal system that a single courageous State may, if its citizens choose, serve as a laboratory; and try novel social and economic experiments without risk to the rest of the country."[4] Although Brandeis had legal restrictions on economic competition in mind, his formula applies equally well to the removal of restraints, social as well as economic. If one approves of the result, or is at least willing to give it a chance, "social experiment" is a happier description than "race to the bottom."

While these legal experiments are in progress, they provide a social safety valve, an outlet for those activities that are elsewhere illegal. Legalized betting on collegiate sports in Nevada, for example, is sometimes justified as providing a legal venue for complaints about tampering with student athletes.[5] Observation of the outcome of these "social experiments" may eventually convince other states to follow their example. In the meantime, these "laboratories" produce "experimental law" not only for their own citizens, but also for those with the time and money necessary to travel to the appropriate legal marketplace. Of course, in a democratic society the existence of "law for the elites" – or, to be more precise, venues for elites to get the law they prefer – increases the pressure on other states to "democratize" the benefit (and not lose out on the profits). What ended the attraction of the "Reno divorce" was the adoption of relaxed divorce laws in other states. Gambling works for Nevada, providing the state with sufficient revenue to maintain a low-tax regime, thereby attracting new residents and businesses, and increasing the pressure on other states to offer gambling opportunities. Without Nevada's legislative power, Las Vegas and much of the state would still be uninhabited desert.

Travel is obviously necessary if actual physical presence is required, as for marriage or divorce. Gambling, too, requires a presence in the state since federal

---

3 As of 2003, almost 200 federally recognized Indian tribes run over 300 gambling facilities in 28 states, generating about $10 billion annually, one-seventh of all legal gambling proceeds. Craig Lambert, Trafficking in Chance, *Harvard Magazine* 33, 40 (July–August 2002).

4 *New State Ice Co.* v. *Liebmann*, 285 U.S. 262, 280, 311 (1932) (Brandeis, J., dissenting).

5 See Chad Millman, *The Odds: One Season, Three Gamblers, and the Death of Their Las Vegas* 186–91 (2001).

law prohibits the placing of bets over means of interstate communication, such as the telephone and internet.[6] But elites do not necessarily need to travel to take advantage of other favorable legal regimes, and in some cases, personal presence may actually be a disadvantage. For trusts located in Delaware, no state income tax is levied if the beneficiaries live in another state. Given the fact that money is easily transmitted within the United States, competition has broken out among the states to secure the trust business of the wealthy by offering better (that is, less restrictive) trust law. There has long been competition for trust business between American states, on the one hand, and foreign nations, particularly small island nations, on the other. What foreign nations could not offer, of course, was the stability and security of American law.

When Delaware repealed the Rule Against Perpetuities as applied to trusts, it freely admitted in the preamble to its statute that the purpose was to keep the state's banks and trust companies competitive. Although repeal cost the federal government estate tax revenue, local interests were better served by attracting capital. Pointing the finger at "several innovative jurisdictions that have abolished the rule," the Delaware statute recited that "several financial institutions have now organized or acquired trust companies, particularly in South Dakota, at least in part to take advantage of their favorable trust law."[7] Determined to beat these states at their own game and "maintain Delaware's role as the most favored jurisdiction for the establishment of trusts," the state went on to authorize the creation of self-settled spendthrift trusts that protect the settlor's assets from the claims of creditors.[8]

The state's power of eminent domain, the power to take private property for public use, can be invoked to provide opportunities for economic development.[9] States compete with one another for investments that bring jobs and higher tax revenue, not at the expense of the federal fisc but at the expense of other states in the federal union. In a unitary nation like England, central administrative control limits competition. Local authorities there have little incentive to compete with one another.

---

6   Interstate Wire Act of 1960, 18 U.S.C. § 1084.

7   1996 Laws of Del., ch. 538 (amending Del. Code Ann. tit. 25, § 503), preamble quoted in Jesse Dukeminier & Stanley M. Johanson, *Wills, Trusts, and Estates* 854 (6th ed. 2000). South Dakota had earlier repealed the Rule Against Perpetuities. S.D. Codified Laws Ann. §§ 43-5-4; 43-5-8. See Stewart E. Sterk, Jurisdictional Competition to Abolish the Rule Against Perpetuities: R.I.P. for the R.A.P., 24 *Cardozo L. Rev.* 2097 (2003).

8   Del. Code Ann. tit. 12, § 3570 ff. (2002). See John E. Sullivan III, Gutting the Rule Against Self-Settled Trusts: How the New Delaware Trust Law Competes With Offshore Trusts, 23 *Del. J. Corp. L.* 423 (1998). Previously, spendthrift provisions were limited to trusts for the benefit of others than the settlor. George T. Bogert, *Trusts* § 40, p. 155 (6th ed. 1987) ("a property owner may not create a spendthrift trust in his own favor"). For the latest development see, John v. Orth, Allowing Perpetuities in North Carolina, 31 *Campbell L. Rev.* 399 (2009) (describing one state's attempt to join the race and the constitutional problem that caused).

9   *Kelo* v. *City of New London*, 545 U.S. 792 (2005).

And in Europe as a whole, the construction of a continental common market has led to restrictions on "state aids" that could distort economic decision-making.[10]

Competition creates a market for laws not only between states in a federal union but also between courts of concurrent jurisdiction operating in the same state. In England before the Judicature Acts of 1873–75,[11] the three common-law courts of King's (Queen's) Bench, Common Pleas, and Exchequer exercised overlapping jurisdiction. Throughout the Middle Ages, a lively competition among these courts, driven by the judges' desire to augment their incomes with fees from the litigants, had produced substantial improvements in justice.[12] The action of ejectment, which began as a tenant's remedy, was made available as a means to try title to land by the toleration of a convenient legal fiction; because of procedural advantages, it relegated the "proper" remedy, the writ of right, to oblivion.[13] The action of trover, which began as a finder's remedy (as its French name implies), became the means to try title to chattels by a similar fiction and won out over the ancient action of detinue, also because of procedural advantages.[14]

In addition, the English Chancery Court, usually known as "equity," was famously available to supplement the common law whenever the legal remedy was inadequate, leaving a legacy that survived the eventual merger in most jurisdictions of law and equity.[15] The trust for a married woman's "sole and separate use" offered wealthy fathers a means to circumvent the male-dominated common law and preserve a daughter's property from her husband and his creditors. The celebrated passage of Married Women's Property Acts in England and America in the mid-nineteenth century democratized the benefits, making them available to all married women.[16]

---

10   Tom Allen, Controls Over the Use and Abuse of Eminent Domain in England: A Comparative View, in *Private Property, Community Development, and Eminent Domain* 75, 88–92 (ed. Robin Paul Malloy, 2008).

11   36 & 37 Vict. c. 66 (1873); 38 & 39 Vict. c. 77 (1875).

12   For a brief survey, see Gray, *Nature and Sources of Law* 32–35. For a facetious summary with a serious intent, see John v. Orth, A Reverie on Medieval Judges, Milton Friedman, and the Supreme Court's Workload, 69 *A.B.A.J.* 1454 (1983).

13   See 3 *Bl. Com.* 199–206.

14   See id. 150–53.

15   See U.S. Const. art. III, § 1 ("The judicial Power of the United States shall be vested in one supreme Court….," i.e., not in separate courts of law and equity as in England at the time); N.C. Const. art. IV, § 13 ("There shall be in this State but one form of action for the enforcement or protection of private rights or the redress of private wrongs, which shall be denominated a civil action…," i.e., not separate actions at law and suits in equity) (original in N.C. Const. of 1868, art. IV, § 1). In England the merger of law and equity was complete by 1875, but a few common law jurisdictions retained separate equity courts much longer. The Australian state of New South Wales maintained the separation until 1972. Patrick Parkinson, *Tradition and Change in Australian Law* 157–58 (2nd ed. 2001). The state of Delaware still does.

16   See Dicey, *Law and Opinion* 371–98. See also N.C. Const. art. X, § 4 ("The real and personal property of any female in this State acquired before marriage, and all property,

In the United States the federal system gave litigants a choice of federal or state courts in many private law actions, at least when the parties were not citizens of the same state. For almost a century after the decision in *Swift v. Tyson* (1842),[17] federal judges exploited this "diversity jurisdiction" to offer litigants a better and national brand of commercial law. Only in 1938 did the Supreme Court in *Erie Railroad v. Tompkins*[18] put an end to this competition, commonly known by the bad name of "forum shopping." Luckily, other forces – national legal education, scholarly treatises, and uniform acts – were by then available to provide the homogenization once provided by the federal courts.

Legal competition occurs not only between states or courts; it even occurs between legal doctrines within the same jurisdiction. Where there are two different means to the same end, lawyers and judges will constantly be required to compare and contrast them, and litigants will advance one or the other as it suits their interests. It is a staple of first-year property law that *inter vivos* gifts of personal property require donative intent, delivery, and acceptance.[19] Of these three, delivery is the most problematic, as the cases amply attest. Left to more advanced property courses is the fact that by a mere oral declaration of trust a donor may transfer beneficial title (the only one that usually matters) without delivery.[20] The roots of the two doctrines lie in the dual sources of Anglo-American jurisprudence. Law, with its tradition of fixed rules and remedies, gave rise to the formal requirements for gifts,[21] while equity, with its emphasis on intention and consequent tolerance of informality, was the home of the trust.

Maintaining the distinction between gifts and trusts has been a recurring preoccupation of judges and property scholars. In the first part of the nineteenth century, a line of English cases threatened to eliminate the legal requirement of delivery altogether by treating almost any manifestation of donative intent as a

---

real and personal, to which she may, after marriage, become in any manner entitled, shall be and remain the sole and separate estate and property of such female, and shall not be liable for any debts, obligations, or engagements of her husband, and may be devised and bequeathed and conveyed by her....) (original in N.C. Const. of 1868 art. X, § 6).

17   16 Pet. (41 U.S.) 1 (1842).

18   304 U.S. 64 (1938) (overruling *Swift*).

19   Brown, *Personal Property* § 38, p. 84.

20   The beneficial title acquired by the donee in a declaration of trust is in one situation inferior to the legal title acquired by the donee of a completed *inter vivos* gift: if the trustee disposes of the property to a purchaser for value and without notice of the equitable interest, the purchaser's title prevails over the donee's title. George T. Bogert, *Trusts* § 165, p. 597 (6th ed. 1987) ("bona fide purchaser rule"). Of course, the beneficiary in such a situation is entitled to enforce a constructive trust on the property acquired by the trustee in exchange for the trust corpus. Rest. 2d Trusts § 202 ("trust pursuit rule").

21   The delivery requirement in the law of gifts has very ancient antecedents and has been related to the comparable requirement in the early law of feoffments, livery of seisin. See *Cochrane v. Moore*, 25 Q.B.D. 57, 65–66 (C.A. 1890).

declaration of trust.[22] Sir George Jessel, himself an influential equity judge, finally put an end to this development in 1874 by ruling that "for a man to make himself a trustee there must be an expression of intention to become a trustee, whereas words of present gift shew an intention to give over property to another, and not to retain it in the donor's own hands for any purpose, fiduciary or otherwise."[23] In America, Professor Austin Scott, a founding scholar of the modern law of trusts, frowned on cases where an intended gift fails for lack of delivery but courts nonetheless "torture," as he put it, "an imperfect gift into a declaration of trust."[24] While nominally concerned with discerning intention – to make a present gift or to create a trust – the real concern seems to be with drawing the proper legal lines.

The effect again is to create law for the elites, this time not in the sense of those with the resources to travel (or send their money) to the most attractive legal marketplace but in the sense of those with the best lawyers. The legally well advised may undoubtedly make gifts without delivery by making an express and well attested declaration that they hold legal title as trustee for the beneficiary-donee. A simple donor of a common law gift, on the other hand, must see to it that there is actual delivery of the item itself (or at least some part or symbol of it) or risk the failure of the transfer.[25] The ironic result of the continued distinction is that courts will enforce an oral declaration that A gives B the equitable interest in a chattel while retaining the *legal* interest, but will not enforce an oral declaration that A gives B the *entire* interest, both legal and equitable.[26]

The alternative of a declaration of trust has not been altogether without effect on the law of gifts. The delivery requirement is subject to constant pressure not only from the increased value now assigned to intention but also from the existence of a parallel gifting procedure that never required delivery. Recent Restatements of the Law reflect the current ambivalence. While the Restatement (Second) of

---

22   *Ex parte Pye*, 18 Ves. Jun. 140, 34 Eng. Rep. 271 (Ch. 1811); *Grant v. Grant*, 34 Beav. 623, 55 Eng. Rep. 776 (Ch. 1865) (placing the case of a husband's gift of personal property to his wife within "that class of cases in which it has been held that, though there is not an absolute delivery, a declaration of trust is sufficient"); *Morgan v. Malleson*, L.R. 10 Eq. 475 (1870).

23   *Richards v. Delbridge*, L.R. 18 Eq. 11, 15 (1874).

24   1 Austin W. Scott, *The Law of Trusts* § 31, p. 321 (4th ed., William F. Fratcher ed., 1987). Scott did allow that in case the intended donee of a failed *inter vivos* gift reasonably relied on the prospective benefit, a constructive trust could be impressed, but he insisted that in such case "equity is not converting an imperfect gift into a declaration of trust, but is merely imposing a duty on the donor in order to prevent unjust enrichment." Id. § 31.4, p. 350.

25   Actual delivery of the donated chattel may be excused if it is too bulky or if, for some good reason, it is not at hand, but some symbol of it must be actually delivered. Brown, *Personal Property* § 41, p. 102. The legal fiction of "constructive delivery" was the common law's way of mitigating the harshness of the delivery rule.

26   See C.B. Labatt, The Inconsistencies of the Laws of Gifts, 29 *Am. L. Rev.* 361, 368 (1895).

Property officially takes no position on whether a gift may be effective without delivery, it does note the fact that "a beneficial interest in personal property can be conferred on another person by an oral declaration of trust even though there is no delivery" and suggests that "the law should recognize, to the extent it has not already done so, that a completed gift of personal property may be accomplished without a delivery by proof of the donor's manifested intention to make a gift."[27] The Restatement (Third) of Trusts straddles the same divide. To the black-letter rule that "if a property owner intends to make an outright gift *inter vivos* but fails to make the transfer that is required in order to do so, the gift intention will not be given effect by treating it as a declaration of trust," the reporter appends the subversive comment that "the preferred interpretation in marginal cases of this type is not that the property owner was merely expressing an intention to make a gift in the future but rather that the owner intended a declaration of trust."[28]

This tension is unlikely to be easily resolved. The judges, who created the delivery requirement in the first place, are reluctant to abandon it, not only because of their professional attachment to traditional doctrine, but also because it gives them added flexibility in the administration of justice. As one court that had occasion to consider the alternatives put it: "Obviously, it would be neither advisable nor wise to abrogate the requirement of delivery in any and all cases of intended *inter vivos* gifts, for to do so, even under the guise of enforcing equitable rights, might open the door to fraudulent claims."[29] The delivery requirement, in other words, provides another line of defense against ambiguous or self-serving testimony about donative intent.

A similar competition, but one with far greater consequences, has affected gratuitous transfers at death. Ordinarily effected by the decedent's last will and testament, the inter-generational transfer of wealth may also be arranged through an ever-lengthening list of will substitutes. The modern will, the product of statutes beginning in the sixteenth century,[30] generally requires a writing, signed by the testator and attested by two witnesses. Recognized centuries before the first Statute of Wills, the joint tenancy in land with its associated right of survivorship long provided an alternative legal means for arranging succession at death.[31] The development of modern banking and the invention of the joint and survivor bank account generalized this to include personal property in the form of deposits, so

---

27   Rest. (2d) Property: Donative Transfers § 31.1, cmt k. This is true, but only in the sense of a gift of the beneficial interest.

28   Rest. (3d): Trusts § 16 (2), cmt d.

29   *Hebrew Univ. Assoc.* v. *Dye*, 223 A.2d 397, 401 (Conn. Super. Ct. 1966) (upholding gift by finding delivery of written instrument). Cf. *Hebrew Univ. Assoc.* v. *Dye*, 169 A.2d 641 (Conn. Super. Ct. 1961) (finding insufficient evidence of express declaration of trust).

30   See Digby, *History of the Law of Real Property* 377–92 (tracing legislation from 1530 to 1837).

31   See Chapter 3, Joint Tenancy: Accounting for Continuity. A joint tenancy in land is not an exact alternative to a will, because a present interest vests in the cotenant at the creation of the estate.

much so that these accounts have been dubbed the "poor man's will."[32] Modern brokerage houses offer the same option for investment accounts.

Insurance companies pioneered the pay-on-death contract, which the banks adapted to their own industry in the form of a deposit account known as a Totten Trust, a nominal trust account, the balance of which (if any) is payable to a designated person at the death of the depositor.[33] So attractive has the pay-on-death designation been that the federal government adopted it for United States savings bonds. A growing number of states now allow a death beneficiary to be named in a deed of land.[34] Instead of judicial supervision of a decedent's estate, will substitutes use the administrative resources of financial institutions, which have emerged as private competitors of the public probate system.

It is the trust, however, that has become the ultimate "will substitute."[35] As befits its equitable origin, the trust may be created with few formalities and allows great flexibility. During life, a settlor may transfer assets into a revocable trust, reserving a life estate and specifying future interests; if unrevoked at death, the trust then disposes of the property. Modern estate planners, astute not to lose the ambulatory potential of testamentary dispositions, generally add a "pour-over will," which transfers to the trust any assets remaining in the settlor's sole name at death. Trust law is typically elite law. The revocable-trust-and-pour-over-will arrangement is for well advised, usually wealthy clients. Without competent advice, settlors of small trusts, often of the do-it-yourself variety, sometimes forget to keep their trust documents current and end up with improperly titled property and poorly maintained records, resulting in unnecessary expense and occasionally unintended consequences.[36]

As with *inter vivos* gifts, the simultaneous existence of a less formal means to the same end has placed tremendous pressure on the more formalized alternative.

---

32   See *In re Estate of Michaels*, 132 N.W.2d 557 (Wis. 1965). See also Note, Disposition of Bank Accounts: The Poor Man's Will, 53 *Colum. L. Rev.* 103 (1953). Unlike the joint tenancy in land, no interest passes to a donee "co-depositor" at the creation of the account, only a power to draw on deposited funds, which explains why the federal gift tax is not imposed until an amount is actually withdrawn by the non-depositing party.

33   *Matter of Totten*, 71 N.E. 748 (1904).

34   See, e.g., Kan. Stat. Ann. § 59-3501; Ohio Rev. Code Ann. § 5302.22.

35   The trust, in its guise as a "use," was available before the first Statute of Wills to provide a functional alternative in equity. See Digby, *History of the Law of Real Property* 330–33. It is an irony of history that the trust (use) was a will substitute before there were wills, and that, after centuries of eclipse by the will proper, it has resumed this role.

36   See, e.g., *Austin, Trustee* v. *City of Alexandria*, 574 S.E.2d 289 (Va. 2003) (holding ineffective a second transfer by a settlor who had previously transferred the same property into a revocable trust); *Secor Investments* v. *Anderegg*, 71 P.3d 538 (Or. 2003) (illustrating the distinct legal personalities of the settlor as an individual and as the trustee of a self-settled *inter vivos* trust); *First Nat'l Bank of Bar Harbor* v. *Anthony*, 557 A.2d 957 (Me. 1989) (holding ineffective an apparent attempt to revoke a revocable *inter vivos* trust by a will).

If simpler will substitutes are available, how can statutory will formalities that might defeat intention be justified? In fact, wills law is now subject to searching criticism and a movement is underway in favor of disregarding "harmless error" in execution, permitting "substantial compliance" with the formalities, or simply granting the judiciary a power to dispense with the necessary forms.[37]

Labels encode conclusions. They do not (or should not) dictate them. The "race to the bottom" is competition to get to a destination we do not wish to reach, while "social experiments" sound at once scientific and courageous. Competition is probably inevitable in a federal system, and may well be desirable. Rather than worry about whether we are in a race to somewhere-or-other, we should concentrate our attention on the end we want to attain, then on the means to achieve it. "Law for elites" has an unwholesome sound in a democracy; only a "savage race," as Tennyson so memorably put it, deserves "unequal laws."[38] But equal laws do not necessarily serve everyone equally well. Seeking the least common denominator, commentators and judges may well be distracted from the real project of providing formal requirements appropriate to the transaction and its likely participants.

---

37   See Unif. Probate Code § 2–503 (harmless error); John H. Langbein, Substantial Compliance With the Wills Act, 88 *Harv. L. Rev.* 489 (1975); John v. Orth, Wills Act Formalities: How Much Compliance is Enough? 43 *Real Prop. Tr, & Est. L. J.* 73 (2008). See also Chapter 9, Intention: The Law of Unintended Consequences.

38   Alfred Tennyson, *Ulysses* (1842) l. 4.

Chapter 11

Fiction: Pious Fraud

A general proposition of some value may be advanced with respect to the agencies by which Law is brought into harmony with society. These instrumentalities seem to me to be three in number, Legal Fictions, Equity, and Legislation. Their historical order is that in which I have placed them.

Sir Henry Maine

To modern Americans "legal fiction" brings to mind the novels of John Grisham or Scott Turow, but to an earlier generation of lawyers the phrase meant a different kind of make-believe. Essentially, legal fiction (in the old sense) meant an irrebuttable allegation of a fact without regard to its truth or falsity. The object could be to secure access to a form of procedure that was speedier, cheaper, or simply more likely to produce the desired result. The old action of trover, to recover the value of personal property wrongfully withheld, began with an allegation that the property at issue had been lost by the plaintiff and found (*trouvé* in Law French) by the defendant who converted it to his own use.[1] Of course, it was really immaterial how the defendant came to possess the item in question; it could have been purchased, or received as a gift – or actually found. The dispute concerned whether the plaintiff was entitled to recover its value from the defendant. The action of trover was the simplest way to get a legal resolution of that dispute.

Likewise, disputes concerning title to real property could be determined by the ancient and cumbersome procedure initiated by the writ of right, but the right to present possession – what really mattered – could be tried much more expeditiously by the action of ejectment. The problem was that ejectment had been designed to resolve questions of a tenant's right to possession, not an owner's. So, a plaintiff involved in a dispute over the right to Blackacre alleged that he had leased the land to a tenant, John Doe, who was ejected by someone claiming authority from the defendant. The caption of the case read "Doe on the Demise [lease] of *Plaintiff v. Defendant*," usually shortened to "Doe on the Dem. of...," or even "Doe d...." Before the defendant's answer could be heard, he had to admit the lease and ejectment, which everyone knew was pure fiction; then the court could proceed to the real issue, whether Plaintiff or Defendant had the better right.[2] These usages were carried over to the British colonies in North America and continued in the newly independent country. In a few states such as New

---

1   3 *Bl. Com.* 151–52.
2   Id. 199–206.

Jersey and North Carolina the name of the fictitious tenant inexplicably mutated to Den, so the caption became "Den on the Dem. of...."[3] It became settled doctrine in America, that "trover is to personalty what ejectment is to realty."[4]

Fictions made available some convenient forms of action. They also unlocked the doors to the common law courts. For six hundred years, the common law was administered by three courts: Common Pleas, King's (Queen's) Bench, and the Exchequer. Originally their jurisdiction was distinct. In general terms, Common Pleas handled – as its name implied – ordinary disputes; King's Bench, more serious controversies; and the Exchequer, disputes concerning the royal revenue. Over time, the various courts enlarged their jurisdiction by allowing fictitious allegations. Although medieval lawsuits usually commenced with an initial filing called a writ, it had early been established that proceedings could be commenced by a bill if the defendant was already within the court's jurisdiction, and King's Bench had jurisdiction over all disputes of whatever kind arising in the County of Middlesex, which encompassed Westminster where the court sat. All that was required to gain access to King's Bench, then, was to file a bill, known as a "Bill of Middlesex," alleging a trespass in Middlesex by the defendant, who was lurking (*latitat*) in another county, and the court had jurisdiction to hear any real cause of action against him. In time, the Bill and its fictitious allegations came to be dispensed with altogether.

Common Pleas responded to the threat and enlarged its own jurisdiction by allowing a fictitious allegation that a defendant who had been summoned had failed to appear and required capture (*testatum capias*), before going on to the real cause in controversy. Not to be left out, the Exchequer expanded its reach by allowing an allegation that the defendant had failed to do justice to the plaintiff by which he was rendered less able (*quo minus*) to pay his dues to the King, again allowing access to the court for the resolution of the real dispute. By the mid-eighteenth century it was the case that the first process in all three courts was based on a fiction: a *latitat* in King's Bench, a *testatum capias* in Common Pleas, and a *quo minus* in the Exchequer.[5] The judges' uncharacteristic eagerness to enlarge their jurisdiction and thereby increase their workload, is explained by the fact that they and their officers were compensated largely out of the fees collected from litigants.[6]

In after years, the most notorious example of the use of fiction to extend jurisdiction was probably *Mostyn v. Fabrigas* (1774),[7] in which the Mediterranean

---

3   See, e.g., *Den on the Dem. of Bayard* v. *Singleton*, 1 N.C. 5 (1787).

4   *Russell* v. *Hill*, 34 S.E. 640, 640 (N.C. 1899). For a discussion of this case, see John *v.* Orth, *Russell* v. *Hill* (N.C. 1899): Misunderstood Lessons, 73 *N.C. L. Rev.* 2031–61 (1995).

5   See 3 *Bl. Com.* 286.

6   See Gray, *Nature and Sources of Law* 32–35.

7   1 Cowp. 161, 98 Eng. Rep. 1021 (K.B. 1774). See Gray, *Nature and Sources of Law* 35 (1st ed. 1909) (describing *Mostyn* as "the most grotesque of these fictions"); Charles

island of Minorca was alleged to be located in central London so that a dispute that arose there could be resolved in the Court of King's Bench. Of course, no one really believed this geographical tomfoolery, or any of the other legal fictions. Lord Mansfield, who participated in the decision of *Mostyn*, had observed in an earlier case that "fictions of law hold only in respect of the ends and purposes for which they were invented; when they are urged to an intent and purpose not within the reason and policy of the fiction, the other party may shew the truth."[8] Nonetheless, legal fiction carried to such an extent attracted increasing criticism in the Age of Enlightenment, and drew the particular ire of that tireless critic of the common law, Jeremy Bentham.[9] Not only did Bentham object to the obscurantism – a charge that is hard to deny – but he was outraged by the idea of "a willful falsehood having for its object the stealing of legislative power by and for hands which could not, or durst not, openly claim it."[10] Stripped of the fictions, what was going on – as Bentham rightly saw – was a violation of separation of powers, law making, not by the legislature, but by the courts.

Not only could convenient fictions overcome jurisdictional obstacles, they could also assist a court in doing justice in individual cases. To create an express easement, a deed was required, but when one person made long-continued use of the land of another in a manner that would normally indicate an easement, the absence of a deed could be excused by alleging that it had been lost. If the landowner had acquiesced in the use for long enough (usually the period set by the statute of limitations for the acquisition of an estate in fee simple by adverse possession), the allegation of the "lost grant" became irrebuttable. Counsel and court were in on the game, fully aware of what was going on. As Lord Mansfield said in open court: "Not that, in such cases, the Court actually thinks a grant has been made; because, it is not probable a grant should have existed, without its being upon record; but they presume the fact, for the purpose and from principle of quieting the possession."[11] To this day, easements acquired by adverse use are said to be acquired by prescription (literally, "previously written").[12]

Allan Wright & Mary Kay Kane, *Law of Federal Courts* § 42, n. 2, p. 258 (6th ed. 2002) (similar).

8   *Morris* v. *Pugh*, 2 Burr. 1241, 1243, 97 Eng. Rep. 811, 811 (K.B. 1761).

9   For a brief biographical sketch, see John v. Orth, Jeremy Bentham: The Common Law's Severest Critic, 68 *A.B.A.J.* 710–15 (1982). For a fuller, more philosophical account, see Gerald J. Postema, *Bentham and the Common Law Tradition* (1986).

10   Quoted in Carter, *Law* 181.

11   *Eldridge* v. *Knott*, 1 Cowp. 214, 215, 98 Eng. Rep. 1050, 1051 (K.B. 1774).

12   See Bruce & Ely, *Easements* § 5:1. See also Jerome J. Curtis, Reviving the Lost Grant, 23 *Real Prop. Prob. & Trust J.* 535 (1988); Mark A. Clawson, Note, Prescription Adrift in a Sea of Servitudes: Postmodernism and the Lost Grant, 43 *Duke L. J.* 845 (1994). *Pace* Lord Mansfield, the ghost of the lost grant continued to haunt the law of easements by prescription since "adverse" use by the claimant was inconsistent with "acquiescence" in the use by the landowner.

A similar technical problem in the law of easements arose if a grantor attempted simultaneously to grant a fee simple and retain an easement in the granted land. Because at common law no one could have an easement in his own land – "so long as there is unity of ownership, there can be no easement"[13] – in order to effectuate intention, the court had to pretend that the grant of the fee by the grantor to the grantee included a simultaneous grant of the easement by the grantee back to the grantor, leading to the baffling distinction in the law of conveyancing between an exception, which excepts (that is, excludes) an interest from a grant, and a reservation, which reserves (that is, in this sense, creates) an entirely new interest.[14]

* * *

Separation of powers is one of the cardinal principles of American constitutionalism, implicit in the structure of the Federal Constitution and explicit in many state constitutions. The North Carolina Constitution of 1776, for example, echoing the Maryland Constitution of earlier the same year, declared "that the legislative, executive, and supreme judicial powers of government ought to be forever separate and distinct from each other."[15] But the verbal triumph of separation of powers in America did not mean the end of law making by legal fiction. As we have seen, the old common law causes of action, such as trover and ejectment, continued in use in the New World. So too did the fiction of the lost grant (easement by prescription) and the strained concept of easement by reservation.

While the precise jurisdictional gambits of the old common law courts found no home in the newly organized American court system, a remarkable new fiction quickly developed in the federal courts to confer jurisdiction where it

---

13   2 George Thompson, *Commentaries on the Modern Law of Real Property* § 352, p. 305 (1980).

14   "A *reservation* is a clause in a deed, whereby the grantor reserves some new thing to himself issuing out of the thing granted, and not *in esse* before; but an *exception* is always of a part of the thing granted, or out of the general words and description in the grant." 4 *Kent Com.* 468. The legal imagination was apparently exhausted by the effort of imagining the grant of an easement from the grantee to the grantor. It could not imagine a reservation in favor of a third party, one not in privity with the grantor and grantee. According to a rule at least as old as Lord Coke, "the reservation must be to the grantors, or some, or one of them, and not to any stranger to the deed." 2 *Bl. Com.* 299. See *Co. Litt.* § 58, p. 47a. The Restatement (3d) of Prop.: Servitudes § 2.6 (2) (2000) rejects the old no-reservations-in-a-stranger rule: "The benefit of a servitude may be granted to a person who is not a party to the transaction that creates the servitude."

15   N.C. Const. of 1776, Dec'l of Rights § 4, carried forward substantially unchanged in N.C. Const. art. I, § 6. See John *v.* Orth, *The North Carolina State Constitution* 41–44 (1993). For a modern case involving this provision, see John *v.* Orth, "Forever Separate and Distinct": Separation of Powers in North Carolina, 62 *N.C. L. Rev.* 1 (1983). See also Md. Const. of 1776, Dec'l of Rights § 6. To the same effect, see Va. Const. of 1776, Bill of Rights § 5; Mass. Const. of 1780, Dec'l of Rights § XXX.

would otherwise have been lacking. By presuming that all the stockholders in a corporation, itself a fictitious person, are citizens of its state of incorporation, federal courts were able to assume jurisdiction over many suits involving the rapidly proliferating new form of business association on the ground of diversity of citizenship. Harvard Law Professor John Chipman Gray early in the twentieth century denounced this fiction as "remarkable for the late date of its origin and for its absurd results."[16]

Bentham and his followers had so blackened the name of legal fiction that the name at least had to go. But a very similar reality remained under the label of "constructive this-and-that." The common law had a sorry history of using construction to extend the reach of the medieval Treason Act[17] by the doctrine of constructive treasons, which Chief Justice John Marshall firmly excluded from federal law in the treason trial of Aaron Burr.[18] In the law of wills, an expansive doctrine of constructive revocation caused wills to fail unnecessarily. Beginning with the reasonable principle that subsequent marriage and the birth of issue impliedly revoked a prior will, the courts had come to find that almost any change in circumstances revoked a will, which Lord Mansfield denounced as "over-strained resolutions" that "had brought a scandal upon the law."[19] Nonetheless, Chancellor Kent reluctantly admitted that this doctrine had crossed the Atlantic and flourished in America.[20]

Still, legal construction (if not legal fiction) served useful purposes. The law concerning gifts of personal property had long ago settled into a rigid pattern: actual delivery of the donated item was required, and delivery meant the complete surrender of dominion and control.[21] But attempted gifts of items that were remote or too large to deliver could be upheld on a theory of constructive delivery, if something that gave access to the thing, such as a key, or if some symbol of it, such as a writing, was actually delivered. The law of landlord and tenant gave the tenant the option of rescinding the lease in case of eviction, and eviction meant ouster by the landlord. But actions short of actual ouster that made continued occupancy very undesirable, and in some cases similar actions by other tenants, came to be accepted by courts as giving rise to the same remedy on a theory of constructive eviction.[22] At common law, fraud required the intentional misrepresentation of a material

---

16   Gray, *Nature and Sources of Law* 35. See also id., 183–86.

17   25 Edw. 3, st. 5, c. 2 (1350).

18   *United States* v. *Burr*, 25 F. Cas. 55, 59–80 (C.C.D. Va. 1807) (No. 14,693) (distinguishing *Ex parte Bollman*, 8 U.S. (4 Cranch) 75, 126 (1807).

19   *Swift d. Neale* v. *Roberts*, 3 Burr. 1488, 1491, 97 Eng. Rep. 941, 942–43 (K.B. 1764).

20   4 *Kent Com.* 530.

21   Modern U.S. Treasury Regulations concerning the effectiveness of gifts for tax purposes restate the common law requirement of complete surrender of dominion and control. Reg. § 25-2511-2(b).

22   See, e.g., *Blackett* v. *Olanoff*, 358 N.E.2d 817 (Mass. 1977) (finding constructive eviction due to a disturbance created by other tenants of the same landlord).

fact, but constructive fraud could be found without intentional misrepresentation in case a statement of a fact was made as of one's own knowledge when such knowledge was actually lacking.[23]

Constructive delivery, constructive eviction, and constructive fraud were all recognized by common law courts to lessen the rigors of common law rules and produce just results, but a constructive something can also be produced by statute. The operation of the recording acts means that a purchaser of real property is charged with notice of whatever is revealed on the face of the record even if the record was not actually examined; it provided constructive notice.[24] And apart from the statute, a court can find constructive notice from facts on the ground that would cause a reasonable person to make inquiries, "inquiry notice."[25] In consequence, the defense of bona fide purchase – that a good faith purchaser takes clear of defects in title unknown to him – is sometimes denied even to one who had no actual knowledge.

Although construction can be a (more or less intended) by-product of a statute, as with the recording acts, it is more commonly used by courts to prevent a statute from producing an inequitable result. The statute of descent and distribution might provide that on the death of a married man survived by a wife and no descendants, the wife is to succeed to all his property. But what if she had murdered her husband? One response has been to allow the legal title to descend to the murderer as provided by the statute and then, in an appropriate proceeding, to impress a constructive trust on the property.[26] In other words, the murderer is treated as a trustee, holding bare legal title for the benefit of others. The trust is, of course, pure fiction, imposed to prevent wrongful gain from bad behavior, a trust *ex malificio*.[27] There was no intention to create it, and the trustee is not given the usual fiduciary powers of control and management. In fact, the trustee may do nothing with the property except whatever is necessary to transfer legal title to the beneficial owner.[28] Despite its name, the constructive trust is merely a remedial device, not properly a trust at all[29] – to the consternation of modern law students, not so inured to legal fictions as their predecessors. Of course, legislation in the form of so-called slayer statutes can reach the same destination more directly.[30]

---

23   See, e.g., *National Academy of Science* v. *Cambridge Trust Co.*, 346 N.E.2d 879 (Mass. 1976).

24   Gray, *Nature and Sources of Law* 36–37.

25   See, e.g., *Sanborn* v. *McLean*, 206 N.W. 496 (Mich. 1925).

26   *In re Estate of Mahoney*, 220 A.2d 475 (Vt. 1966).

27   See James Barr Ames, Can a Murderer Acquire Title by His Crime and Keep It?, in *Lectures on Legal History and Miscellaneous Legal Essays* 310 (1913) (originally published in *American Law Register*, 1897) (developing theory that legal title passes to a murderer subject to a trust *ex malificio*).

28   George T. Bogert, *Trusts* § 77, p. 287 (6th ed. 1987) (constructive trustee's "sole duty is to transfer title and possession to the beneficiary").

29   See Cardozo, *Judicial Process* 42.

30   See, e.g., N.C. Gen. Stat. § 31A-1ff. See also Unif. Probate Code § 2-803 (1990).

In addition to the historic common law courts, there was also a court of chancery or equity, with jurisdiction generally supplemental to that of the law courts. This opened the possibility of further fictions under the name of "equitable this-and-that," a possibility made even more likely when law and equity came to be administered by the same court. Where a child was raised by persons other than her parents who did not follow the statutory procedures for legal adoption, it might be equitable (in the general sense of "fair") to treat the child as if she had been adopted; thus was born the concept of equitable adoption.[31]

Equity courts had jurisdiction over disputes concerning transfers of property because the remedy at law (damages) was presumed to be inadequate, since any given parcel of land is unique. Equitable conversion, so-called, confers equitable title on a purchaser from the moment an enforceable contract for the sale of land is executed. In other words, the purchaser under a still executory contract is treated in equity as if the transaction had actually closed because the contract is specifically enforceable.[32] Not only can equitable conversion allow a contract to be treated as a grant, it can also allow personal property to be treated as real property. When condemnation replaces land with money, the money is held by the same title as the realty, which can have significant consequences if the land had been held by a married couple in tenancy by the entirety, a form of ownership based on the fiction that "the two become one." Just as the land could not have been sold or otherwise dealt with by one spouse alone, so the money is held *in solido*, inseverable by the act of either spouse and with an indefeasible right of survivorship.

Mortgage law, too, is marked by the equity court's special role in real estate transactions. Although originally structured as a defeasible transfer – in many states it still bears the marks of its origin – the mortgage has been hedged about over the years with an elaborate series of protections for the borrowing landowner. But a distressed borrower might succumb to a lender's demand that he waive these protections, or that he allow the transaction's true nature to be disguised as an outright sale. Equity will pierce the veil and look through to the reality – doing justice by means of a fiction, the equitable mortgage.

* * *

Legal fiction began as a means to add flexibility to the law in an age when statutes were few and far between. Grown accustomed to the practice, judges continued to use it to address the problems inevitably generated by the clash between the operations of a rule-based system and the demands of individual justice. A rule is settled, whether by precedent or statute, that comes to seem unduly restrictive. A gift is intended, but the item to be given is not (or cannot be) actually delivered. A tenant leaves premises that have been made functionally, if not actually, untenable by the landlord. A person in a position to know misstates a fact on which another

---

31   See, e.g., *Lankford* v. *Wright*, 489 S.E.2d 604 (N.C. 1997).
32   Cardozo, *Judicial Process* 38–39.

reasonably relies. A person who acts as a parent fails to comply with the terms of the adoption statute. A person with the opportunity to get information from the record fails to examine it. An heir takes title to property that rightfully should pass to someone else. A person obligated to purchase real property has not yet actually been tendered the deed. A borrower has tried to surrender legal protections incident to a mortgage.

Legal development by precedent is of no help in these cases. The law has already reached its outermost limit. There was really no delivery, eviction, fraud, or notice. The child was not legally adopted. Legal title has not yet passed; no mortgage was actually given. It is no longer possible to say that these cases are like the others in all essential details, the necessary predicate for the application of precedent or a statute. But justice demands a similar result. So, fictions in the form of legal or equitable constructions are pressed into service. If the cases are not really alike, then a court will simply pretend that they are.

Of course, legal fiction is not the only device to handle the clash between inflexible rules and just results. A person with only a limited interest in real property such as a life estate is duty-bound to let it pass unchanged to the holder of the future interest. Any changes in the physical condition of the land is "waste." But what if the change is beneficial and restoring the property to its previous condition would actually be destructive of value? Fiction is of no particular help here, so the effect of the rule must be nullified by a different device. Waste it is and waste it remains, but a new form of waste is recognized: "meliorating waste," waste that does not waste (that is, diminish) the property, but actually improves it, and so does not merit the consequences of real waste.[33] Thus the rule is preserved and justice is done.

Sometimes the root of the problem is a statutory requirement of form, as with the law prescribing the form of adoption. The Statute of Frauds requires a writing "signed by the party to be charged therewith" for "any contract or sale of lands, tenements or hereditaments, or any interest in or concerning them."[34] What is to be done in the case of a deed poll, signed only by the grantor and accepted by the grantee, but including covenants to be performed by the grantee? How is the grantee who never signed to be held liable for any violations of the covenants? It has been seriously suggested that perhaps the grantee can be said to have adopted the grantor's signature as the grantee's own: "Acceptance by the grantee... amounts to an adoption of the signature of the grantor as that of the grantee also, so that the requirement of the statutes of frauds as to signature is considered satisfied."[35] Of course, the straightforward approach is simply to dispense with the statutory requirement of a signature in this case. "A grantee, by acceptance of a deed, becomes bound by conditions, etc., contained therein, even though he

---

33   See, e.g., *Melms* v. *Pabst Brewing*, 79 N.W. 738 (Wis. 1899).
34   29 Car. 2, c. 3, § 4 (1677).
35   2 *Am. L. Prop.* 408.

has not signed the deed. The delivery and acceptance of a deed takes covenants contained therein out of the operation of the statute of frauds."[36]

What about ill-advised or unadvised parties who enter into an oral contract for the sale of land? The equitable doctrine of part performance allows the court to enforce the contract despite the Statute of Frauds if actions such as a change in possession, payment, and the making of improvements have taken place.[37] The chancellor's conscience is salved by the reasoning that these objective acts are referable only to both parties' understanding that a binding contract had been made – thereby satisfying the policy behind the statute: securing reliable evidence of intention. What if a person makes an unqualified conveyance in due form but subject to an oral agreement to reconvey under certain conditions? Technically void, the oral agreement can nonetheless be enforced under a theory of constructive trust if necessary to prevent fraud, a further instance of a trust *ex malificio*.[38]

Similarly, an oral grant of an easement fails under the statute, but entry by the grantee is no trespass because the grant can at least function as a license, which is not subject to the requirement of a signed writing. If improvements are made by the grantee in reasonable reliance on the validity of the easement, the licensor can be estopped to revoke the license (at least so long as necessary for the grantee to recoup on the investment).[39] Of course, an irrevocable license is indistinguishable from an easement, the only difference between an easement and a license being the revocability of the latter. In consequence, although easements cannot be created orally, an oral easement coupled with reasonable reliance can become an irrevocable license – or, to make a long story short, an easement "by estoppel."[40]

Again, the Statute of Frauds requires a writing for leases of more than a certain period.[41] What is to be done in case of an innocent failure to comply? The court

---

36   See, e.g., *Harris & Gurganus* v. *Williams*, 246 S.E.2d 791, 794 (N.C. App. 1978). Accord Restatement (3d) of Prop.: Servitudes § 2.7 cmt g (2000).

37   See Zechariah Chafee, Jr. & Edward D. Re, *Cases and Materials on Equity* 549–50 (5th ed. 1967).

38   See, e.g., *Hieble* v. *Hieble*, 316 A.2d 777 (Conn. 1972).

39   See, e.g., *Stoner* v. *Zucker*, 83 P. 808 (Cal. 1906). On the duration of the estoppel, *compare* 2 *Am. L. Prop.* 321 ("The irrevocability . . . extends only so far as necessary to protect the licensee in the expenditures made by enabling him to realize upon them.") *with* Restatement (Third) of Prop.: Servitudes, ch. 4, Intro. Note, at p. 496 ("The first Restatement of Property took the position that irrevocable licenses... have a shorter duration, based on the period of time necessary to amortize the expenditures that gave rise to creation of the easement. A similar result could be reached in a particular case under § 4.3, but only if the circumstances suggest that the parties intended or reasonably expected that result. Otherwise, the irrevocable license is treated the same as any other easement.").

40   See Bruce & Ely, *Easements* § 6:1.

41   29 Car. 2, c. 3, §§ 1–3 (1677) (leases of more than three years "from the making thereof"). Some statutes preserve the three-year period, see, e.g., N.C. Gen. Stat. § 22-2 (2003), but most reduce the period to one year. E.g., Va. Code Ann. § 11-2 (2006).

can recognize the creation of a periodic tenancy instead.[42] While not achieving all that the parties intended to accomplish (as with part performance), this result at least gives both parties legal rights, and the tenant some security of tenure. Ironically, periodic tenancies are exempt from the Statute of Frauds because the longest period allowed is one year; yet, unless timely notice is given by either party, the tenancy may endure for as long as (or even longer than) the term of the unenforceable oral lease.[43]

The Statute of Wills allows revocation by physical act, if done with the requisite intent, the *animus revocandi*. What if a testator who has a validly executed will revokes it and executes another instrument which is intended to replace it but which is, for one reason or another, defective? In order to effectuate intention a court may disregard the revocation and assume that it was meant to be conditional on the validity of the replacement. To avoid the name (if not the reality) of legal fiction, the device is known to generations of law students as "dependent relative revocation."[44]

Finally, the Statute of Wills prescribes a specific form for the execution of a will, usually the signature of the testator witnessed by two disinterested witnesses. What to do about innocent failures to comply? Strained constructions upholding technically defective wills have been resorted to[45] – the reverse of the "over-strained resolutions" concerning constructive revocations that Lord Mansfield long ago found so scandalous. Latterly, it has been proposed to disregard the formal requirements altogether. The Uniform Probate Code, in a section captioned "harmless error," would allow the probate of an informally executed will if a judge is convinced by "clear and convincing evidence that the decedent intended the document… to constitute… the decedent's will…."[46] The vestigial requirement of a "document" may be the next to go, as videotaping and computer files become commonplace.[47] In other words, here we pass beyond the realm of rules – real,

---

42   Geldart, *Introduction to English Law* 84 ("[A]t common law a lease which ought to be made by a deed but is not will not completely fail of effect, if possession is taken and rent paid under it; the tenant will be treated as tenant from year to year upon the terms of the lease so far as they are applicable to such a tenancy.").

43   Latterly, as leases are increasingly conceptualized as contracts, it has been held that part performance may also be applicable in the case of leases. See, e.g., *Corder* v. *Idaho Farmway, Inc.*, 986 P.2d 1019 (Idaho App. 1999).

44   See Atkinson, *Wills* § 88, p. 452 (describing it as the "fiction of conditional revocation").

45   See, e.g., *In re Snide*, 418 N.E.2d 656 (N.Y. 1981) (allowing probate of will not signed by testator when error resulted from mistaken execution of mutual wills by husband and wife).

46   Unif. Probate Code § 2–503 (1990, as amended 1997). Although captioned "harmless error," this section really grants a dispensing power. See Chapter 9, Intention: The Law of Unintended Consequences.

47   See *Rioux* v. *Coulombe*, 19 Est. & Tr. Rep. 2d 201 (Quebec 1996) (probating electronic will under provincial statute allowing substantial compliance with Wills Act).

fictional, constructive, or equitable – and into the realm of discretion, the judge to do justice on the facts of each individual case, reminiscent of the authority which, according to the medieval Council of Constance, inheres in the Church, to "grant indulgences for reasonable causes."[48]

* * *

We have seemingly wandered far from the ancient legal fictions allowing allegations of facts known to be false. But our path has actually brought us close to the heart of the matter. The Rule of Law, humanity's best effort so far to produce justice on a regular basis, requires rules, but because of their rigidity and generality, rules can produce injustice in individual cases. Making and changing rules is the very definition of legislation, but the legislature is constrained to make rules with only prospective effect, and in any event the legislature is not in permanent session and cannot be expected to address every imaginable (and unimaginable) contingency. The judges have responded from time immemorial with fictions and constructions of one sort or another. The larger fiction, of course, is that the judges are not legislating. Perhaps, as critics since the days of Bentham have maintained, it is time to abandon this pretense and insist on candor. But it is a fact that so long as there have been rules, there have been legal fictions, allowing slightly different cases to be shoehorned into existing patterns. And legal fictions will persist – until, that is, we are ready to abandon the Rule of Law altogether and simply allow the judges to resolve every dispute "on its merits."

---

48   The comparison is drawn from Brooks Adams, *The Theory of Social Revolutions* 92 (1913).

Chapter 12
Labels: Argumentative Jargon

Items of jargon can also be usefully argumentative…, designed as they are to point out the absurdity of the designated doctrines.

W. Barton Leach

In an introductory property course a significant amount of time is usually devoted to the classification of interests in real property.[1] Estates in fee simple and for life are defined and analyzed; the defunct estate in fee tail may be briefly mentioned. Future interests are divided into those a grantor may retain – reversion, possibility of reverter, and right of re-entry (a.k.a. power of termination) – and those transferred to a grantee – remainder and executory interest. Vested and contingent remainders are compared and contrasted, and the intricacies of vesting explored, whether indefeasibly vested, vested subject to partial divestment ("subject to open"), or vested subject to complete divestment. Questions on the final examination are often in the form of "pin the label on the interest."

The basic vocabulary of property law is centuries old. The Man of Law in Chaucer's *Canterbury Tales* was already speaking the language in the fourteenth century: "*Al was fee symple to hym in effect.*"[2] Age brings with it ample scope for confusion. Words of similar sound and appearance – reversion, possibility of reverter – have distinctly different meanings. Time and technicality have created ambiguities: "purchase," as in "words of purchase," does not mean quite the same thing as in "vendor and purchaser."[3] Familiar words can have unexpected meanings. "Limitation," as in "words of limitation," describes the estate created by a grant. A "particular estate" is any that is less than a fee simple. "Determine" can mean to end, as in fee simple determinable. "Conversion," as in "trover and conversion" is a tort; as in "equitable conversion," it is a title. Apparent paradoxes abound: "heirs" do not take under a will,[4] and "no one is the heir of the

---

1   See Joanne Martin, The Nature of the Property Curriculum in ABA-Approved Schools and Its Place in Real Estate Practice, 44 *Real Prop., Tr. & Est. L.J.* 385 (2009).

2   *The Canterbury Tales* (late 14th century), I (A) 328, in *The Works of Geoffrey Chaucer* 20 (2nd ed., F.N. Robinson ed., 1957).

3   "Words of purchase" describe the grantee of an estate. "In this sense, one may be a purchaser even though he or she is a donee." Cribbet, *Property* 254. The law of vendor and purchaser concerns the sale and purchase of real estate.

4   See Cribbet, *Property* 258 ("Heirs are those who take the property under the relevant statutes of descent."). Those who take under a will are technically legatees (of personal property) and devisees (of real property), although today "devise" may be used

living."[5] But the problems of traditional terminology are more apparent than real. Clarity comes with careful definition. There are right and wrong answers to the questions on the exam.

Bizarre terminology in the law of property is not limited to estates and future interests. "Demise" is another name for a lease, as well as for a death.[6] A tenancy "for years" can last no more than a month.[7] The rent "reserved" in a lease means the amount the tenant must pay.[8] Covenants in leases may be "independent," meaning that breach of a covenant by one party does not relieve the other party of the duty to perform. The assignee of a lease and the landlord can be in "privity" – privity of estate – without any contact whatsoever. "User" in the law of easements can mean the use itself or the person who makes the use, and "reservation" is actually a form of grant.[9] An easement acquired by prescription never had anything to do with a script or writing. "Premises" can be a place, as well as a logical predicate.[10] "Occupy" can mean to take possession of a chattel, as well as to reside somewhere (as, on the premises).[11]

Once away from the time-crusted labels for estates and future interests and archaic terms, ambiguity – often attributable to parallel legal and non-legal usages – may permit a play on words, allowing lawyers and judges to achieve their desired results. "Burden" in the law of easements can mean either the legal burden that a right of way imposes on the title to a servient estate (an encumbrance) or the practical burden that the use imposes on the land. Whether a right of way is used little or not at all, it remains a burden on title. But increasing passage over the right

---

interchangeably to refer to testamentary succession to personal or real property. See Dukeminier, *Wills, Trusts, and Estates* 32–33.

   5   *Nemo est haeres viventis.* (No one is the heir of the living.) 3 *Bl. Com* 224.

   6   "The usual words of operation in [a lease] are, 'demise, grant, and to farm let; *demisi, concessi, et ad firmam traditi.*'" 2 *Bl. Com.* 317–18.

   7   See Restatement of Property § 19, p. 48 (a tenancy for years has a duration fixed "in units of a year or multiples or divisions thereof"). One property casebook draws the obvious conclusion: "In spite of its name, this type of lease can be for any definite period of time, whether it is for one day or 100 years." Cribbet, *Property* 475.

   8   *Reddendum*: clause in conveyance in which grantor "doth create or reserve some new thing to himself out of what he had before granted." 2 *Bl. Com.* 299.

   9   The reservation of an easement is the fictitious grant by the grantee of an estate in fee simple to the grantor of the estate. See 4 *Kent Com.* 468 ("A *reservation* is a clause in a deed, whereby the grantor reserves some new thing to himself issuing out of the thing granted, and not *in esse* before...."). For this reason, reservation in the law of leases means the creation of an obligation to pay rent to the landlord.

   10   Premises came to mean a place because of where the legal description of land appeared in a deed. "*Premises*: matters previously stated: as *a*: the part of a deed preceding the habendum... stating names of parties, consideration, capacity, and land to be conveyed... [also] specified piece of land." *Webster's Third New International Dictionary* s.v. (1966).

   11   "Occupancy is the taking possession of those things which before belonged to nobody." 2 *Bl. Com.* 258.

of way, even though within the scope of the easement, increases the perceived burden. In a leading case, the Washington Supreme Court allowed an easement appurtenant to one parcel to serve an adjacent parcel by finding that despite the obvious additional burden on the title – the easement was now appurtenant to two parcels instead of one – there was "no increase in the burden," because "there was no increase in the volume of travel on the easement."[12] *Presto chango*, a burden is a burden, yet not a burden.

By a rule dating from the age of Shakespeare, extrinsic evidence is admissible to explain an ambiguity in the terms of a will, but only if it is "latent," not "patent."[13] The distinction between the two is between an ambiguity that appears on the face of the will (patent) and one that appears only when the terms of the will are applied to the facts on the ground (latent). The distinction is subject to manipulation in the interests of justice. An Illinois court held that the death of a devisee before the testator, ordinarily a cause for the gift to lapse, created a latent ambiguity and admitted extrinsic evidence relating to the testator's probable intention in such case.[14] Was the devise in a California will "to the university in Southern California known as the U.C.L.A." a latent or a patent ambiguity?[15]

Similar games may be played by those seeking to change existing law. The historic torts of alienation of affections and criminal conversation are trivialized as the "heartbalm torts." Statutes of descent and distribution that allow inheritance by collateral heirs of remote degree are criticized by labeling those heirs "laughing heirs," who feel no pang of sorrow at the death of the decedent, but only joy at the unexpected windfall.[16] The bad name for intention that seeks to extend its reach too far is control by the "dead hand" (mortmain). Calls for repeal of estate and inheritance taxes are routinely described as seeking the end of "death taxes." More generally, competitive law reform by various states, usually in the form of repeal of or reduction in legal restrictions, is denounced as a "race to the bottom."[17]

Lawyers are by long experience aware of the thaumaturgic power of words. The law concerning the proper execution of wills is undergoing a dramatic upheaval, yet the degree of change is concealed behind benign phrases. Statutes prescribing the formalities required for the execution of valid wills, like statutes prescribing formalities for the legal effectiveness of other documents, require compliance. Yet

---

12 *Brown v. Voss*, 715 P.2d 514, 518 (Wash. 1986). See Chapter 6, Easements: Playing a Word Game.

13 See Francis Bacon's Maxim 23: *Ambiguitas verborum latens verificatione suppletur; nam quod ex facto oritur ambiguum verificatione facti tollitur.* (Latent ambiguity may be supplied by evidence; for an ambiguity which arises by proof of an extrinsic fact may, in the same manner be removed.) Broom, *Maxims* 608.

14 *Dawson v. Yucus*, 239 N.E.2d 305 (Ill. App. 1968).

15 *In Estate of Black*, 27 Cal. Rptr. 418 (App. 1962) (latent).

16 See David F. Cavers, Change in the American Family and the "Laughing Heir," 20 *Iowa L. Rev.* 203 (1935). Excluding remote collaterals, of course, increases the chance that the property will escheat to the state, giving it the last laugh.

17 See Chapter 10, Competition: The Race to the Bottom.

the occasional egregious case of hypertechnicality in the application of the wills acts, causing the failure of wills apparently intended to be valid, has led to the notion that these acts require not only compliance, but "strict compliance." So, at one time, it was suggested that only "substantial compliance" should be required.[18] Latterly, it has been argued that even that is not a relaxed enough standard, and "harmless error," a phrase imported from civil and criminal procedure, has been officially proposed as the proper standard for the execution of wills.[19] On the merits, of course, it is hard to object to a rule that allows for disregarding "harmless errors," so long as it continues to prevent harmful ones.

Ambiguity can be used to produce a desired result, arguably just. Shifting nuance and anodyne appellations can help to transform a traditional body of law, perhaps for the better. But labels can also be, as Harvard Law Professor W. Barton Leach admitted, "usefully argumentative."[20] When American courts began to admit disabling restraints on alienation of equitable interests in private non-charitable trusts, the development was criticized as protecting spendthrift beneficiaries from the consequences of their own improvidence.[21] But the "spendthrift" label did not cause that device to be repudiated; instead, it is today a term of art, used by trust lawyers and legislative drafters alike.[22]

Until recently, settlors of trusts were barred from using disabling restraints to protect themselves from their own creditors, but as self-settled spendthrift trusts have gradually begun to gain acceptance, they have been rechristened "asset protection trusts."[23] In this case, the usefulness of the jargon is that it works to

---

18   See John H. Langbein, Substantial Compliance with the Wills Act, 88 *Harv. L. Rev.* 489 (1975).

19   See John H. Langbein, Excusing Harmless Errors in the Execution of Wills: A Report on Australia's Tranquil Revolution in Probate Law, 87 *Colum. L. Rev.* 1 (1987); Unif. Probate Code § 2-503: Harmless Error (amended 1990), 8 U.L.A. 146 (1998); Restatement (Third) of Prop.: Wills and Other Donative Transfers § 3.3 (1999). Cf. Fed. R. Civ. P. 61, Fed. R. Crim. P. 52.

20   W. Barton Leach, Perpetuities: The Nutshell Revisited, 78 *Harv. L. Rev.* 973, 991 n. 78 (1965).

21   A spendthrift is defined as "*1:* one that spends or uses improvidently or wastefully *2:* one who spends his estate (as by drinking or gambling) so as to expose himself or his family to want or suffering or to becoming a charge upon the public." *Webster's Third New International Dictionary* 2190 (1966). See generally John Chipman Gray, *Restraints on the Alienation of Property* 262 (1883) ("The general introduction of spendthrift trusts would be to form a privileged class, who could indulge every speculation, could practice every fraud, and, provided they kept on the safe side of the criminal law, could yet roll in wealth.").

22   See, e.g., Unif. Trust Act § 103(16) ("Spendthrift provision means a term of a trust which restrains both voluntary and involuntary transfer of a beneficiary's interest.").

23   See Stewart E. Sterk, Asset Protection Trusts: Trust Law's Race to the Bottom? 85 *Cornell L. Rev.* 1035 (2000) ("the notion that property owners ought to be able to protect themselves against their own profligacy, at the expense of their creditors, has been much harder to swallow").

conceal rather than to point out the reality. Perhaps settlors prefer not to describe themselves as "spendthrifts."

The most dramatic use of "argumentative jargon" to undercut existing law is the way law professors made the common law Rule Against Perpetuities ridiculous as part of their project to reform it. The Rule, which might more accurately be labeled the "rule against remote vesting," began to take shape in the seventeenth century and reached its classic expression in the formulation of John Chipman Gray in the nineteenth century: "No interest is good unless it must vest, if at all, not later than twenty-one years after some life in being at the creation of the interest."[24] The Rule, which is applied as of "the creation of the interest," voids an interest that is not certain, under any imaginable contingency, to vest within the "perpetuities period."[25]

When Professor Leach wanted to point out the "absurdity" of requiring prospective application of the Rule Against Perpetuities – what he called the "might-have-been rule"[26] – he relied on derogatory labels. One of the Rule's greatest strengths, the certainty provided by voiding remote interests *ab initio*, was also one of its potential weaknesses. Because any possibility of remote vesting was fatal, bizarre and unlikely eventualities could cause the failure of benign interests. The common law's conclusive presumption of fertility until death, regardless of age or sex – a source of certainty in applying the Rule – was ridiculed as the "fertile octogenarian rule," by which a class composed of a woman's children could not be presumed closed until her death, regardless of her present age, so any gift over after the death of her last surviving child – as to "her issue then living" – would vest too remotely (and so be void).[27] Covering the other end of the age continuum was the "precocious toddler rule," by which even a very young child was conclusively presumed to be presently capable of reproducing.[28] The unlikely

---

24　Gray, *Rule Against Perpetuities* § 201, p. 191 (capital letters in original). For a discussion of the Rule's early development, see George L. Haskins, 'Inconvenience' and the Rule for Perpetuities, 48 *Mo. L. Rev.* 451 (1983). For John Chipman Gray's role in the Rule's later development, see Stephen A. Siegel, John Chipman Gray, Legal Formalism, and the Transformation of Perpetuities Law, 36 *Miami L. Rev.* 439 (1982).

25　Interests subject to the Rule – contingent remainders, executory interests, and remainders vested subject to open – must be certain to vest either in interest or in possession within the period allowed by the Rule. That is, a contingent remainder must turn into a vested remainder or vest in possession; an executory interest must vest in possession; and a remainder vested subject to open must become indefeasibly vested (the "all or nothing rule"). For the latter, see Dukeminier, *Wills, Trusts, & Estates* 686–88.

26　Leach, Perpetuities Reform: London Proposes, Perth Disposes, 6 *U.W. Austl. L. Rev.* 11, 14 (1963–64)

27　Leach, Nutshell Revisited, 78 *Harv. L. Rev.* at 992. The common law presumption of fertility is best exemplified by the leading case of *Jee v. Audley*, 1 Cox 324, 29 Eng. Rep. 1186 (Ch. 1787), actually involving a septuagenarian. For the details of the case, see Simpson, *Leading Cases* 76–99.

28　See *Re Gaite's Will Trusts*, [1949] 1 All Eng. Rep. 459 (Ch.) (recognizing the rule, but validating the gift in question on the ground that a child born to so young a person

possibility that a beneficiary might marry a woman not alive at the creation of the interest who might then outlive him was caricatured as the "unborn widow rule," making interests contingent on surviving a named man's "widow" invalid.[29]

Once the game was begun, it was not hard to identify other events of uncertain duration and make fun of them accordingly. A will devising property to "my issue alive at final distribution of my estate" postpones vesting for an indefinite time. Unexpected developments or inexcusable delay by the executor could conceivably exceed the perpetuities period. A funny name to describe this situation would be the case of the "slothful executor."[30] "The magic gravel pit" parodies the result in the English case of *In re Wood* (1894), in which a will directed that gravel pits be operated by trustees until exhausted, then sold with the proceeds to be distributed to the testator's issue then living. At the testator's death it was, of course, impossible to know for certain how long the pits would be productive, so again vesting is postponed for a period that could conceivably outlast some life in being at the creation of the interest plus twenty-one years.[31] A devise to such members of a testator's family alive at the end of World War II, then in progress, made vesting dependent on an event of indefinite date. Could this be "the war that never ends"?[32]

This is a game that any number can play. Consider "the birthday present that blows up": a devise in trust to A for life, then to such of A's children as reach their respective twenty-first birthdays. Because the common law conceptualized birthdays as the first day of the following year of a person's life, the ultimate gifts in this devise could vest more than twenty-one years after a life in being at the creation of the interest: twenty-one years plus one day.[33]

Having made prospective application of the Rule ("at the creation of the interest") a source of amusement, Professor Leach's proposed solution was simply to allow retrospective application; that is, to restate the Rule – "No interest is good unless it vests [not 'must vest'] if at all not later than twenty-one years after some life in being at the creation of the interest" – in other words, to wait for the expiration of the perpetuities period and see if the interest actually had vested by

---

would necessarily be illegitimate and so disqualified). For the label, see Leach, Nutshell Revisited, 78 *Harv. L. Rev.* at 992.

29   See Gray, *Rule Against Perpetuities* § 214, p. 208 (describing it as "a mistake which has been often made"). For the label, see Leach, Nutshell Revisited, 78 *Harv. L. Rev.* at 992.

30   See Dukeminier, *Wills, Trusts, & Estates* 685–86.

31   [1894] 3 Ch. 381 (pits were in fact exhausted in six years). For the label, see Dukeminier, *Wills, Trusts, & Estates* 686.

32   *Brownell v. Edmunds*, 209 F.2d 349 (4th Cir. 1953) (holding devise void). For the label, see Dukeminier, *Wills, Trusts, & Estates* 686. For an attempt to imagine a war that never ends, see Joe Haldeman, *The Forever War* (1974).

33   For the label, see Dukeminier, *Wills, Trusts, & Estates* 686; W. Barton Leach, The Careful Draftsman: Watch Out! 47 *A.B.A.J.* 259 (1961).

that time. A few states, beginning with Pennsylvania in 1947,[34] adopted this "wait-and-see" reform of the Rule – to applause from Professor Leach.[35] The approach was eventually endorsed by the second Restatement of Property in 1983.[36]

Retrospective application, as Professor Leach well knew, would not eliminate all the games that could be played with the Rule Against Perpetuities. Taking advantage of the Rule's use of the measure "*some* life in being at the creation of the interest" – not limited to the life of a beneficiary or of a person related to a beneficiary – English conveyancers had developed the "royal lives clause," vesting the contingent remainders twenty-one years after the death of, for example, "all lineal descendants of Queen Victoria now living."[37] Leach produced a republican version: "'to such of my children and more remote issue as shall be living 21 years after the death of the survivor of R, S, T, U, V, W, X, Y, and Z' (these being nine healthy babies selected at random)."[38]

Other law professors now took up the cause of improving the Rule Against Perpetuities. Rather than continue to allow games to be played with the "life in being" relevant to the application of the reformed Rule, they proposed a rule that required interests to vest within 90 years, an estimate of "the average period of time that would traditionally be allowed by the wait-and-see doctrine."[39] This variation, in other words, was to restate the Rule: "No interest is good unless it vests not later than ninety years after [not 'twenty-one years after some life in being at'] the creation of the interest." This alternative, incorporated in the Uniform Statutory Rule Against Perpetuities, was promulgated by the National Conference of Commissioners on Uniform State Laws in 1986, only three years after the Restatement Second had adopted the wait-and-see variation of the common law Rule Against Perpetuities.

Although the Uniform Statutory Rule was at first adopted by a significant number of states, it too was quickly overtaken by even more radical change. Once the reformers demonstrated that the ancient Rule was vulnerable, it was only a matter of time before its very existence began to be questioned. By a happy (or

---

34   Pa. Stat. Ann. tit. 20, § 6104(b) (2002).

35   W. Barton Leach, Perpetuities in Perspective: Ending the Rule's Reign of Terror, 65 *Harv. L. Rev.* 721 (1952) (approving the Pennsylvania legislation).

36   Restatement (Second) of Prop.: Donative Transfers § 1.4 (1983).

37   *In re Villar*, [1929] 1 Ch. 243.

38   W. Barton Leach, Perpetuities in a Nutshell, 51 *Harv. L. Rev.* 638, 642 (1938). Leach later increased the number of babies and eliminated the random selection in his original version. See 6 *Am. L. Prop.* § 24.16, p. 52 ("a dozen or so healthy babies chosen from families noted for their longevity").

39   Lawrence W. Waggoner, The Uniform Statutory Rule Against Perpetuities: The Rationale of the 90-Year Waiting Period, 73 *Cornell L. Rev.* 157, 162 (1988) (reporting rationale of drafters of the Uniform Statutory Rule). The English Law Commission estimated that a skilled conveyancer, using a royal lives clause, could stretch out the period as long as 125 years. The Rules Against Perpetuities and Excessive Accumulations, Report No. 251, p. 723 (1998).

unhappy) coincidence, in 1986 – the year USRAP was promulgated – Congress amended the tax code to provide for a tax on assets in excess of an exempt amount transferred at death at each generation, either in the form of the traditional estate tax or a new "generation skipping transfer tax."[40]

Since then, lobbied by lawyers and bankers seeking the business of establishing and servicing well-funded trusts,[41] twenty-three states have repealed the Rule Against Perpetuities in any of its forms – common law, wait-and-see, Uniform Statutory Rule – as applied to beneficial interests in trusts if the trustee has a power of sale.[42] In vain, the Commissioners on Uniform State Laws declared the movement "ill-advised."[43] The object of the latest reform, of course, is to permit perpetual or nearly perpetual trusts funded with the amount exempted from taxes. Popularly known as "dynasty trusts," such trusts can preserve property for the benefit of a settlor's descendants from generation to generation forever, that is, in perpetuity. If care is taken in setting up the trust, no estate or generation skipping

---

40   Tax Reform Act of 1986, Pub. L. No. 99–514, 100 U.S. Stats. 2085 (1986). In 2009 the exemption is $3.5 million per transferor.

41   See Dukeminier & Krier, The Rise of the Perpetual Trust, 50 *U.C.L.A. L. Rev.* 1303, 1315–16 (2003).

42   E.g., N.C. Sess. Law 2007-390, captioned "An Act to Repeal the Statutory Rule Against Perpetuities as it Applies to Trusts Created or Administered in This State and Codify the Law Regarding the Power of Alienation for Trusts Created in North Carolina" (adding N.C. Gen. Stat. § 41-23 and amending § 41-15). Its constitutionality is being challenged. *Brown Bros. Harriman v. Benson*, No. 08-CVS-13456 (N.C. Super. Ct. Feb. 26, 2009) (upholding constitutionality), appeal filed, Notice of Appeal, No. 08-CVS-13456 (N.C. Ct. App. Mar. 5, 2009). See Orth, Allowing Perpetuities in North Carolina, 31 *Campbell L. Rev.* 399 (2009).

As of 2008 the following states allowed perpetual or nearly perpetual trusts. Additional states may have joined the list since then.

States permitting perpetual trusts: Alaska Stat. §§ 34.27.051, 34.27.100; Ariz. Rev. Stat. § 14-2901A; Del. Code Ann. tit. 25, § 25, § 503; 765 Ill. Comp. Stat. §§ 305/3(a-5), 305/4(a)(8); Me. Rev. Stat. Ann. tit. 33, § 101-A; Mich. Comp. Laws §§ 554.91 – 554.94; Md. Code Ann., Est. & Trusts § 11-102(b)(5); Mo. Rev. Stat. § 456.025; Neb. Rev. Stat. § 76-2005(9); N.H. Rev. Stat. Ann. § 564:24; N.J. Stat. Ann. §§ 46:2F-9–46:2F-11; N.C. Gen. Stat. 41-23; Ohio Rev. Code Ann. § 2131.09(B); 20 Pa. Cons. Stat. § 6107.1(b)(1); R.I. Gen. Laws § 34-11-38; Va. Code Ann. § 55-13.3(C). *See also* D.C. § 19-904(a)(10).

States permitting very long trusts: Colo. Rev. Stat. § 15-11-1102.5 (1,000 years); Fla. Stat. § 689.225 (360 years); Nev. Rev. Stat. § 111.1031 (365 years); Tenn. Code Ann. § 66-1-201(f) (360 years); Utah Code Ann. § 75-2-1203 (1,000 years); Wash. Rev. Code § 11.98.130 (150 years); Wyo. Stat. Ann. § 34-1-139 (1,000 years).

In 1986 three states already permitted perpetual trusts: Idaho Code § 55-111; S.D. Codified Laws §§ 43-5-1, 43-5-8; Wis. Stat. § 700.16(1)(a).

43   National Conference of Commissioners on Uniform State Laws, Uniform Statutory Rule Against Perpetuities Is Law in 26 States: Move of a Few States to Abolish the Rule in Order to Facilitate Perpetual (Dynasty) Trusts Is Ill-Advised (press release, Jan. 2000), quoted in Dukeminier, *Wills, Trusts, & Estates* 722.

transfer tax on the exempt amount or its accumulations will be due until and unless the trust terminates and the principal is finally distributed.

It was Professor Leach's simple faith that the Rule Against Perpetuities had been rendered unnecessary by the advent of income and estate taxes and that such legislative amelioration of its complexity as occurred was the result of "uncompensated and often frustrating activity by university law faculties."[44] He unaccountably underestimated the possibility that the wealthy and powerful would find a way to entail their estates for the benefit of their descendants forever.[45] In its hour of need, the Rule Against Perpetuities found no defenders among those entrusted with preserving it as a restraint on the dynastic impulse. The chamber of horrors Leach and his successors had so effectively associated with the Rule brought it into disrepute and helped clear the way for would-be dynasts to create perpetual trusts.

---

44   Leach, Perpetuities Reform: London Proposes, Perth Disposes, 6 *U.W. Austl. L. Rev.* at 12, 16.

45   See Hirsch, Inheritance: United States Law, in 3 *Oxford Internat'l Ency. of Legal History* 235, 239 (2009) (describing dynasty trusts as "a sort of throwback to entail").

Chapter 13
Second Thoughts: Full Enlightenment?

We now come to the last stage in our inquiry concerning what has actually governed the conduct of men in society. This is the stage of full enlightenment, such as is exhibited in Europe and the United States at the present day....

James C. Carter (1905)

When Oliver Wendell Holmes, then a justice of the Massachusetts Supreme Judicial Court, delivered the address at the dedication of a new law school building at Boston University that was later published as "The Path of the Law," he touched upon – among many other topics – the then burning issue of employer liability for injuries sustained by workers in the course of their employment. "It is conceivable," he told his audience, "that some day in certain cases we may find ourselves imitating, on a higher plane, the tariff for life and limb which we see in the *Leges Barbarorum*."[1] The learned reference was to collections of customary law from the Dark Ages, literally the "laws of the barbarians," that aimed to stamp out private vengeance by imposing on the party responsible for an injury a duty to pay the victim or his family a fixed amount, so much for an eye, a hand, a foot, etc.[2] This was Holmes at his most Olympian, marking the resemblance between barbaric law and progressive proposals to establish a cost-effective administrative system to replace litigation and compensate workers injured in industrial accidents – so much for an eye, a hand, a foot, etc.[3] It was also Holmes at his most impish, assuring his complacent late nineteenth century listeners that if "some day" and "in certain cases" they ever did imitate the *Leges Barbarorum*, it would surely be "on a higher plane"!

The need for legislation to deal with the cost of accidents was created by the associated common law doctrine of assumption of the risk and the fellow servant rule,

---

1   10 *Harv. L. Rev.* 456, 467 (1897).

2   The Leges Barbarorum were contrasted with the Leges Romanae, the laws of the Romans. The earliest Anglo-Saxon legal compilation was the Laws of Ethelbert, promulgated about 600 A.D., described in Harold Berman, *Law and Revolution: The Formation of the Western Legal Tradition* 54 (1983).

3   See, e.g., The North Carolina Workers' Compensation Act, N.C. Gen. Stat. § 97-31 (16) (12) (14) (providing compensation for the loss of an eye equal to "sixty-six and two-thirds percent of the average weekly wages during 120 weeks"; for the loss of a hand, "sixty-six and two-thirds percent of the average weekly wages during 200 weeks"; for the loss of a foot, "sixty-six and two-thirds percent of the average weekly wages during 144 weeks").

dating from the early days of industrialization, which insulated employers from liability if the injured worker had assumed the risk of accident in return for compensation or if the proximate cause of the injury was the fault, not of the employer, but of another employee or "fellow servant."[4] The rigor of the rules had eroded over the course of the nineteenth century as plaintiffs' lawyers came up with ingenious arguments to allow juries to nullify the rules' effect by finding that employers were really the ones at fault for employing unskilled workers, failing to supply proper equipment, or providing inadequate supervision.[5] As Holmes knew from his experience on the bench at the end of the century, "in such cases the chance of a jury finding for the defendant [employer] is merely a chance, once in a while rather arbitrarily interrupting the regular course of recovery" by the injured worker.[6]

The common law rules, the legal system's first response to a problem that ballooned in importance as the pace of industrial development quickened and the risk of accidents increased, were in need of repair or replacement. England, the home of the common law and the world's first industrial nation, responded with legislation in 1897, the year Holmes spoke.[7] In America, federalism led to a fragmented and slow-motion response, with the federal government acting in the first decade of the twentieth century to deal with injuries in interstate commerce[8] and states slowly following suit with statutes dealing with injuries in local industries over the next four decades.[9] Further complicating the process in the United States was the need for legislation to run the gauntlet of judicial review, with several early workers' compensation statutes being held unconstitutional.[10]

---

4   Both doctrines can be traced to *Farwell* v. *Boston & Worcester RR*, 35 Mass. (4 Metc.) 49 (1842). See also, for England, *Priestley* v. *Fowler*, 3 M. & W. 1, 150 Eng. Rep. 1030 (Exch. 1837). For a poem ridiculing the fellow servant rule, see Edgar Lee Masters, "Butch Weldy" in *The Spoon River Anthology* (1915). See also John v. Orth, The Law in Spoon River, 16 *Legal Studies Forum* 301–32 (1992).

5   See generally Lawrence M. Friedman & Jack Ladinsky, Social Change and the Law of Industrial Accidents, 67 *Colum. L. Rev.* 50 (1967).

6   10 *Harv. L. Rev.* at 467.

7   60 & 61 Vict. c. 37 (1897).

8   Act of June 11, 1906, ch. 3073, 34 Stat. 232 (Federal Employers' Liability Act) (FELA) (carriers in interstate commerce liable to employees for injuries caused by defective equipment or negligent supervision), amended by acts of April 22, 1908 (ch. 149, 35 Stat. 65) and April 5, 1910 (ch. 143, 36 Stat. 291).

9   Beginning with New York in 1910, thirty-seven states had passed workmen's compensation statutes by 1917. In 1948 Mississippi became the last state to adopt a workmen's compensation statute. Latterly the name of the statutes has been changed, in the interest of gender-neutrality, to Worker's Compensation Act. E.g., N.C. Sess. Laws 1979, c. 714, § 1.

10   Employers' Liability Case, 207 U.S. 463 (1908) (holding 1906 FELA unconstitutional because it applied to intrastate as well as to interstate carriers); Employers' Liability Case, 223 U.S. 1 (1912) (upholding FELA as amended); *Ives* v. *South Buffalo Railway Co.*, 94 N.E. 431 (N.Y. Ct. App. 1911) (holding N.Y. Workmen's Compensation Act unconstitutional for violation of the due process clauses of state and federal constitutions);

The pattern of rule and reaction is not limited to the law's response to the problem of liability for industrial accidents. It repeats as the passage of time reveals dissatisfaction with results in other situations, whether because of deeper analysis, accumulated experience, or the force of contrary opinion. No area of the law offers more examples than property law because of its extraordinary longevity. For centuries, while torts and criminal law were underdeveloped and contract law was most noticeable by its absence, property law was elaborated by an intricate interaction of developing case law and interfering legislation. One of the first statutes in the English lawbook, *De Donis Conditionalibus* (1285),[11] the root of the fee tail, was enacted to overturn a line of common law decisions that frustrated the donors' intent to tie up property in their descendants. The oldest treatise on English property law was Littleton's *Tenures* from about 1481, greatly elaborated by Sir Edward Coke's celebrated *Commentary upon Littleton* from 1628, while the first English book on contracts would not appear until the late eighteenth century,[12] and treatises on tort law were delayed more than sixty years after that.[13]

The joint tenancy and its associated right of survivorship, dating from the thirteenth century, functioned as a will substitute in a world before wills.[14] Originally intended to keep estates intact to facilitate the collection of feudal incidents, the joint tenancy was actually used to subvert that purpose by facilitating the development of feoffments to uses, separating the legal title (held by feoffees in joint tenancy) from the equitable title of the beneficiaries. So widespread was this practice that it came to be assumed that grants to two or more persons were intended to be in joint tenancy, rather than in tenancy in common. Abolition of the feudal incidents eliminated the need to avoid them, but by then the use (or, as it was then coming to be called, the trust) had proved its utility in other ways. The presumption in favor of joint tenancy had outlived its purpose (except as to trustees) and became instead a trap for the unwary.[15] Without the advice of skilled conveyancers, grantees could end up with an estate whose operation they did not understand and whose results they did not want – "a manifest injustice," as the North Carolina General Assembly put it in 1784, "to the families of such as happen to die first."[16]

New York Central RR. v. *White*, 243 U.S. 188 (1917) (upholding Act reenacted after amendment of N.Y. Const.).

11   13 Edw. 1, c. 1 (1285). For its background and subsequent history, see John v. Orth, Does the Fee Tail Exist in North Carolina? 23 *Wake Forest L. Rev.* 767, 773–78 (1988).

12   John Joseph Powell, *Essay upon the Law of Contracts and Agreements* (1790). See P.S. Atiyah, *The Rise and Fall of Freedom of Contract* 103 (1979).

13   Francis Hilliard, *The Law of Torts* (1859). See G. Edward White, *Tort Law in America: An Intellectual History* 4 (1985); S.F.C. Milsom, *A Natural History of the Common Law* 13 (2003).

14   See Anne L. Spitzer, Joint Tenancy with Right of Survivorship: A Legacy from Thirteenth-Century England, 16 *Tex. Tech. L. Rev.* 629 (1985).

15   See Chapter 3, Joint Tenancy: Accounting for Continuity.

16   Act of 1784, ch. 22, § 6, reprinted in 24 *The State Records of North Carolina* 574 (Walter Clark ed. 1904).

The common law's response was characteristically devious: applying a relaxed presumption in wills as opposed to deeds,[17] and as to the latter, strictly applying the technical requirements of the so-called four unities to avoid the application of the presumption.[18] The final remedy was legislative. States that confronted the issue first, such as North Carolina and Pennsylvania, abolished the right of survivorship as an incident of joint tenancies,[19] while states that dealt with the issue later, such as Illinois and Iowa, discovered a simpler solution: reverse the presumption.[20] The second legislative thought was better than the first. There was no reason not to allow the creation of a joint tenancy with right of survivorship if the parties knew what they were getting into and wanted it. States in the first group eventually caught up, Pennsylvania by a fairly prompt judicial gloss that the statute only applied in the absence of clearly expressed intention to the contrary,[21] North Carolina by an amendment to the statute two centuries later.[22]

Wills law provides some of the best examples of second, third, and more thoughts on the most expedient rule. A creature of statute, not of the common law, the will first became possible with the adoption of the Wills Act of 1540.[23] Indicative of the complex interaction of statute and common law that would follow, experience over more than a century with evidentiary problems led to further legislation. The Statute of Frauds of 1676, best known to lawyers today for its provisions concerning contracts and leases, had a section on wills requiring, in quaint fashion, a writing with "three or four credible witnesses,"[24] the germ of the modern written attested will. Applying standard common law rules on witness competency, the courts then proceeded to invalidate wills witnessed by persons who benefited as devisees or legatees in the will. To remedy this in turn, parliament in 1752 adopted the so-called purging statute, widely copied in American states.[25] Drafted on the assumption that the testator's primary intention was that the will be valid, the statute saved it by purging interested witnesses (and their spouses) of their interests. Thus was the will saved, but oftentimes at the expense of invalidating

---

17   See 2 *Bl. Com.* 193.

18   Although really a description of the nature rather than the creation of the joint tenancy, the Doctrine of the Four Unities – that joint tenants must at all times have "one and the same interest, accruing by one and the same conveyance, commencing at one and the same time, and held by one and the same undivided possession," id. at 180 – could function in the hands of an astute judge as a screen to prevent the recognition of unwanted joint tenancies by finding some defect in the unities.

19   N.C. Gen. Stat. § 41–2; Pa. Stat. Ann. tit. 68, § 110.

20   765 Ill. Comp. Stat. § 1005/1; Iowa Code Ann. § 557.15.

21   *Arnold* v. *Jack's Executors*, 24 Pa. 57 (1854).

22   See John *v.* Orth, The Joint Tenancy Makes a Comeback in North Carolina, 69 *N.C. L. Rev.* 491 (1991) (describing amendment to N.C. Gen. Stat. § 41–2).

23   32 Hen. 8, ch. 1 (1540).

24   29 Car. 2, c. 3, § 5 (1676).

25   25 Geo. 2, ch. 6, § 1 (1752). E.g., Mass. Gen. Laws ch. 191, § 2; N.C. Gen. Stat. § 31-10.

the very gifts that had been its primary purpose. New legislation was required and is today slowly making its way through the state legislatures.[26]

Wills are delayed-action documents, executed one day to be effective later, often much later, when the testator dies.[27] What if the testator's situation changes but the will remains the same? At common law, subsequent marriage and the birth of issue revoked the will.[28] The rationale was that the ordinary testator would want in such circumstances to make new provisions, that failure to do so was most likely the result of inattention, and that in such cases the results produced by the canons of descent (that is, by intestate succession), favoring close family members, would probably be preferable to the unamended will. That did not go far enough for some, and further legislation was adopted: subsequent marriage alone should be sufficient to revoke a will by operation of law.[29] But then, why should the law revoke the will at all? Why not provide for an "overlooked" spouse in other ways? So pretermitted spouse statutes sprung up, reserving a share of the estate for the spouse but otherwise leaving the will in effect.[30]

Divorce (like the will itself) was unknown to the common law, so divorce had no necessary effect on wills. But what if a testator died leaving unchanged a will providing for a now ex-spouse? Again it was difficult to imagine that the ordinary testator intended this result. Legislation ensued, revoking such testamentary dispositions.[31] But what about gifts to the relatives of ex-spouses, such as former in-laws or step-children? And what about provisions in favor of ex-spouses in all those proliferating means to pass property at death other than by will, "will substitutes" like revocable trusts, pay-on-death contracts, joint and survivor bank accounts? More legislation.[32]

---

26   E.g., Cal. Prob. Code § 6112 (allowing interested witnesses but raising a rebuttable presumption that their devises were procured by duress, menace, fraud, or undue influence). See also Unif. Probate Code § 2-505 (1990) (accepting interested witness as competent).

27   Wills are said to be "ambulatory," that is, inoperative until the testator's death; in consequence, they are capable of disposing of property acquired after execution. The same characteristic is referred to in the Bible: "For where a testament is, there must also of necessity be the death of the testator. / For a testament is of force after men are dead: otherwise it is of no strength at all while the testator liveth." Heb. 9: 16–17 (KJV).

28   2 *Bl. Com.* 502. Indeed, the common law went further: *any* change in testator's circumstances could revoke the devise. For a survey of the cases, see 4 *Kent Com.* 528–31. Lord Mansfield criticized these results and announced his opinion that "constructive revocations, contrary to the intention of the testator, ought not to be indulged; and that some over-strained resolutions of that sort had brought a scandal upon the law." *Swift* v. *Roberts,* 3 Burr. 1488, 1491, 97 Eng. Rep. 941, 942–43 (K.B. 1764).

29   E.g., Conn. Gen. Stat. § 45a-257.

30   E.g., Fla. Stat. § 732.301. See also Unif. Probate Code § 2-301 (1990, as amended 1993).

31   E.g., N.C. Gen. Stat. § 31-5.4.

32   See Unif. Probate Code § 2-804 (1990, as amended 1997) (revoking gifts by will or will substitute to relatives of ex-spouse as well as to ex-spouse).

What if a will beneficiary dies before the will becomes effective at the death of the testator? Gifts *inter vivos* or testamentary cannot be given to a dead person, so the gift lapses, that is, fails. But is that the correct inference to draw from a testator's failure to provide a substitutionary gift in the original will or to add a codicil taking account of the change caused by the death? Legislation was adopted to prevent the effect of the lapse of a gift to a named individual but only if the individual was closely related to the testator and died leaving issue.[33] In the case of a gift to a class, such as a gift to "grandchildren," the common law had provided a sort of anti-lapse protection by providing for distribution among any surviving class members, a sort of "right of survivorship." As the number of class members got smaller, the potential share of each got bigger until final distribution at the testator's death. Was this what the testator likely intended? Or should the anti-lapse statute be amended to apply in the case of class gifts as well? Still more legislation.[34]

The list could be extended with examples of other attempts involving repeated legislative efforts to effectuate presumed intent in cases in which a testator failed to make express provision – statutes concerning pretermitted children,[35] ademption by extinction,[36] ademption by satisfaction[37] – although not all gaps are filled. And in some cases deliberately so; that is, in some cases the testator's actual intention is known, not merely presumed, but crossed nonetheless. The right of survivorship associated with the joint tenancy can be severed by *inter vivos* conveyance of an undivided share, but not by provision in a will, no matter how plainly expressed. As one respected casebook puts it:

> A large number of joint tenants select the tenancy precisely because of the high degree of assurance that there will be no entanglement with probate. To continue this assurance, the right of testamentary disposition must be denied, and the few attempts by ignorant testators to devise their part of joint tenancy property must fail.[38]

---

33   E.g., Tex. Probate Code Ann. § 68.

34   E.g., 2001 N.C. Sess. Laws 83 (*adding* to N.C. Gen. Stat. § 31-42(a) "In the case of the class devise, the issue shall take whatever share the deceased devisee would have taken had the devisee survived the testator" *the words* "in the event the deceased class member leaves no issue, the devisee's share shall devolve upon the members of the class who survived the testator and the issue of any deceased members taking by substitution.").

35   E.g., Fla. Stat. § 732.302; N.C. Gen. Stat. § 31-5.5. See Unif. Probate Code § 2-302 (1990, as amended 1993). Pretermitted children are those born after the execution of a will and left unprovided for.

36   E.g., Unif. Probate Code § 2-606 (1990, as amended 1997). Ademption refers to those situations in which the subject of a specific gift indicated in a will is absent from the estate at testator's death, either because it was parted with *inter vivos* (ademption by extinction) or because it was given during life to the intended donee (ademption by satisfaction).

37   E.g., N.C. Gen. Stat. § 29-24.

38   Dukeminier, *Wills, Trusts, & Estates* 345.

The juridical conscience is salved by the thought that such attempts are "few" and the disappointed testators "ignorant," so the frustration of their clearly expressed intention is not so barbaric after all.

What should be the result if a married person deliberately excludes a spouse from the provisions of a will? The common law's solution to the problem of providing for the surviving spouse (whether there was a will or not) was dower for the widow and curtesy for the widower. Dower was a life estate in one-third of all estates of freehold of which the husband was seized during the marriage,[39] while curtesy was a life estate in all the estates of freehold of which the wife was seized during the marriage, but only on condition that live issue had been born to the couple.[40] For obvious reasons neither estate was convenient except in situations of large and stable landownership, the common law's presumed original position. Even then, both were routinely avoided by private arrangements in the form of strict settlements.

In modern times curtesy was eliminated and dower extended to both sexes, but this eventually proved unsatisfactory. At last, even the old name was erased, replaced by a statutory elective share, granting the surviving spouse the right to demand a portion of the decedent's estate. At first applicable only to property passing by will, the elective share has been progressively (but unevenly) extended to property passing outside the will by various will substitutes. Constantly tinkered with by further legislation in an effort to afford more perfect equity and now exhibiting a bewildering array of forms in various states, the modern elective share defies generalization – so much so that one widely used casebook posts a prominent warning: "Caution. There is no subject in this book on which there is more statutory variation than the surviving spouse's elective share."[41] The operation of federal tax law has actually prompted a revival of life interests for surviving spouses, usually widows, in the form of "qualified terminal interest property," QTIP for short, leading one scholar to describe the effect as "the new federal law of dower"[42] – a return, if not quite to the laws of the barbarians, at least to the laws of the Middle Ages.

And what should be the result if a person named in a will murders the testator? It is difficult to imagine a testator intending the gift to stand under such circumstances. And public policy seems to demand that the wrongdoer be deprived of the benefit. "No one should profit from his own wrong."[43] But can this untoward result be prevented by common law, or is legislation required? At first, some courts gamely tried,[44] but eventually the legislatures stepped in. Experience with the so-

---

39   2 *Bl. Com.* 129.

40   2 *Bl. Com.* 126. For an historical explanation of why curtesy was greater than dower, see S.F.C. Milsom, *A Natural History of the Common Law* 60–61 (2003).

41   Dukeminier, *Wills, Trusts, & Estates* 425.

42   Mary M. Wenig, Taxing Marriage, 6 *S. Cal. Rev. L. & Women's Stud.* 561 (1997).

43   Cal. Civ. Code § 3517 ("No one can take advantage of his own wrong."); N.C. Gen. Stat. § 31A-15 ("no person shall be allowed to profit by his own wrong.").

44   See the celebrated common law case of *Riggs* v. *Palmer*, 22 N.E. 188, 190 (1889) ("No one shall be permitted to profit by his own fraud, or to take advantage of his own

called slayer statutes has revealed a host of problems. What is to be done with the gift to the murderer? What if the crime was manslaughter rather than homicide? What if no prosecution is possible because the murder was immediately followed by the suicide of the murderer? – in which case no earthly profit was aimed at (or gained) by the crime. What of so-called "mercy killings" in which the "victim" requests death at the hands of a loved one in order to shorten a lingering and painful death? And what about will substitutes benefiting the murderer? Particular problems arise with the application of the slayer statutes to joint tenancies with right of survivorship since the theory of the joint tenancy, which long predated the Wills Act, does not conceptualize the effect of the death of one joint tenant as passing any interest to the survivor.[45] Even more complicated are cases involving powers of appointment. What if the slayer was a taker in default of appointment and the victim was the donee of the power, now forever unable to appoint the property away from the taker in default? More and still more legislation.[46]

Second and subsequent thoughts are not unique to the legislature. The judiciary, too, regularly rethinks the law, although the process is somewhat harder to observe. Part of the problem is the slippery nature of the common law itself. Although it originated in England centuries ago, the common law has been (sort of) domesticated in America. "The common law of England," Justice Joseph Story declared on behalf of the United States Supreme Court in 1829, "is not to be taken in all respects to be that of America."[47] And, a few years later, he added that the decisions of courts concerning the common law "are often reexamined, reversed, and qualified by the Courts themselves, whenever they are found to be either defective, or ill-founded, or otherwise incorrect."[48]

Early in the twentieth century in an apparent attempt to stabilize the common law and perhaps insulate it from further legislative meddling, the legal establishment commenced the project that resulted in the monumental Restatements of the Law.[49] Although the project seemed to call only for the reduction to black letter of the basic common law rules, the Restaters did not confine themselves to stating

---

wrong, or to found any claim upon his own iniquity, or to acquire property by his own crime."). See also Ronald Dworkin, *Taking Rights Seriously* 23 (1978) (discussing *Riggs*).

45 See Chapter 3, Joint Tenancy: Accounting for Continuity.

46 E.g., 84 Okla. Stat. Supp. 1975 § 231 (effective June 12, 1975) (amending slayer statute to prohibit slayer from "receiv[ing] any interest in the estate of the victim…, or as a surviving joint tenant").

47 *Van Ness* v. *Pacard*, 27 U.S. (2 Pet.) 137, 144 (1829).

48 *Swift* v. *Tyson*, 41 U.S. (16 Pet.) 1, 18 (1834). For an essay reflecting on the consequences of this view of the common law operating within a system governed by a written constitution, see John v. Orth, Can the Common Law Be Unconstitutional? in *How Many Judges Does It Take to Make a Supreme Court? And Other Essays on Law and the Constitution* ch. 3 (2006).

49 The Restatements were meant to satisfy "[t]he desire of the legal profession for an orderly statement of our Common Law." *The Restatement in the Courts* 1. The first Restatements appeared from 1932 to 1957.

(or "restating") whatever rule was applied by the majority of courts but chose instead the rule they judged most logical or best.[50] The adoption of minority rules made the Restatements a vehicle for legal innovation,[51] and the Restaters became, like the poets, "unacknowledged legislators."[52] Having themselves had second thoughts about some settled doctrines, the first Restaters unintentionally invited still further thoughts, "re-Restatements."[53] The result has been Second and even Third Restatements, as later generations of Restaters think yet again.

* * *

Shortly after Holmes pointed out the "path of the law" at Boston University, the eminent lawyer James C. Carter prepared lectures for delivery at the Harvard Law School, the culmination of his lifelong campaign to defend the common law against legislative codification.[54] Concluding his survey of law's "origin, growth, and function," Carter complacently announced: "We now come to the last stage in our inquiry concerning what has actually governed the conduct of men in society. This is the stage of full enlightenment, such as is exhibited in Europe and the United States at the present day...."[55] This fatuous statement is simply an unguarded expression of a sentiment that is (and always has been) current in some circles, mainly academic: the belief that after their second or third or more thought that the final thought would have been thought.

The point, of course, is not that our law should become like that of the Medes and the Persians, which, if the Bible is to be taken literally, "changeth not."[56] There is no reason not to think again and again about improving the existing rules, while at the same time recognizing the value of stability. What really deserves a second thought is the notion that at the next term of court or the next meeting (or perhaps the one after that) of the particular drafting committee, whether of state

---

50   The Restatements represented "the considered opinion of those constructing it, of the way in which the law would be decided in the light of decisions by the courts." Id. 8.

51   See David Thomas, Anglo-American Land Law: Diverging Developments from a Shared History – Part III: British and American Real Property Law and Practice – A Contemporary Comparison, 34 *Real Prop., Prob. & Tr. L.J.* 443, 479 (1999).

52   See Percy Bysshe Shelley, A Defense of Poetry (1821) ("Poets are the unacknowledged legislators of the world.").

53   See Grant Gilmore, *The Death of Contract* 67 (1974) (asking "Why should there be a second series of Restatements?").

54   Carter, *Law* 66. Intended for delivery in early 1905, the lectures were never actually delivered because of Carter's untimely death. For Carter's place in American legal history, see Bernard Schwartz, *Main Currents in American Legal Thought* 337–46 ("James C. Carter: Written Law – 'Victorious upon Paper and Powerless Elsewhere'"); 353–63 ("Legal Thought in Action: Carter versus [David Dudley] Field") (1993).

55   Carter, *Law* 66. For repeated references to "the present enlightened age," see id. 115, 119.

56   Esther 1:19 (KJV).

legislators or of academic experts, the final stage of "full enlightenment" will have been reached.

What history teaches is not some simple and simply applied rule for future behavior, nor is it only the clichéd notion that "everything changes," or, as Carter would have put it, "progresses." Instead, by showing with specificity how things have changed – how often, how incompletely, how ultimately unsatisfactorily they have changed – history informs our thoughts about future change and leads us to abandon the pursuit of the *ignis fatuus* of "full enlightenment." Something Holmes said earlier about consistency in the law is also true of the quest for legal perfection:

> The truth is, that the law is always approaching, and never reaching, consistency.
> It is forever adopting new principles from life at one end, and it always retains
> old ones from history at the other, which have not yet been absorbed or sloughed
> off. It will become entirely consistent only when it ceases to grow.[57]

What deserves another thought, in other words, is the thought that our last thought is the last possible thought. Holmes knew better.

---

57   Holmes, *Common Law* 32.

Afterword

It is difficult to draw general conclusions from a small number of specific cases, although that has never stopped the common law from trying. A few generalizations, based on the preceding reappraisals of individual topics in the law of property, may be hazarded here. All the reappraisals involve areas in which the role of statutes has been tangential and the role of the judges central. The task assigned to the common law judges was to resolve the disputes that were brought to them, so the common law was built out of solutions to specific problems, rather than according to a legislative master plan. Over time, these solutions developed into general rules, which took on a life of their own as they were periodically restated to respond to changed circumstances and as they were affiliated with other rules, derived from solutions to other problems.

Because the disputes that were brought to the judges seemed worth fighting over at the time, the foundations of the common law rules were always practical and contemporary, but rules have a tendency to remain after the reason for them has ceased. Inertia is a powerful force in law, as in nature. No very great study of property law is required to show that some of its basic rules are old, very old, dating back hundreds of years. Major doctrines of everyday importance must evolve or die, but more obscure doctrines, usually of minor significance can sometimes outlive, even for centuries, the causes that gave them birth, bypassed by careful legal drafting or paralleled by new rules opening new possibilities. This can happen, as examination of the hoary Rule in Shelley's Case demonstrates, because of professional conservatism and the institutional structure of the common law legal system, in which judges make law but (usually) defer to the legislature to change it.

More often, ancient rules survive because they deal with perennial problems of social and economic organization. Among the oldest concepts of property law, the right of survivorship associated with the joint tenancy, originated to serve feudal purposes yet endures long after the decline of the society that called it into being, serving new and unforeseen social needs. The problem changed; the solution remained the same. When the subsequent recognition of wills provided an orderly means to direct succession to property at death, the right of survivorship did not disappear but was left in the common law storehouse of legal rules. Statutes eventually jettisoned the inconvenient historical baggage like the presumption in favor of joint tenancy and the obstacle to sharing individual ownership with another co-owner in joint tenancy. So modified, joint tenancy has continued to this day, a hardy alternative to testation, a "will substitute."

Similarly, the form of concurrent ownership in which married couples in many states still take title to real property, tenancy by the entirety, is also of ancient origin, but its survival into the modern world required rather more profound modifications before it could be suited (more or less) to contemporary understandings of marriage and the rights of women. Male domination obviously had to go, but the golden opportunity it offered for asset protection and probate avoidance made tenancy by the entirety too attractive to lose. It is also a hardy survivor, able to withstand even the growing recognition of same-sex marriage.

Made by the judges in the first place and tinkered with over the years by statutes, the common law of property is still subject to periodic reworking by the judiciary, nowadays often in a more dynamic relationship with the legislature. The civics-book theory of separation of powers – the legislators make the laws, the judges apply them – is only approximately correct. The law of landlord and tenant, for example, that had remained static for so many centuries was rather rapidly overhauled when reform-minded judges reconceptualized what had been a conveyance as a contract and imported more or less suitable rules from that area of the law. Faced with an abandoning tenant, landlords – at least of residential tenancies – now must mitigate damages, just like a party to a contract faced with a breaching counterparty. Similarly, the implied covenant of merchantability in contracts for the sale of consumer goods became in the law of property the implied covenant of habitability – again, at least in residential tenancies. In this case, the legislative role was to catch up with the judiciary and generalize the new rule by adopting statutes.

While separation of powers does not prevent judicial law-making, it does affect the way judges make law. Rare today is the judicial *pronunciamento* of entirely new rules, such as the landlord's duty to mitigate damages or the implied covenant of habitability in residential leases. More common is a surreptitious modification of received law. Words may be manipulated to produce desired results, as with the classification of property as previously "lost" or "mislaid" in the law of finding, or the play on the meaning of the word "burden" in the law of easements. A host of examples of law reform by other means may be grouped under the heading "legal fiction," now more politely described as "constructive" or "equitable" doctrines. Further changes in the law are promoted by law reformers on the bench or off it – some of them legal academics – who use emotive labels as part of their campaign for favored legal results. Who would want to see a will fail because of a "harmless error" in execution? Or a trust fail because of the possibility of a "fertile octogenarian"?

Law must be relatively stable so ordinary people can live their lives without too many surprises, and legal professionals can manage the huge apparatus efficiently. But law must also change in large or small ways to accommodate new institutions and understandings. Why law changes when it does is a question commonly dismissed with off-hand references to logic or social and economic development, without explanation of why logic suddenly became more persuasive or why only certain social and economic developments are accommodated, or accommodated so quickly. Explanations seem more necessary in case of departures from precedent than in cases of maintaining existing rules, even in changed circumstances.

Rationales giving prominence to extrinsic factors are useful in minimizing the perceived role of judicial choice in selecting the rule to be applied, but they necessarily conceal the considerations that determine which factors to recognize, and when. Whether continuing to apply old rules in new situations or overturning existing concepts, the judges are nonetheless making new law, inviting further reappraisals.

Usually a congeries of reasons explains the change, not least among them a desire to conform the rule to popular beliefs and practices and to encourage good social customs, as with the implied covenant of habitability in the sale and lease of residential property. An increasing emphasis on respecting individual intention, even at the expense of complicating or sacrificing well-known rules, has led to an increasing willingness to grant judges more discretion in deciding cases, in the careless belief that they will "do the right thing." Rules that offered a high degree of predictability of result at the expense of occasionally defeating intention have come under particular pressure – from the relatively insignificant Rule in Shelley's Case to the monumental Rule Against Perpetuities.

Another force of change, this one not particularly connected to perceptions of social policy, is the pressure of jurisdictional competition. Legal systems constantly borrow from one another – from the historic interchange of concepts and vocabulary between the great legal systems of English common law and Roman civil law, to the enriching interaction between common law and equity, to the inglorious rivalry between American states to secure lucrative legal business. The resulting legal marketplace may be no more than a racecourse for those seeking the least restrictive alternative, whether it is in the public interest or not, or it may be a laboratory for those striving to develop more serviceable rules.

After such a survey of topics in the law of property, it is impossible – for me, at least – to conclude that property law is a coherent whole. In its state at any given time, it could never have been the product of a single mind or institution. What we call property law is, instead, a collection of originally ad hoc solutions to specific problems, ossified or adapted over time, and imperfectly associated with solutions to other specific problems, all united only by their general concern with the eternal problem of *meum et tuum*, mine and thine.

Table of Cases

Croker v. Marquis of Hertford, 4 Moo. P.C. 339, 13 Eng. Rep. 334 (P.C. 1844)
Crowder v. Vandendeale, 564 S.W.2d 879 (Mo. 1977)
Dawson v. Yucus, 239 N.E.2d 305 (Ill. App. 1968)
Dearman v. Bruns, 181 S.E.2d 809 (N.C. Ct. App. 1971)
Den on the Dem. of Bayard v. Singleton, 1 N.C. 5 (1787)
D'Ercole v. D'Ercole, 407 F. Supp. 1377 (D. Mass. 1976)
Doctor v. Hughes, 122 N.E. 221 (N.Y. 1919)
Dolley v. Powers, 89 N.E.2d 412 (Ill. 1949)
Doyle v. Andis, 102 N.W. 177 (Iowa 1905)
Duke of Norfolk's Case, 3 Ch. Cas. 1, 22 Eng. Rep. 931 (Ch. 1682)
Dumpor's Case, 4 Co. Rep. 119, 76 Eng. Rep. 1110 (K.B. 1603)
Erie Railroad v. Tompkins, 304 U.S. 64 (1938)
Eldridge v. Knott, 1 Cowp. 214, 98 Eng. Rep. 1050 (K.B. 1774)
Employers' Liability Case, 207 U.S. 463 (1908)
Employers' Liability Case, 223 U.S. 1 (1912)
Estate of ________. See name of party.
Ex parte ________. See name of party.
Faison v. Middleton, 88 S.E. 141 (N.C. 1916)
Farwell v. Boston & Worcester RR, 35 Mass. (4 Metc.) 49 (1842)
First Nat'l Bank of Bar Harbor v. Anthony, 557 A.2d 957 (Me. 1989)
Fisher v. Wigg, 1 Salk. 391, 91 Eng. Rep. 339 (K.B. 1701)
Foster v. Reiss, 112 A.2d 553 (N.J. 1955)
Foundation Devel. Corp. v. Loehmann's, Inc., 788 P.2d 1189 (Ariz. 1990)
Gaite's Will Trusts, Re, [1949] 1 All Eng. Rep. 459 (Ch.)
Gardner, In re, 202 S.E.2d 318 (N.C. Ct. App. 1974)
Goodridge v. Dept. of Public Health, 798 N.E.2d 941 (Mass. 2003)
Grant v. Grant, 34 Beav. 623, 55 Eng. Rep. 776 (Ch. 1865)
Hammer v. Hammer, 633 S.E.2d 878 (N.C. Ct. App. 2006)
Hannah v. Peel, 1 K.B. 509 (1945)
Harris & Gurganus v. Williams, 246 S.E.2d 791 (N.C. App. 1978)
Hartley v. Ballou, 209 S.E.2d 776 (N.C. 1974)
Hawes v. Hawes, 1 Wils. 165, 95 Eng. Rep. 552 (Ch. 1747)
Hebrew Univ. Assoc. v. Dye, 169 A.2d 641 (Conn. Super. Ct. 1961)
Hebrew Univ. Assoc. v. Dye, 223 A.2d 397 (Conn. Super. Ct. 1966)
Hieble v. Hieble, 316 A.2d 777 (Conn. 1972)
Hill v. Schrunk, 292 P.2d 141 (Or. 1956)
Hillyer, In re Estate of, 664 So.2d 361 (Fla. 1995)
Hopkins v. Hopkins, 1 Atk. 591, 26 Eng. Rep. 371 (Ch. 1738)
In re ________. See name of party.
Ingalls v. Hobbs, 31 N.E. 286 (Mass. 1892)
Ives v. South Buffalo Railway Co., 94 N.E. 431 (N.Y. Ct. App. 1911)
Jackson v. O'Connell, 177 N.E.2d 194 (Ill. 1961)
Javins v. First Nat'l Realty Corp., 428 F.2d 1071 (U.S. Ct. App., D.C. Cir.), cert.
    denied, 400 U.S. 925 (1970)

Jee v. Audley, 1 Cox 324, 29 Eng. Rep. 1186 (Ch. 1787)

Jenni v. Gamel, 602 S.W.2d 696 (Mo. Ct. App. 1980)

Johnson v. Johnson, 279 P.2d 928 (Okla. 1954), 424 P.2d 414 (Okla. 1967)

Jones v. Green, 337 N.W.2d 85 (Mich. App. 1983)

Kelo v. City of New London, 545 U.S. 792 (2005)

Keron v. Cashman, 33 A. 1055 (N.J. Eq. 1896)

Keyes v. Guy Bailey Homes, Inc., 439 So.2d 670 (Miss. 1983)

King v. Greene, 153 A.2d 49 (N.J. 1959)

Klatzl's Estate, In re, 110 N.E. 181 (N.Y. 1915)

Kline v. 1500 Massachusetts Ave. Corp., 439 F.2d 477 (U.S. Ct. App., D.C. Cir. 1970)

Lake v. Craddock, 3 P. Wms. 158, 24 Eng. Rep. 1011 (Ch. 1732)

Lankford v. Wright, 489 S.E.2d 604 (N.C. 1997)

Lewis v. Pate, 193 S.E. 20 (N.C. 1937)

Libby Hill Seafood Restaurants, Inc. v. Owens, 303 S.E.2d 565 (N.C. Ct. App. 1983)

Louisiana Health Serv. & Indem. Co. v. McNamara, 561 So.2d 712 (La. 1990)

Loveman v. Lay, 124 So. 2d 93 (Ala. 1960)

Lowry's Estate, In re, 171 A. 878 (Pa. 1934)

Lusk v. Broyles, 694 So.2d 4 (Ala. 1997)

MacPherson v. Buick Motor Co., 111 N.E. 1050 (N.Y. 1916)

Mahoney, In re Estate of, 220 A.2d 475 (Vt. 1966)

Mahoney v. Grainger, 186 N.E. 86 (Mass. 1933)

March, In re, 27 Ch. D. 166 (1884)

Matter of Totten, 71 N.E. 748 (1904)

McAvoy v. Medina, 11 Allen (Mass.) 548 (1866)

Melms v. Pabst Brewing, 79 N.W. 738 (Wis. 1899)

Michael, In re Estate of, 218 A.2d 338 (Pa. 1966)

Michaels, In re Estate of, 132 N.W.2d 557 (Wis. 1965)

Michalski v. Michalski, 142 A.2d 645 (N.J. 1958)

Miller v. Cannon Hill Estates, Ltd., 2 K.B. 113 (Eng. 1931)

Morgan v. Malleson, L.R. 10 Eq. 475 (1870)

Morris v. McCarty, 32 N.E. 938 (Mass. 1893)

Morris v. Pugh, 2 Burr. 1241, 97 Eng. Rep. 811 (K.B. 1761)

Mosser v. Dolsay, 27 A.2d 155 (N.J. Ch. 1942)

Mostyn v. Fabrigas, 1 Cowp. 161, 98 Eng. Rep. 1021 (K.B. 1774)

Mustain v. Gardner, 67 N.E. 779 (Ill. 1903)

National Academy of Science v. Cambridge Trust Co., 346 N.E.2d 879 (Mass. 1976)

National Lead Co. v. Kanawha Block Co., 288 F. Supp. 357 (S.D.W. Va. 1968)

New State Ice Co. v. Liebmann, 285 U.S. 262 (1932)

New York Central RR v. White, 243 U.S. 188 (1917)

Nolan v. Paramount Homes, Inc., 518 S.E.2d 789 (N.C. Ct. App. 1999)

North Carolina Bd. of Architecture v. Lee, 142 S.E.2d 643 (N.C. 1965)

Wollard v. Smith, 94 S.E.2d 466 (N.C. 1956)
Wood, In re, [1894] 3 Ch. 381

Table of Constitutions and Statutes

Nevada Constitution
Nev. Const. art. I, § 21
Nev. Const. art. 11, § 3

New Mexico Constitution
N.M. Const. art. XII, § 4

North Carolina Constitution
N.C. Const. of 1776, Dec'l of Rights § 4
N.C. Const. of 1868, art. IV, § 1
N.C. Const. of 1868 art. X, § 6
N.C. Const. art. I, § 6
N.C. Const. art. IV, § 13
N.C. Const. art. IX, § 10(1)
N.C. Const. art. IX, § 10(2)
N.C. Const. art. X, § 4

North Dakota Constitution
N.D. Const. art. IX, § 1

Oklahoma Constitution
Okla. Const. art. X, § 32

Oregon Constitution
Or. Const. art. VIII, § 2

South Carolina Constitution
S.C. Const. art. XIV, § 3

South Dakota Constitution
S.D. Const. art. VIII, § 2

Virginia Constitution
Va. Const. of 1776, Bill of Rights § 5

Washington Constitution
Wash. Const. art. IX, § 3

Wisconsin Constitution
Wis. Const. art. I, § 14
Wis. Const. art. IX, § 3
Wis. Const. art. X, § 2

Wyoming Constitution
Wyo. Const. art. 7, § 2

United States Statutes
Northwest Ordinance, 1 Stat. 50
Interstate Wire Act of 1960, 18 U.S.C. § 1084
Federal Employers' Liability Act, Act of June 11, 1906, ch. 3073, 34 Stat. 232
Act of April 22, 1908, ch. 149, 35 Stat. 65
Act of April 5, 1910, ch. 143, 36 Stat. 291
Tax Reform Act of 1986, Pub. L. No. 99-514, 100 Stat. 2085

Alabama Statutes
Ala. Code § 35-4-230

Alaska Statutes
Alaska Stat. § 34.15.110
Alaska Stat. § 34.27.051
Alaska Stat. § 34.27.100

Arizona Statutes
Ariz. Rev. Stat. § 14-2901A

Delaware Statutes
Del. Code Ann. tit. 12, § 3570
Del. Code Ann. tit. 25, § 25
Del. Code Ann. tit. 25, § 503

California Statutes
Cal. Civ. Code § 1214
Cal. Civ. Code § 1710.2
Cal. Civ. Code § 3517
Cal. Prob. Code § 6112

Colorado Statutes
Colo. Rev. Stat. § 15-11-1102.5

Connecticut Statutes
Conn. Gen. Stat. § 45a-257
Conn. Gen. Stat. § 45a-436
Conn. Gen. Stat. § 47-14a

Delaware Statutes
1996 Laws of Del., c. 538
Del. Code Ann. tit. 25, § 25

Del. Code Ann. tit. 25, § 503

Florida Statutes
Fla. Stat. § 689.225
Fla. Stat. § 732.301
Fla. Stat. § 732.302

Hawaii Statutes
Haw. Rev. Stat. § 523A-21

Illinois Statutes
Ill. Ann. Stat. ch. 76, para. 1
765 Ill. Comp. Stat. § 305/3(a-5)
765 Ill. Comp. Stat. § 305/4(a)(8)
765 Ill. Comp. Stat. § 1005/1
765 Ill. Comp. Stat. § 1025/15

Idaho Statutes
Idaho Code § 55-111

Indiana Statutes
Ind. Code Ann. § 32-1-2-8
Ind. Code Ann. § 32-34-1-30

Iowa Statutes
Iowa Code, § 556F
Iowa Code Ann. § 557.15

Kansas Statutes
Kan. Stat. Ann. § 59-3501

Louisiana Statutes
La. Civ. Code Ann. art. 2669
La. Civ. Code Ann. art. 3412
La. Rev. Stat. 9:164

Maine Statutes
Me. Rev. Stat. Ann. tit. 33, § 101-A
Me. Rev. Stat. Ann. tit. 33, § 1962

Massachusetts Statutes
Mass. Gen. Laws Ann. ch. 191, § 9

Michigan Statutes
Mich. Comp. Laws Ann. § 554.45
Mich. Comp. Laws §§ 554.91 – 554.94

Maryland Statutes
Md. Code Ann., Est. & Trusts § 11-102(b)(5)

Missouri Statutes
Mo. Rev. Stat. § 456.025

Nebraska Statutes
Neb. Rev. Stat. § 76-2005(9)

Nevada Statutes
Nev. Rev. Stat. § 111.1031

New Hampshire Statutes
N.H. Rev. Stat. Ann. § 551:10
N.H. Rev. Stat. Ann. § 564:24

New Jersey Statutes
N.J. Stat. Ann. §§ 46:2F-9 – 46:2F-11

New York Statutes
N.Y. Estates, Powers and Trusts Law § 6-2.2
New York Est., Powers & Trusts Law § 5-3.3
N.Y. Estates, Powers & Trusts Law § 7-1.9
N.Y. Personal Property Law §§ 251-258

North Carolina Statutes
Act of 1784, c. 22, § 6
N.C. Sess. Laws 1979, c. 714, § 1
N.C. Gen. Stat. § 1-50
N.C. Gen. Stat. § 1 534
N.C. Gen. Stat. § 22-2
N.C. Gen. Stat. § 29-14
N.C. Gen. Stat. § 29-24
N.C. Gen. Stat. § 30-3.1
N.C. Gen. Stat. § 31-5.4
N.C. Gen. Stat. § 31-5.5
N.C. Gen. Stat. § 31-42
N.C. Gen. Stat. § 31A-1
N.C. Gen. Stat. § 31A-15
N.C. Gen. Stat. § 39-13.6

N.C. Gen. Stat. § 39-50
N.C. Gen. Stat. § 41-2
N.C. Gen. Stat. § 41-6
N.C. Gen. Stat. § 41-6.3
N.C. Gen. Stat. § 41-15
N.C. Gen. Stat. § 41-23
N.C. Gen. Stat. § 42-3
N.C. Gen. Stat. § 42 41
N.C. Gen. Stat. § 42 44
N.C. Gen. Stat. § 47 18
N.C. Gen. Stat. § 97-31
N.C. Gen. Stat. § 116B-7
N.C. Gen. Stat. § 116B-64

Ohio Statutes
Ohio Rev. Code Ann. § 169.08(D)
Ohio Rev. Code Ann. § 2131.09(B)
Ohio Rev. Code Ann. § 5302.22

Oklahoma Statutes
84 Okla. Stat. Supp. 1975 § 231

Pennsylvania Statutes
Act of 1812
Pa. Stat. Ann. tit. 20, § 6104
Pa. Cons. Stat. tit. 20, § 6107.1(b)(1)
Pa. Stat. Ann. tit. 68, § 110

Rhode Island Statutes
R.I. Gen. Laws § 34-11-38

South Dakota Statutes
S.D. Codified Laws Ann. § 43-5-1
S.D. Codified Laws Ann. § 43-5-4
S.D. Codified Laws Ann. § 43-5-8
S.D. Codified Laws Ann. § 43-41B-22

Tennessee Statutes
Tenn. Code Ann. § 66-1-201(f)

Texas Statutes
Tex. Probate Code Ann. § 68

Utah Statutes
Utah Code Ann. § 75-2-1203

Vermont Statutes
Vt. Stat. Ann. tit. 27, § 2

Virginia Statutes
Va. Code Ann. § 11-2
Va. Code Ann. § 15-15.3
Va. Code Ann. § 55-70.1
Va. Code Ann. § 55-13.3(C)

Washington Statutes
Wash. Rev. Code § 11.98.130

Wisconsin Statutes
Wis. Stat. § 700.16(1)(a)

Wyoming Statutes
Wyo. Stat. Ann. § 34-1-139

District of Columbia
D.C. § 19-904(a)(10)

England & United Kingdom
Statute of Gloucester, 6 Ed. 1, c. 5 (1278)
De Donis Conditionalibus, 13 Ed. 1, c. 1 (1285)
Statute Quia Emptores, 18 Ed. 1 (1290)
25 Edw. 3, st. 5, c. 2 (1350)
36 Ed. 3, c. 15 (1362)
Statute of Uses, 27 Hen. 8, c. 10 (1535)
31 Hen. 8, c. 1 (1539)
Statute of Wills, 32 Hen. 8, c. 1 (1540)
32 Hen. 8, c.32 (1540)
Statute of Tenures, 12 Car. 2, c. 24 (1660)
Statute of Frauds, 29 Car. 2, c. 3, § 1 (1677)
Statute of Frauds, 29 Car. 2, c. 3, § 2 (1677)
Statute of Frauds, 29 Car. 2, c. 3, § 3 (1677)
Statute of Frauds, 29 Car. 2, c. 3, § 4 (1677)
Statute of Frauds, 29 Car. 2, c. 3, § 5 (1677)
Statute of Frauds, 29 Car. 2, c. 3, § 17 (1677)
25 Geo. 2, ch. 6, § 1 (1752)
Judicature Act, 36 & 37 Vict., c. 66 (1873)
Judicature Act, 38 & 39 Vict., c. 77 (1875)

Married Women's Property Act, 45 & 46 Vict., c. 75 (1882)
60 & 61 Vict., c. 37 (1897)
15 Geo. 5, c. 3, § 41(1) (1925)
15 Geo. 5, c. 3, 46 (1925)
Law of Property Act, 15 & 16 Geo. 5, c. 20, § 39(6), sch. I (1925)
Law of Property Act, 15 & 16 Geo. 5, c. 20, § 131 (1925)

Index